Footnotes to A Fairytale
A Study of
THE NATURE OF EXPRESSION IN THE ARTS

ABOUT THE AUTHOR

William J. Bonville completed his undergraduate work at Bethany College, Bethany, W. Va., and received his M.A. in philosophy from Columbia University in New York City. He was appointed to a University Scholarship for doctoral studies at the University of Colorado, Boulder, Colorado. At Columbia, he concentrated in the field of the philosophy of art, preparing his thesis under the direction of the late Irwin Edman. At Colorado, he continued his work in philosophy and art criticism, and studied the psychology of affect under the late Karl Muenzinger. A native of Leominster, Massachusetts, he resides in Pasadena, California.

Footnotes to A Fairytale

A Study of
THE NATURE OF EXPRESSION
IN THE ARTS

W. J. BONVILLE

Foreword by
Dr. Stanley L. Levine

WARREN H. GREEN, INC.
St. Louis, Missouri, U.S.A.

Published by

WARREN H. GREEN, INC.
8356 Olive Boulevard
St. Louis, Missouri 63132, U.S.A.

© 1979 by W. J. BONVILLE

Library of Congress Catalog No. 79-50183
I.S.B.N. No. 0-87527-192-8

Printed in the United States of America

By the same author

Something of A Woman
a novel

FOREWORD

BY

Dr. Stanley L. Levine

The past few hundred years have been the age of logic, science, reasoning and analysis. We have seen the birth of science and the application of the scientific method to all aspects of life. This scientific age, however, has not been void of all nonscientific progress. The area most prevalently associated with non-scientific determinations is the aesthetic. Today, at least, beauty cannot be measured, weighed, formularized or created by the numbers. Beauty yet can be experienced and felt. And so, with the aesthetic, we find that concepts are evolved through philosophic analysis and synthesis.

If we look to the past, we can see how the study of aesthetic, of beauty, has searched for classification and how difficult it has been to explain with scientific approaches. In *The Nature of Expression in the Arts,* the aesthetic and the scientific have been innovatively associated by the author, William J. Bonville, to the extent possible with our present state of knowledge. The result is a creative, progressive beginning that will be further refined with time and enlightenment.

Reviewing the past, we observe that man has been vitally concerned with aesthetic, the expressions associated with beauty, especially in the arts. Most of the great minds since antiquity have pondered the questions, "What makes a painting beautiful?", "What makes a dance or a piece of music beautiful?", "What makes a poem beautiful?", or "What makes a play beautiful?" Taken together, these questions seek means to identify those ingredients of beauty that determine why one expression in the arts is beautiful and another is not. Many theories have been developed. None have been sustained in the test of time, although many have contributed to the evolution of modern thinking. *The Nature of Expression in the Arts* is a contribution to furtherance of that evolutionary process.

In this book, Bonville presents a comprehensive study of the nature of expression in the arts. He deals with primary human insights into beauty as well as with the interpretation of various abstract aesthetic theories associated with specific periods of the past and present. He shows us how the often considered simple idea of beauty in reality encompasses a complex myriad of aesthetic forces approachable through diverse disciplines involving philosophical, psychological, physiological, sociological, and communication concepts.

The book begins with a fairytale about a knight in ancient times, who comes across a statue. The knight is overwhelmed by its beauty, and yet is perplexed by the fact that it is only a piece of wood—but seems to be more than that. He feels its beauty, but doesn't know why. It is from this primary human experience that Bonville departs upon his study and analysis of beauty and the nature of expression in the arts.

Bonville's approach is historical in nature as he establishes the ground for aesthetic inquiry. Then each later chapter addresses a specific aspect of aesthetic and makes a developmental analysis of the concepts. The antecedent ideas are drawn from the writings of many outstanding contributors to the field: Plato, Socrates, Bacon, Baumgarten, Kant, Tolstoy, Pater, Jung, William James and many others. Although each chapter is concerned with a different aspect of aesthetic, there is an intricate development of argument leading to formulation and reinforcement of various key concepts concerning expression in the arts.

Within this framework, Bonville has a remarkable capability to define and resolve opposing theories and to extract the significant contributions contained in them. This he accomplishes through critical analysis and creative interpretation. Through Bonville's provocative insights and his Gestalt approach, the reader comes to realize that no one existing theory is all inclusive and that an eclectic approach is advisable—and that is precisely what Bonville does. Through keen insight and careful analysis he molds and supports the determination of the central concepts for understanding the nature of expression in the arts. His position is constantly supported by philosophical and psychologial analysis as well as the results of neurological and biological research.

This specific character of this study—the conceptual unification of philosophical analysis and scientific research, the subjective orientation of analytical psychology with the objective researches of the neurosciences, the correlations such as of Aristotle's "universal statements" with modern concepts of genetics and ethology—was most striking to me in Bonville's work. It shows concern not only for the science and methodologies of the old Age of Enlightenment that brought us to the age of logic, science, reasoning, and analysis; it reveals a similar awareness of the intrinsic nature of affect natural to that Enlightenment, but generally ignored in our unbridled enthusiasm for the works of intellect. This interests me because a primary area of my own work is pointed toward seeking methodologies to release a greater awareness of these hidden affections and the value contents natural to them. For in the world as I see it, exactly this awareness is required if we are to achieve what might be called the inner side of the old Enlightenment. For, in my view, the next two thousand years are destined to become the age of the New Enlightenment, the age in which feelings will gain prominence. Problem solving, planning, and implementation will rely more on the inner knowing, meditative experience and right brain activities of individuals. This will *not* replace scientific approaches but will supplement them to provide more viable, humanistic solutions to individual and sociological problematic situations.

The Nature of Expression in the Arts is a significant study performed with care and excellence. Bonville's contribution to the philosophy of art and aesthetics lies in combining the evolution of the idea of expression with current scientific probings into the affective inheritance of man. The application of science qualifies the implications of philosophic thought. The book also adds provocative new dimensions to communication theory, the theory of emotions, and the description of the nature of human consciousness.

Throughout the book, caution is given to accurately present opposing points of view and, with analysis, to extract the ideas significant to resolution of problems in the field of aesthetics. For those readers interested in delving into the holistic concept of the nature of expression in the arts, this book will challenge your mind and stimulate your interest in further explorations in the field.

Stanley L. Levine
Newport Beach, California
September 1978

Dr. Levine has an international reputation as a specialist in learning systems and the psychology of learning. His current research interest is in the affective phenomena underlying psychological adaptation, and in derivative methodological implications for development and test of techniques facilitating expansion of personal awareness and perceptions of worth.

In recent years an adjunct professor at the University of Southern California and at Chapman College, Orange, California, his principal work is as an educational consultant, serving Government and private institutions at home and abroad, including recent work in the remoteness of Tabriz, Iran, at the University of Azerabadagan.

Dr. Levine is a graduate of Brooklyn College in physics, and received his Ed.D. from the University of Southern California. A frequent contributor to professional journals and publications, he is author of several texts in mathematics, electronics, and computer applications to learning systems.

INTRODUCTION

Expression in the arts is regarded by modern philosophy as that singular quality of meaningfulness that marks one's experience of art.

Our subject is expression in the arts.

Our objective is to explore the basis for a new understanding of the phenomenon of expression, one that effectively reconciles ancient and modern theories by an inquiry into the roles of intellect and affect in the aesthetic experience.

Our approach begins where one phase of art begins, with a fairytale.

Since fairytales and art in one form or another appeal to virtually everyone, then in the best of all possible worlds this study of expression in the arts surely would appeal to everyone. In practical fact we cannot pretend that it does or even that it ought. Most of us would rather enjoy our art than analyze it, just as eating a fine dinner is more to be relished than the excellence of its description on a menu. Yet, when aesthetic and gastric appetites are satisfied and quiet moments are found for the luxury of contemplation, more than a few curious souls are wont to reflect on the hows and whys and wherefores of their experiences of things of art.

What follows is offered for such reflection. Here is grist for student or aficionado of ideas, whether he comes to the matter of expression from the side of philosophy or from the arts, and arrives with a full belly or the equally physical sense of captivation that one gains from a good book, a painting, or an evening at the theater.

The fairytale provides a kind of ostensive definition of the subject. A simple device, yet the tale implicates all the issues perennially at stake in aesthetic theory. Not that we here intend to develop a full-blown, systematic philosophy of art or the compleat aesthetics; rather, if art is a lunar madness possessing the elect of man, this is a finger pointing at the moon. It is the basis for a modern philosophy of art and provides touchstones for an aesthetics relevant to emerging understandings of man's affective inheritance.

Every student knows that theories of expression have dominated recent aesthetic theory, yet the germination of those theories out of root concepts going back to the birth of Hellenic sophistry goes unremarked. The development of the idea of expression out of those roots is a history waiting to be written. Chapters of this book address salient features of that history, but only in general outline. Our interest is less in the history than in the ideas. As Aristotle instructed so long ago, the historical perspective of an idea is important if not essential to understanding. A view of history shows where we are and whence we came along the way of ideas. Seeing the road behind we are less apt to invent old wheels already cast off or improved upon by those who passed before.

Men have long noted the quality of meaningfulness that characterizes experience of the arts. The ancients devised a theory that remained vogue without substantial improvement for more than two thousand years. Aesthetic meaning was explained in terms of intellect. As most familiarly recounted in the *Dialogues*, meaning in the arts was said to come of the contemplative intellect beholding the Divine Ideas represented in the work of art.

Where aesthetic was described as a contemplative, intellectual experience, feeling was banished from serious theoretical consideration. That we do have vivid feelings in our experience of art was not denied. The fact of feeling was taken to be quite beside the theoretical point. With such an approach to aesthetic, feelings needed more to be explained away than understood for any significant role they might play in the experience of art. In short, aesthetic was imputed to have an ideational essence and thus be intellectual in nature.

About two hundred years ago, within the ideational fabric of the Romantic revolution, the notion developed that aesthetic meaningfulness is a matter of feeling possessing the character of idea. This notion became the germ of the modern concept of expression in the arts, which asserts that the aesthetic meaning which is the essence of expression is in no way related to intellectual meaning. Indeed, intrusion of intellect into the moment of aesthetic was held to be disruptive, harmful to the quality of the experience, able even to destroy its possibility. That aesthetic experience often is associated with rather complex intellectual operations became a fact that needed to be explained away or ignored rather than understood for any role such processes might actually play in the experience.

The most striking feature of the comparison of ancient and modern viewpoints, other than their polar opposition, is that each recognizes that the qualities of both ideation and feeling are involved in the actual experiences people have of the arts. Each side also finds cause to reject one or the other aspect of the experience from theoretical consideration when formulating theory. The consistent appearance of this pattern in the history of ideas lends the impression that one or the other approach to aesthetic theory is taken only because a coherent theory is easier to attain if one doesn't have to cope with all the facts. In other words, a philosophy of art or an aesthetics is easier to develop if one doesn't have to deal with the problems of integrating two kinds of aesthetical facts – ideas and feelings – into a single system of theory.

A study of this theoretical opposition reveals another peculiarity. Each side is able to say some meaningful things the other is unable to say at all, or maybe not so well. This suggests that a measure of the truth is revealed from each side of opposition, and that an improved approach to aesthetic theory would tend to subsume something from both sides.

To follow the suggested approach, one would have to stipulate, first of all, that both ideas and feelings operate together in aesthetic experience, with the function of each being a necessary condition for the appearance of aesthetic. To explain this possibility, we might hypothesize that intellect and affect have complementary functions that achieve an operational unity in the moment of aesthetic. Such a notion would be radical enough in light of current theory, but it appears insufficient as the basis for a satisfactory explanation. The immediate problem is that one must postulate an operational parallelism between discrete functions of the mind in generation of aesthetic experience. We thereby are thrust up against one of the most ignored but enigmatic questions of psychology, to wit: How do thoughts and feelings interact?

The psychologist asserts that there is such interaction, and he trots out a dazzling display of physiological descriptions of the hormogenic foundations of feeling and the cerebral bases for thought. Yet the twain never quite meet except as an indemonstrable assertion which thus turns out to be as mythological as the Fates, rather than a description of scientific fact. From such sources we find then that the possibility of a psychological description of aesthetic experience – a psychological phenomenon – based on prevailing theories of psychology appears to be out of the question. But if we cannot discover a satisfying description of aesthetic in general psychological theory concerning the reciprocal influences of thought and feeling, whither shall we go?

The analytical philosopher might turn to the methods of logic. But logic only talks about talk itself and creates (or clarifies, as the case may be) another part of the problem men have when they try to cope with aesthetical problems. Men don't seem quite able to talk about thoughts and feelings in the same way at the same time as matters of either mind or experience. That is, not without great confusion of terms and semantic connections. At best we are left on one hand with the psychological facts of aesthetic, and on the other with rules about what we can say about them in terms of the structure of the linguistic medium selected.

While logic may be helpful as method for straightening out one's thinking in terms of the instrument of language, the true object of investigation lies in the concrete aesthetical facts and not in the words used to symbolize them. Since those facts, after all, are psychological, we again turn our interest toward psychology. Our objective remains to find a way to meet the requirements of our initial stipulation; i.e., that both ideas (in the sense of thoughts as opposed to impressions) and feelings operate together in aesthetic experience.

If we are to avoid the problem inherent to a theory based on functional parallelism, the sole avenue of inquiry remaining, it would seem, is to regard intellect and affect as a single, unified process in aesthetic experience. But saying, like wishing, doesn't make it so. What we have achieved is simply a point of view. Yet it is one that can be tested against the data and assumptions of science as well as the facts of aesthetic experience and the conventions of language and thought related to the event, expression. Much of this book is, therefore, directed into just that enterprise, leading to and giving warrant to the conclusion that expression – the only unique feature of aesthetic as experience – is ideation experienced as feeling, and not merely feeling with the quality of idea as some modern theories have it.

Now, if one wishes to base his understanding of expression on nothing more than a formula, there is little more to be said. The nature of expression in the arts is understood properly as ideation experienced as feeling. A skeptic, however, would have us do more than supplant one formula with another, particularly when one must look closely to notice the difference between them. So, to establish a foundation of argument and fact validating the brief assertion that expression is ideation experienced as feeling, and to discern the principal implications of what it means for that assertion to have validity, we here undertake an inquiry intending to identify the pertinent data and locate the terms and language suitable for argument demonstrating the validity of the formula.

The task, as shall be seen, takes us along paths of inquiry often remote from those followed by the standard studies of aesthetics and the philosophy of art. In consequence, we will cover a range of material not included ordinarily in works of this kind. Equally, some of the "standard" materials will at times be given an unconventional treatment; and principal among that is the psychological material common to current aesthetic theory.

Aesthetic, virtually since the name was coined, has been mired down in a faculty psychology bequeathed to us by the prestigious Kantian analyses. The vaunted analytic and dialetic of aesthetic judgment in his *Critique of Judgment* is, in effect, descriptive psychology made the basic for logical analysis. Because global behaviors of consciousness may be described in particular terms (e.g., imagination), Kantian psychology attributed to the psyche itself the faculty (e.g., imagination) in functional rather than descriptive terms. No matter that now psychology has "officially" escaped adherence to "faculty" theories, the literature of aesthetics (and psychology too) persistently exhibits a naive form of the faculty theory. That is, in the literature we find a psychologic form of the reification problem so long latent in the naive use of language. The ways of thought characteristic of faculty psychology persist and indeed even prevail in the literature in question.

Now one cannot contest that the traditional terms of psychology (e.g., imagination) continue to be useful linguistic tools for describing aspects of human behavior. For example, there seems no reason to deny the meaningfulness of the statement, "Art is imagination." The statement is common to the literature of the philosophy of art and psychology, and there is a characteristic behavior pattern apparent both subjectively and objectively deemed by consensus as appropriately designated by the term "imaginative." By the same token, to say that art is imagination, and to define imagination solely in terms of its global appearance as behavior, leaves aesthetic theory grounded upon a faculty psychology in fact if not in name, if that term describing that characteristic global behavior is taken to mean anything more than the sheer appearance of that behavior. In other words, while there is no reason to abandon the term as it applies to the typical behavioral construct called "imagination," there is also no reason to impute to the term a meaning that goes beyond its purely descriptive application to that characteristic construct. Neither is there any reason to let the matter drop there, perhaps with an agreement that there is such a limit to the operational meaning of the term, "imagination." We can move the investigation to another level where the life processes that underlie those behavioral events may be brought into question.

The term, "expression," presents an investigator with the same kind of problem. One cannot doubt that the term, "expression," has a measure of meaning relative to the experience one has of art, for it is used commonly in the literature of criticism, art theory, and aesthetics. In that literature, however, the term is used to describe what are in fact several quite different behaviors, often with little or no awareness evident that such differences in usage exist, along with their correlative meanings. We also find the term used as if "expression" is itself a faculty of the mind, or perhaps the product of some psychic faculty, such as imagination. So, if we reject the notion of a faculty psychology, we must at the same stroke reject these notions of expression. We must treat "expression" as a behavioral description, then advance beyond that description only by an extension of inquiry into other levels of discourse dealing with other kinds of data than the gross behaviors of expression in the arts.

At the same time, we cannot ignore that the natural beginning of such an inquiry as we propose, is found exactly in those grosser behaviors, for they are what first appear to the eye. They are what suggest the questions on which an inquiry is based, and provide the material that gives substance to the endeavor. Describing those behaviors, we find them as varied as the men who inhabit the earth. What appears as an essential attribute in one instance is often lacking in another. Yet, certain nuances pervade man's experience of art throughout the ages, nuances that have become a ground for a kind of consensus of what one talks about when one discusses art or the art experience.

Our first task is to explore that consensus to find some of the language, terms, and ideas in the company of which an inquiry of this nature might be expected to proceed, particularly as they relate to the idea of expression in the arts. To commence the work such that we all have a common understanding of the idea in question, let us clarify the subject by means of a device that trades on expression itself – a fairytale.

TABLE OF CONTENTS

Footnotes to A Fairytale

A Study of
THE NATURE OF EXPRESSION IN THE ARTS

Chapter 1

THE KNIGHT'S TALE

Once upon a time, a young knight-errant was riding through a dark, forbidding wood. As he went along he chanced upon a small glade, in the center of which stood a low mound of earth. Atop the mound was a little figure, carved of wood.

The figure was of an old man who sat cross-legged, elbows on knees, chin on fists, head and shoulders stooped in fixed contemplation. His face was wrinkled and stolid beneath shaggy brows and long, unkempt hair. His body was half-clad in the pelt of an animal.

The knight approached the figure cautiously, his sword held ready, fearful he had come upon some demon in disguise. But as he reined up near the wooden image and was able to see it clearly, he became indefensibly fascinated by what he saw. Indeed, so fascinated he was unaware of sheathing his sword and dismounting.

Initially, the knight's gaze was quizzical, then perplexed until a slight smile of pleasure drove the frown from his brow. Suddenly curious, he reached out to touch the figure and the spell was broken. He nudged it to test its weight, walked about it that he might examine each detail in order to understand what he was looking at. Then it occurred to him that something was missing. Something he had observed only moments before was gone.

The knight stepped back for a larger view of the figure. Again he found it, though he knew not precisely what. Then he lost it again as he began thinking about it, retaining nothing more than the awareness that he had seen . . . . . something.

Upon an impulse, the knight grasped his sword. Poised to attack the bewitching little image, an afterthought stayed his hand. It was, after all, rather a pleasing enchantment, not in the least diabolical. So instead the knight lifted the little figure up across his saddle and rode off to the castle of his lady fair.

At the lady's castle, the knight carried the figure into the Great Hall and placed it where the light through the casements was brightest and the details of the figure stood in sharp relief. Presently, responding to the knight's messenger, the lady entered the Hall. Upon spying the figure she stopped short with pleased surprise, held spellbound for long moments while the knight waited impatiently for her to speak.

"Tis my gift to you, my lady," the knight prompted hopefully.

"How beautiful," the woman breathed at last. "How beautiful it is."

The knight turned to glance skeptically at the figure. It had not occurred to him that the statue was beautiful. For him, only his lady deserved that name. But as he turned his attention to the figure of the old man his perplexity returned.

"It's bewitching," he suggested.

"Entrancing," the woman replied in a whisper, still caught in the spell cast by the stolid old wooden man.

"But why?"

"Why?" asked his lady in return, puzzled that he should ask such a question.

"Why is it," he explained, "that there is something more to that little statue than is really there? It is only a bit of wood carved to appear as a man, yet. . ." The man hesitated, trying to phrase words to tell her what he wished to say.

He could only gesture toward the statue as if to say, "There, that is what I am trying to tell you."

"Yes, I see what you mean," the woman murmured thoughtfully. "There is something more."

"But what is it?"

"It's. . . It's a story."

"A story?" the knight enquired, again studying the wooden figure as he considered the matter. "Yes," he agreed, "but what does it say?"

"Well," the lady began, "it says. . . . It says. . . . Something. Oddly, I don't really know what. That is, I can't tell you. But you seem to feel the same way about it, so I don't really have to tell you. Do I? Honestly?"

There was indeed no need. The knight and his lady were of a single mind in the presence of the little wooden man.

So ends our tale of the knight and his lady fair. We ought to add only that they lived happily ever after and, with the passing of years, the "something more" for them so ineffably attached to the little wooden image became "more and more."

The enigmatic "something more" experienced by the knight and lady, and by all of us more times than we can remember, has perennially puzzled people since some ancient age when art broke free from ritual magic in the minds of men. Deep in regions of the heart, however, the break was never complete. Today as before men find a haunting, magical quality somehow attached to things of art. Call it "bewitching," as the knight did. Call it "entrancing," as did his lady. Use a whole host of descriptors, each one appropriate within the many varied experiences the arts make possible. No matter how described it comes down to this: Experiences of art occur with stirring qualities of feeling, a kind of excitement, a nervous excitation somehow different from experiences of "ordinary life" and "the world in general."

Unlike our feelings about ordinary things and events, and our expectations and fulfillments associated with them, art generates overtones of feeling which somehow seem detached from the natural materials and events in which art is embodied. The feelings may appear so loosely associated with the object – so intangibly ethereal – that the feelings seem even to have another source outside nature and self. Add to this that gripping possession of consciousness that art achieves and we find the reason why the ancients came to call the experience of art a divine madness.[1]

Conventionally, one hears this "madness" attributed only to the artist. In consequence, when problems or art are discussed, attention is focused upon the artist. He is the creative one among us. His art is proof enough that he possesses a power denied his lesser fellows. Learn to understand his creativity and its object and the whole nature of art and aesthetic experience will be clarified. Such is the promise, at least. Unfortunately, the promise remains unfulfilled.

No one need deny the appearance that the artist has more intimate connections with things artistic than do other people. The object of art is of his making, after all. That factual evidence of his creative initiative conclusively disallows any doubt that the artist has powers either lacked or insufficiently developed by the rest of us. Yet, to insist that all will be understood when we understand the artist can only invite failure simply because analysis of the artist does not bring into question all the facts of art. The principal further fact is the audience who recognizes the work of the artist as art. While the nature of the artist's power remains moot, whether called divine madness or genius, in the final analysis one must also admit that a measure of the same genius (whatever it may be) resides in each of us. If it did not, the artist would go unrecognized. Real creativity is demanded no less of his public else they may not follow his artistic initiative. Even more, in the act of following, his public also find themselves swept up in a divine madness of their own – fully enchanted as were the knight and his lady in the presence of the little wooden man.

---

[1] In *Enthusiasm and Divine Madness*, Josef Pieper objects to "madness" as a proper translation of what Plato meant by "mania." Today, he says, "the word connotes unsoundness and irrationality." (p 49) In contrast, Plato used "mania" to mean "a being-beside-oneself, a loss of command over oneself, surrender of autarchic independence and self control; a state in which we are not active but passive." (p 49) It is a state of "being filled by God," (p 50) or "enthusiasm." He admits, however, that the modern meaning of "enthusiasm" is too debased to be a valid translation of Plato's meaning today.

Enchanting as art is, said the ancients, art can only be transporting us beyond the mundane plane of existence. A muse has possessed us, bestowing upon us a taste of a divine nature otherwise denied our ken. Or so the story goes. Today we are able to look behind that story. There is more to be told than that. Perhaps another story. Maybe only a way of seeing the notion of the divine madness as something else: a charming myth often told by poets, or by poets masquerading as philosophers. But like so many myths it has its spark of truth. The poetic truth of myth in our more sophisticated age finds only a new term. Instead of divine madness or the transport of the muse, we say "expression."

The new term is not necessarily any more meaningful than the old "divine madness." They are simply different terms for that experience of meaningful feeling shared by the knight and his lady. Both the ancient sage who described it as a madness of divine origin, and the modern who explains it psychologically as an expression of some deep-seated human need, are speaking mythologically. We say that because the characteristic felt significance marking the experience of a work of art is little better understood today than it was in ancient Athens. The principal difference between the ancient and modern terms for the experience is that each term tends to suggest quite different kinds of questions.

Accepting the facticity of the phenomenon called the divine madness, we may enquire into it with the question, "What is the nature of the divine madness?" As of yore the reply would be, "It is the Divine Muse possessing us," which doesn't really tell us terribly much no matter what may be our religious or theological leanings. In this vein Josef Pieper remarked, "When such matters as these [Plato's concept of the divine madness] come up, we realize how much we lack a theological and philosophical doctrine of the arts, in terms of which we could examine this Platonic thesis, as well as others, with some adequacy."[2] What we really need is to avoid the impasse with a new set of terms and another question.

The new set of terms comes out of the modern use of the word "expression" when describing the experience of art. In those modern terms, the question leading into the nature of man's experience of art becomes phrased as, "What is the nature of expression in the arts?"

The phrase, "expression in *the* arts," immediately begs the question of art itself. It implies concern only for the jealously limited cadre of the fine arts, an implication borne out in fact by the literature of art throughout the ages. The traditional view of the arts in the western cultures, that is to say, holds that the fine arts are essentially different from the remainder of human activities.

---

[2]*Ibid.*, p 64.

There is alleged to be a fundamental split between aesthetic and practical experience, a distinction which corresponds to the division between the fine and practical arts. Such a distinction in turn leads to a theoretical differentiation between the experience of the connoisseur and that of the layman. Little wonder then that artists typically appear bent on creating works completely alien to the experience of the work-a-day man in the street, while art critics tend to laud an *Art* which despite its appeal to the aesthetes is generally viewed with bafflement by ordinary people. By the same token, those same critics vigorously deny the aesthetic quality or worth of things that ordinary people tend to enjoy.

In the light of a deeper view, the opinions of the critics are quite puzzling. In effect they contest an hypothesis implicit in the idea that the experience of art is marked by the "something more," or expression, felt by the knight and lady. The hypothesis is that an object is art if and only if meaningful expression results from one's experience of it. If mere bafflement results, the alleged art of the ultrasophisticated critic cannot be art at all. Equally, if the ordinary man finds expression in something outside the realm of art recognized by the critic, then that critical realm is false and our leading question must be: "What is the nature of expression in art?" with "art" understood to include all that appeals aesthetically to the unsophisticated consciousness.

The long tradition of Western thought tends to deny the foregoing argument. Today as always, aestheticians, regarding the tastes of critic, artist, and cultivated aesthete as the proper measure of aesthetic quality, overlook or deem irrelevant the vulgar tastes of ordinary folk. Socrates justified their viewpoint long ago, asserting that *hoi polloi*, ruled by passion and ignorance, ought not be reckoned with when determining what is proper for individuals or societies. Instead, Socrates advised, refer only to the man who has cultivated in himself the harmonies of his soul and contemplatively envisioned the Idea which is Beauty. Such a man and no other is the legitimate judge of what is to be considered as art.

The wisdom of Socrates to this day is used to explain as well as sanction the variances between vulgar and sophisticated taste. Yet there is a basic fault in the parochial narrowness of such a view. It denies legitimacy to the unpolished aesthetic experience which constitutes vulgarity while ignoring the fact that every aesthete was a vulgar child who achieved catholicity of taste. No aesthete can escape his human, vulgar condition. Sophistication rests upon and grows out of the broad base of vulgarity. The vulgar and the cultivated are cut from the same cloth. The latter is but a specialized development of the former. So there is no basis for maintaining that the experience of art is available only to the degree that one achieves the attributes of the cultured aesthete. The aesthetic is like life. In terms of the creative realization of art, all men have a share though their discovered shares may be different.

Considered as described above, that art moulded of precise intricacies and sophisticated materials which baffle the crowd does indeed qualify as art. Such art in fact elicits the experience of expression for some people – the sophisticated aesthetes. That art which pleases the crowd also qualifies, and for exactly the same reason. It elicits the experience of expression for some people, no matter how coldly it may be greeted by the professional critics.

All this adds quite another dimension to any answer we might give to the question: "What is the nature of expression in the arts?" The answer must embrace a folk melody as well as a fugue, *Dick Tracy* along with *Finnegan's Wake*. With Leo Tolstoy we must grasp the significance of the homely aesthetic sense of the peasant and the imaginative fancies of the child. Faced by such evidence the great artist humbled himself to the point of rejecting his own creations. "What is art?" he pondered. His answer turned out to be as parochial as that of Socrates, although diametrically opposed.

The failures of both Socrates and Tolstoy sprang from the same source. They dismissed the evidence of their own experience in their haste to develop a concept of art having objective values which directly supported their concepts of justice. The intermediate figure of the problem, aesthetic experience as such, was too hastily put aside after cursory admission of its facticity. The point is that for us there is no art unless there is aesthetic experience. Only with the experience may we know there is art.

Each in his own way, Socrates and Tolstoy, asked; "What is art?" Each failed because he sought an ultimate answer out of a proximate question. Their question should have been, "What is the nature of the aesthetic experience by which one identifies the object of art?" The answer to that question subsumes all questions concerning art beyond the technical problems of the respective media. The answer implies a whole spectrum of further answers concerning art in relationship to other disciplines, such as a sociology of art or a psychology of aesthetic. The answer further is bound up with a total philosophy of man, his world, his knowledge of self and world, and his feelings about them.

As to what the aesthetic experience ostensibly is, taken in its operational context, the experience is neither more nor less than what the knight and his lady discovered it to be. All things else to be said about it are but footnotes to a fairytale.

Chapter 2
PROBLEMS OF AESTHETIC

In the tale of the knight and his lady, the aesthetic experience had the quality of being a "story," albeit one they could not tell. Nor did it have to be told. Each could "see" the story in the presence of the wooden man. Together they shared an experience of felt meaningfulness—a pervasive, gripping feeling which possessed a peculiar character of significance.

That feeling of meaningfulness is known as expression in the arts. That feeling, however, must be recognized as but a part of their total experience. If nothing else, they were engaged in looking at the wooden figure. The lady called it beautiful. The aesthetic experience, then, appears to include several quite different factors. First there is the experience of looking at and perceiving an object of art. There is also the discovery of qualities said to be beautiful, which implies an aesthetic judgement. Then there is the felt meaningfulness called "expression."

Of those three major aspects of the experience, the latter two depend upon the prior process of perception. Because of this indisputable fact, aesthetic theory has focused upon the perceptual element of the experience, sometimes to the point of denying the legitimacy of the other factors. Even the name given to the experience we have of things of art, "aesthetic" experience, reflects the priority of perception. The root meaning of "aesthetic" is perception, and its specific meaning is "perception of the beautiful."

"Aesthetic experience," then, means "the experience of perceiving beauty." Since that experience is singularly marked by qualities of feeling, "aesthetic" has also come to mean "feeling," specifically those feelings peculiar to the experience of beautiful things. With this meaning, "aesthetic experience" is able to be described as "the experience of feelings attendant to the perception of beauty," and consequently as a particular kind of affective experience rather than as a modality or kind of perception.

Not everyone accepts that evolution of the meaning of "aesthetic." Some authorities insist that "aesthetic" applies only to the perceptual act when applied to beautiful things. An advantage of that position is its implicit assertion of a direct correlation between aesthetic quality and the objective characteristics of things called beautiful. This leads to the notion that all issues concerned with aesthetic judgement are resolvable in terms of objective standards of taste and empirically derivable principles of art.

In contrast to such a view, those who understand "aesthetic" principally in terms of feeling assert that aesthetic judgement hinges upon the quality of the feelings experienced. The act of perception is necessary but never the less incidental to the achievement of feelings. The fundamental issue of aesthetics thus concerns the source and nature of the feelings. Some hold that aesthetic is comprised solely of sensuous qualities. Others insist upon the necessary involvement of emotions, else the experience never could achieve the character of affect peculiar to aesthetic. Others posit what in effect is another kind of affect unique to aesthetic, such as the "aesthetic emotion" of Clive Bell.

Such disagreements about what "aesthetic" really means, and proper usage of the word, are symptomatic of the many fundamental problems of aesthetic which historically became matters for theoretical dispute. Another important source of controversy, long remarked, is that the aesthetic experience does not necessarily come from encounters with the same things. Even when it does, the experience is so much a matter of feelings and, after all, a strictly private affair, people are able to talk about their experiences only with great ambiguity. Literal meaning seems at best a mere approximation of the aesthetic meaning one actually discovers in the experience. As a result, there are grounds for meaningful debate about the differences and likenesses between the experiences different people have of things of art.

Still another problem is that aesthetic experience often has pronounced psychological side effects which persist beyond the strictly aesthetic moment and have repercussions in other behaviors operating other than aesthetically in the world. There is also the opposite circumstance where other behaviors reciprocally flavor the aesthetic, at times so powerfully that aesthetic questions tend to be referred elsewhere for final answers. Finally, there is the perplexing problem of feeling itself. No one knows very much about feelings or how we have them. Even their subjective appearance lacks the definiteness and stability of other phenomena of consciousness such as percepts and concepts. Yet, the whole of life is shot through and through with feeling, so the aesthetic is hardly unique for the affective qualities it lends to the living of our lives. The aesthetic, because of its specific relationship to things of beauty, appears merely to be more definitive and more stable than feelings in general.

Then there are the problems of theorizing itself. Approaches to aesthetic almost universally have attempted to draw some principle or system of thought from another field and extend it into the domain of aesthetics. The unspoken purpose was axiomatic demonstration of previously determined principles rather than analytical discovery of aesthetical principles from the data proper to aesthetics. Of course, there is nothing necessarily wrong with such purpose or the consequent approaches to art and aesthetic. If one assumes a fundamental unifying principle of being or knowing, such approaches are fully justified and not at all surprising. The fault comes when aesthetic data are ignored and aesthetics or the philosophy of art are shaped to fit some other need than exploration of the actual facts of aesthetic. The approaches to aesthetic from the side of morality are particularly apt to such a failing – and this too is not surprising. Moral consciousness has an axe to grind. It takes sides in approaching man and his world. Moral Philosophy is an idealized extension of that basic moral experience and therefore is no less partial.

Given the complexities deriving from any one of these basic problems, we begin to appreciate not only the diversity of aesthetic theory but also the long history of controversy in artistic circles and among the critics. Consider one example: The problem of the interactions between aesthetic and other behaviors. Here is the root of the long debate over the legitimacy of the doctrine of art for art's sake, the banning of books in Boston, moralistic criticism of the arts, and even politically oriented criticism such as the critic in *Pravda* is expected to write concerning the banned works of Evgeny Evtushenko.

The impact of the arts upon human behavior has been recognized since ancient times. The earliest serious inquiries into the nature and function of the arts stemmed from awareness of the conflicts between aesthetic and moral experience. The classic instance of the shaping of aesthetic theory on the basis of moral philosophy is the progress of the dialectic in Plato's *Republic*. Socrates and his cronies formulated principles of individual and social morality, or justice, and used them as the basis for banning practically everything of aesthetic consequence from their ideal state.[1] The irony of Socrates, of course,

---

[1]   The moralistic approach in the *Republic* is based on a metaphysical concept of art. Art is said to imitate the eternal forms of things. Socrates argues that this imitation is less true than false, showing how the work of art is twice removed from the true form and merely copies a single aspect of that form. Even worse than its remoteness from truth, however, is that art as commonly valued or judged does not amount to anything very important after all. As Socrates explains, "The excellence, or beauty, or truth of every structure, animate and inanimate, and of every action of man, is relative to the use for which nature or the artist has intended them" (Book 10, 601D). When it comes to judgements of art, however, the criterion of excellence is not whether the imitation (and by definition the intent is imitation of a form) is any good (true) or not, but on whether people like it or not. That, Socrates argues, certainly cannot be the proper way to criticize or justify art for it places judgement on the level of sense perceptions and feelings, which are baser powers of the soul. Art, by such a measure, appeals to us with charming but unadulterated nonsense. Such art not only fails to elevate humanity but debases man by its false examples and its appeal to his lower nature. For the sake of truth and justice something must be done to make art serve its proper role.

is well known. By the same token there is no doubt that his argument was somehow the measure of actual tendencies of popular Athenian thought. Part of the importance of the dialogue, therefore, is its perennial timeliness. The Athenian critics, condemning the immoral behaviors alleged of the gods in song and story, are allied with religious moralists of all ages. They were as dismayed as any proper Bostonian by the manner in which some artists treated society's most revered themes. Like some Soviet critic, Socrates and his friends insisted that art with contents inconsistent with their theories of the ideal state is seditious and needs be critically disparaged and politically suppressed. In this they were not only like the modern masters of socialist realism, but also akin to the bishops at the Second Council of Nicea in the eighth century.

At Nicea, the assembly decreed that churchmen, not painters, would decide what is to be painted and how. Painters would supply only the skills of their eyes and hands, working humbly in service of Mother Church. Similar dicta were established by the Council of Trent in 1563, becoming a powerful tool of the Inquisition for rallying artists to serve the counter-reformation. Even the most prestigious artists in the south — just as in Russia today — turned their talents into weapons of propaganda. The enemy then was the protestant and not the capitalist. Some artists served through faith, others through economic incentive. Others made what compromises were necessary with authority so as to retain some private avenue of free expression in their artistic enterprise.

These few examples, spanning two millenia, typify how art criticism historically has been predominantly if not wholly moralistic. Yet, the lyrical freedom of poetic inspiration has been no less universally asserted. Poetic souls eternally lament the constraints of moral criticism and insist upon the freedom of the artist to find his own object in his own way. In the nineteenth century this historic sentiment found expression in the phrase, "art for art's sake."[2]

The merits of that doctrine need not be debated at this juncture — no more than we ought now take sides with some theory which asserts that art is completely subject to moral principles. For us, such opposing views are merely facts cognate of the more fundamental behavioral fact that there are interactions between aesthetic and other experiences.

Art must be stripped of all that is bad by applying strict censorship. Only hymns to the gods and eulogies on the acts of great men will be tolerated or encouraged. All the rest — poets and poetry to the fore — must go. "For. . .if you allow the honeyed muse to enter. . .not law and reason of mankind. . .but pleasure and pain will be the rulers of our state." (Book 10, 607A) Artists must be disciplined and art channeled to serve the common good, lending an edifying influence abetting the goals of individual and social justice.

[2] The English equivalent to *"l'art pour l'art."* The phrase was coined by a French literary critic named Fourtoul in 1835 to characterize the theory of art expounded by the noted poet and novelist, Theophile Gautier, in the preface to his *Mademoiselle de Maupin*.

Practically no one today denies that interaction. Instead, everyone argues for the intimate connections between aesthetic and other behaviors. Everything about aesthetic is said to be bound up somehow with all the other aspects of our psychological life. But the consensus is more one of assertion than of real understanding, and in the end there is remarkably little agreement upon anything when one digs into the problems central to aesthetic theory. There is, however, a kind of historical consensus as to what the central problems are. No matter how little agreement there is about solutions, these problems can be identified as basic notions, or themes, perennially basic to the course of any inquiry. The aesthetic experience:

— Is similar to experience in general, yet is peculiarly distinctive. Disagreement arises in defining both the relatedness and the disjunction.

— Is universal, although controversy has centered on whether that universality applies only to aesthetic experience as such, or to the experience of particular aesthetic objects, forms, or media. In part derivative from probings into these questions, the aesthetic experience:

— Is thought to be contingent upon individual psychic potential, whether intrinsic or in situation, and upon assimilation by the individual of social and cultural materials which are conditional to enablement of the experience.

— Has relevance to morality, in that the aesthetic is affected by and itself affects moral experience. Debate ensues as to whether moral and aesthetic experience have an essential connection or not, and upon the theoretical consequences from the respective alternatives. This recognized interaction between the moral and the aesthetic historically has been the primary motive for inquiry into art and aesthetic.

— Reveals no determinate relationship between what is done and what is experienced which is sufficient to explain or account for the experience. That is, while there appears to be a necessary connection between the object of art and our aesthetic experience, the experience has qualities which we cannot explain in terms of that object. Recognition of these enigmatic qualities was the root source for the myth of the divine madness, and also for metaphysical approaches to aesthetic theory, approaches which dominated aesthetic inquiry until just recently.

— Is marked by feeling. Current thought generally holds that aesthetic is purely a matter of affect or at least essentially so. Older positions saw affect as incidental to and not central to the experience as such, and even as a negative influence lending distractions to the purity of the experience.

— Is endowed with meaning. The nature of this meaningfulness characteristic of the aesthetic experience is the subject of extensive debate, yet there is general agreement that aesthetic meaning is unique within the remaining scope of human experience, for it:

— Is non-logical, if not alogical, relative to the structures adopted by intellect for the construct and use of meaning. Because of that phenomenon of aesthetic meaning, however, tradition from ancient times sought to explain that meaningfulness in terms of some special function of intellect. This tradition was virtually abandoned in the nineteenth century in favor of notions of meaning operative solely upon the level of affect, thereby explaining why the experience defies intellectual encompassment and:

—Cannot be translated meaningfully into linguistic terms. At least the translation cannot occur without doing violence to and in effect destroying the particular significance entailed in the aesthetic experience. Because of that quality of meaning, the aesthetic experience related to art thus:

—Makes possible a unique mode of communication between men; that is, a language of feelings or emotion. There is disagreement about how such communication occurs, and as to its communicative fidelity. But because art is a means of communication, although only generically related to instrumental languages, aesthetic experience:

—Is to some degree learned similar to the way one learns other languages, and therefore is educable for obtaining heightened intensity, diversity, or accessibility of objective sources.

Taken in sum, the preceding assertions contain every idea crucial to shaping the history of aesthetic and the philosophy of art. Among them is found our own ideational focal point, the sense of there being a "story" in the experience of art. In modern aesthetic theory that felt quality of meaningfulness, or the sense of "story" in the experience of the thing of art, is called expression.

Theoretical emphasis on the notion of meaningfulness in the arts is hardly unique. The predominance of theories of expression among the most prestigious philosophies of this century cannot be ignored. The modern vogue of the idea, however, scarcely justifies more than scholarly interest in its various manifestations. What is truly provocative is the realization that the idea of meaningfulness in the experience of art, central to modern theories of expression, is as old as philosophy itself. It has been a notion persistent throughout the history of ideas. All that changed as the centuries rolled was the way in which that characteristic sense of meaning was described.

The ancients described the aesthetic experience as a kind of divine madness that makes possible a peculiar kind of knowing or awareness. There is, said the sages, a cognition of meaning in the experience. They explained such meaning as a product of the contemplative intellect viewing the eternal Ideas through the window of art. In the modern mind, that sense of meaningfulness became known as "expression," defined as an experience having a core of feeling possessing the character of idea.

What is remarkable, then, is how man's concept of aesthetic idea not only persisted from ancient times until now, but underwent a polar reversal.

Aesthetic idea lately became a matter of feeling, in contrast to earlier views which held it to be a product of intellectual process. Such a reversal suggests at least that the development of the idea of meaning in the arts deserves inquiry into its history. At most, it implies that the idea of meaning in the arts, persisting but changing, is the key to understanding aesthetic and the artistic enterprise.

Taking the key in hand, the next chapter examines the conventional meanings of "expression," and uses the evolution of those meanings as the vehicle for approaching the historical development of the idea of meaning in the arts.

Chapter 3

THE MEANINGS OF EXPRESSION

The story of the knight and his lady focuses upon an experience familiar to us all. The tale thus draws upon our common experiences to clarify for each of us the idea of expression as the felt meaningfulness that comes of our encounters with things of art. Those familiar with the literature of aesthetics, however, recognize that this one notion fails to explain all uses of the word, "expression." There are two other meanings for the word, each distinct from the idea of expression as feeling with a quality of meaning.

Expression also applies to the artistic act, the activity of expressing. Another usage permits "expression" to signify the character of that activity, usually as defined by the qualities of the product of that activity, the object that art is to others. In this instance, "expression" refers neither to the activity of art as such, nor to the felt significance resulting from the experience of that activity. Rather, it refers to aspects of the personality of the artist, to essential qualities of human nature, or to idealized concepts of the human condition in the world, that underlie and are responsible for the individualized form of a particular instance of art. Expression in this sense means those features of the activity of art which are symptomatic of the character of the artist in particular or of the nature of man in general.

Those three meanings, different as they are, have an implicit union in the idea of expression as it originated in common parlance. "Expression," that is, contains the idea of the representation of something else* and that idea is essential to each of the three meanings of expression, which we can briefly restate as: (1) the activity that is expressive; (2) the signification in or by the act of the root sources or modifiers of the activity; and (3) the subjective, felt con-

---

* This idea is intrinsic also to the meanings of "expressionism" in the literature of art (as differentiated from the literature of aesthetics). Diverse artistic tendencies fall under the single term, expressionism, only because they share the premise that art is "non-imitative" of things. Instead, art is "expressive," meaning representational. Art is said to represent not things, but intangibles such as feelings, emotions, or ideas; or it constructs "representational images" or the "expressive character" of things, or spiritual essences, and so on.

sequence of the activity. In terms of the root meaning of expression, then the first derivative meaning may be said to refer to the act of representing, the second to what is represented, and the third to the consequence of the representation as an affective experience.

The first meaning is implicit in or necessary to being able to talk about either the second or third meanings. The third meaning, the subject of our fairy tale, is of fairly recent origin. The second meaning is ancient and has had a long and powerful influence upon the development of aesthetic theory. As to what is signified, or represented, by expression understood in that second term, philosophical opinion has changed throughout the centuries. Older thought held that art expresses the divine forms of being and the truths of God. Today art is said to express the nature of man. Midway between these notions, we find Winckelmann asserting that while art rests on the beauty resident in the eternal forms, this "pure beauty" occurs in "a state of action and of passion, which we comprehend in art under the term *expression*."[1]. Among the moderns we find Walter Pater, who described expression as "The impress of a personal quality, a profound expressiveness. . . . by which is meant some subtler sense of originality—the seal on a man's work of what is most inward and peculiar in his moods, and manner of apprehension.[2]

Winckelmann does not represent the transitional phase between old and new ideas of expression. This is true in part because he held that expression, no less than form, is resident in the beautiful object, and thus is feeling represented rather than feeling experienced. In part, it is true because he believed that the representation of the passions detracted from the pure beauty of form. Indeed, the ideal expression is "decorum," a condition where one finds "no trace of emotion." Beauty is undisturbed by feeling.

The transition to the humanistic notion of expression as the representation of human nature appears to stem from the work of the fifteenth century Florentine, Marcilio Ficino. An avowed Platonist, viewing the thoughts of man as conceptions in the human mind of the Divine Thought that creates the world, Ficino yet saw art to represent not Divine Thought, but the limited spiritual achievements that are man's. "In pictures and buildings," he wrote, "the intention and the judgement of the artist shine forth. The disposition and, as it were, the figure of his soul can be seen in them. Thus the soul represents itself in these works, as the face of a man looking in a mirror represents itself in the mirror."[3]

Whether expression is of divine or human nature, of eternal truths or the finite virtues of a man's soul, these notions have a single common denomin-

---

[1] *Writings on Art*, Winckelmann, p 119.
[2] *The Renaissance*, p 59.
[3] *The Philosophy of Marcilio Ficino*, P.O. Kristeller, p 119.

ator. To say that art reveals the image of a man's soul or, as Pater phrased it, "what is most inward and peculiar in his moods," implicitly asserts that central to the idea of expression is the notion of meaning. In other words, because there is expression, art means more than what it literally "says" or physically "is." The idea of meaningfulness, central to the third meaning of expression, is therefore no modern invention of thought. It has origins older than the *Dialogues*, where the "meaning" in art was dealt with as a very real question, albeit in terms of intellect.

Perhaps the modern notion of expression really began with Aristotle, since the aesthetic union of meaning and feeling was first recognized by him. Aristotle, that is, clearly understood that meaning associated with feeling is the essential ingredient of the experience of tragedy. That is not to say he developed the equivalent to a modern theory of expression, for he did not. Yet, he did make the understanding of meaning a crucial factor in the experience characterizing the dramatic art of tragedy, insisting upon the necessary function of meaning as the source of the essential feelings of fear and pity.

The Aristotelian emphasis upon the necessary appeal of art to the understanding for the evocation of feeling is generally unappreciated by the historians and text writers. Yet, in formulating that idea, Aristotle provided the initial assertion of the bond between intellect and affect in aesthetic experience. Unfortunately, the long dominant Platonistic tradition, literally following the Socratic example, condemned or at best discounted the importance of the "base influence" of affect and separated thought from feeling in the appreciation of art.

The essence of art, for Platonism, became the function of art as a vehicle for the contemplative intellect to gain access to and meditate upon the eternal Ideas. Art theory was dominated by variations upon that theme for two thousand years. Artists, when they thought about their work, followed after the philosophers. No matter what artists were actually doing to satisfy the affective tastes of their public, their notions of art were pinned to the coattails of systematic philosophy. The so-called Classical Tradition of art, with its emphasis upon form and edifying content, had no other source than man's preoccupation for more than two millenia with metaphysical Ideas and moral imperatives intrinsic to the rational order of being.

That people happened to enjoy the feelings associated with the experience of art was never ignored. There was no doubt of it, although feelings were at best deemed only incidental to the experience. At worst they had to be purged because they interfere with the true ideational essence of aesthetic. The central appeal of art is to intellect alone. Meaning in art is rooted in the contemplative intellect and shorn of affect.

Given that uncontested theoretical foundation of aesthetic upon intellectual meaning, the prevailing concepts of art could not fail to become mere addenda to moral and metaphysical principles. No real split was postulated between aesthetic and intellectual knowing. There was but an operational distinction between means of knowing, both of them intellectual. The truths of art therefore could be no different in kind from the truths of logic or reason. Furthermore, since both Platonist and Aristotelian asserted the fundamental unity of truth, goodness, and beauty in being, then the essential relevance of metaphysical principles, moral precepts, and logical truths to the meaningfulness and value of art is hardly unexpected. Expression in the arts therefore could only be a matter of the intellectual apprehension of truths. The idea of expression as affective meaning became possible only after the Romantic break away from the classical philosophies of form. As long as expression in art was imitation of divine Ideas, whether Platonic or Christian or Transcendentalist, little attention could be focused on that lower part of the soul where feeling resides.

The iconoclastic materialism of Francis Bacon is probably the germinal source of the nuances of thought that became the idea of expression as felt meaningfulness. At the beginning of the seventeenth century, Bacon set the temper and direction of English thought forever after, and took the first step in breaking with the old idea that intellectual awareness of idea is central to the experience of artistic meaningfulness. That step involved a change in the concept of the mind and its objects, although it did not revise the notion that the function of intellect is at the root of meaningfulness in our experiences of art.

Bacon rejected the idea that the meaningfulness characteristic of art stems from contemplation of the divine forms. It originates rather in the data of the senses, just as all knowledge does, and is a product of the processes of mind. In Bacon's description, the imagination, working with the materials of sense, derives the principles of reason from the realm of particulars. The imagination, creative and poetic in nature, is the true source of all knowledge. It releases the mind from bondage to particulars so that it may discover the airy realm of intellect.

Through an analysis of fable, Bacon attempted to demonstrate his thesis that intellectual meanings are the product of the poetic imagination.[4] Unfortunately, his concept of aesthetic meaning was given little serious notice in English philosophy, which practically ignored the theory of art for more than a century thereafter. The problems of the imagination raised by Bacon were matters of continuing philosophical importance, but primarily if not solely in

---

[4] Consult Anderson's *The Philosophy of Francis Bacon*, p 56 ff, for an excellent analysis of Bacon's interpretations of the fables.

terms of the issues of knowing and being, compared to which problems of art are rather paltry indeed. Yet, this is hardly surprising once we grasp the spirit of the times. Men were able suddenly to flex new intellectual muscles provided by the concepts and methods of the new science. In their enthusiasm for searching out "real" truths made accessible to understanding by their new science, they came to regard the products of art as inconsequential in comparison, "only fictions." As Basil Willey documented in excellent detail in his study, *The Seventeenth Century Background*, this milieu of the science enthusiast engendered even a current of antagonism toward the affective excesses of art in general and poetry in particular. He quoted from the work of Thomas Sprat, a savant of the period, who wrote that art is "in open defiance against Reason: Professing not to hold much correspondence with that; but with its Slaves, the Passions; they give the mind a motion too changeable, and bewitching, to consist with right practise."[5]

Continental philosophy at the time showed equally scant concern for art and aesthetics, sharing the English opinion that problems of art were not problems of philosophy proper or of the new science. That is not to say that questions of art were not discussed in learned circles, for they most certainly were, and often with warmth and favorable sentiments. For theoretical purposes, however, the period almost slavishly accepted the Renaissance restatements of classical authority, albeit with an increased Aristotelian temper that resulted in the neoclassical concern for defining "rules" for art. See, for example, Philip Sidney's *An Apology for Poetry*, posthumously published in 1595, and Corneille's *Discourses*, appearing circa 1660. But it was more than the Aristotelian penchant for "rules" and the authority of the ancients that produced the neoclassical temper. It came out of the character of the age itself, where the idea of Nature, expressed in the new science, became the dominant motif in the workings of the mind of Western Man. Newton had shown how all the world operates in accord with fixed laws. God became the maker of natural laws, the cosmic mechanic. In such terms science could be, as Bacon phrased it, the study of God's Works. Religion, by the same token, could become the study of God's Words.

In the initial phase of the new age of science, then, there arose a mood of optimism about the absolute knowability of virtually all things pertaining to the natural realm. In this intellectual milieu, art could be considered to be subject to rules no less stringent than those applying to the rest of the world, and no less a part of nature. And since knowledge of Nature was shown by Newtonian science to be accessible to reason and good sense, then the rules of art must be equally accessible to human understanding. Further, since great

---

[5]*Op. Cit.*, p 212.

art has existed in all ages, such art must partake of the natural rules applying to art. One thus could not doubt that the ancient sages (e.g., Aristotle) must have achieved a measure of understanding of those rules. And such is the argument of Dryden in 1677 in his *Apology for Heroic Poetry and Poetic Licence*. Given our capacity for reason and good sense, and aided by the wisdom of Aristotle and other wise men of old, we can examine the great works of art that have delighted all ages and discover the rules for their creation. The key rule, in his estimation, is that all are imitations of Nature. Such imitation, however, is hardly realism as we understand the term. Rather it is "heroic imitation," where aesthetic decorum and the appearance of rational values and edifying character are paramount qualities.

The demonstrated power of analytical science, then, is seen to have spawned a radical faith in reason that was expressed in the neoclassical interpretation of the experience of art. But analysis is only one phase of the new science, no matter its tremendous power. The observational and inventive aspects of that science were merely slower to be understood in terms of their overall implications, both methodologically and relative to their perceptual and imaginative underpinnings. And these provided the fundamental issues for John Locke and British empirical philosophy thereafter. But the trace of history that we seek lies elsewhere.

At about the turn into the eighteenth century, the European intellectual scene was marked by a growing popular interest in sense perception and feelings. It appeared first in England. It arose as a response to the issues raised by the new psychology derived from the viewpoints of empirical philosophy and its specialized concern for matters of sense perception and imagination. In effect, the new attention given to matters of sense allowed a new appreciation of — or perhaps better, a conscious awakening to — the role of feelings, both sensuous and imaginative, in the experience of art. The vulgar taste for affective charm, always present in folk tales and melodies, became respectable among cultural aristocrats. Within a half century this new awareness led to the vogue of the sentimental novel, with the Gothic novel achieving its peak of popularity. Romantic poetry blossomed and the gay colors and sentimental moods of such painters as Romney and Reynolds and Gainsborough won the hearts and pocketbooks of the aristocracy.

The most significant consequence of the new awareness of feeling was the development of the psychological approach to art theory, a development that occurred in England outside the mainstream of philosophy. Spokesman and principal innovator of this new approach was Joseph Addison, notably in his essays on *The Pleasures of Imagination*. In that series, appearing in 1712, Addison made what is fundamentally a psychological analysis of the art experience, the first such analysis to be written in terms typical of a modern

psychology. We find there the assertion that the pleasure obtained in the experience of art is a legitimate end in itself, a pleasure that stems principally
from the imaginative activity of the mind.

While Addison's theories in particular and the trend of English empirical
thought in general brought the "pleasures of imagination" more and more into discussions of art, there was hardly any rush to incorporate it into the
philosophical mainstream or to abandon the older principles drawn from
classical authority. David Hume, nearly fifty years later, hardly more than
dabbled in the problems of art, and his meager essays on the subject are more
important because of his reputation than for their contributions to the field.
Indeed, a whole century after Addison was needed to accomplish the change.
In the meanwhile, the new viewpoint came more to be accommodated with
the old rather than taking its place. Particularly illuminating in this regard are
Joshua Reynolds' *Discourses on Art,* spanning the years from 1769 to 1790.

In the early discourses, the classical temper thoroughly dominates. In
Discourse IV Reynolds describes the "presiding principle" which regulates
every part of Art as "General Ideas," out of which comes perfect form, which
in turn "gives what is called the *grand* style."[6] Excellence of form constitutes
both beauty and expression. That is, beauty *and* expression are understood as
qualities of the objective form appealing to the mind through its conceptions
of "general ideas."

By 1776, in *Discourse VII,* the notions of an affective appeal based on both
imaginative and sensuous qualities of the experience appeared in his theories.
Still, Reynolds felt obliged to reassert that the guiding principle of his
discourses was that art "is not the industry of the *hands,* but of the mind,"[7]
since good taste by nature is "rational and systematic"[8] and "The natural ap-
petite or taste of the human mind is for *Truth.*"[9]

While Reynolds thus restates his allegiance to the classical temper, he then
goes on to instruct that the appeal of art to the rational aspect of the mind
through the "general ideas" is but the chief and not the sole basis for the effects
of art. Art also appeals "to the imagination and the passions."[10] Yet, these are
not regarded as truly separate bases for appeal, since each in its own way is an
appeal to the mind. Specifically, each has "an appeal to common sense
deciding upon the common feelings of mankind."[11]

The crucial theoretical matter here is that while Reynolds at this point in his

---

[6]*Op. Cit.,* p 57.
[7]*Ibid.,* p 117.
[8]*Ibid.,* p 118.
[9]*Ibid.,* p 122.
[10]*Ibid.,* p 131.
[11]*Ibid.,* p 131.

life still believed in "the reality of a standard of taste, as well as in corporeal beauty," taste came to have its basis in "the uniformity of sentiments among mankind."[12] That is, in common "affections" of the mind, feelings if you will, stemming from the pleasures of sense and of imagination.

The novel preoccupation of the English with the affective pleasurableness of art was slow to attract attention on the continent, where rationalism reigned. The continent, however, was the scene of the next great conceptual advance, the accomplishment of the young Alexander Baumgarten.

A singular misfortune in the course of philosophy is that the achievements of Baumgarten are obscured by the historical proximity of Immanuel Kant, his pupil and lifelong admirer, and Christian Wolff, his teacher. In the histories, Baumgarten is awarded brief mention as the chief heir to Wolffian rationalism and the ancestral inspiration of Kant's early philosophy. More comprehensive texts also remark that Baumgarten coined the term "aesthetic" and invented a new branch of philosophy, "aesthetics." Little or nothing is usually said of Baumgarten's ideas on aesthetics or any other subject, since Wolff had made the final comprehensive statement of the older German rationalism for which Baumgarten was in his time the principal caretaker, and Kant took prestigious command of the new field of philosophy invented by Baumgarten. Kant analytically defined the problems and limits of aesthetics within the structure of a philosophical system that as an edifice of thought rivals the grand perspectives of Aristotle and Acquinas.

Despite the central position awarded to aesthetic in the Kantian philosophy, the influence of Kant upon the advancement of aesthetic theory probably resulted in more harm than benefit. He left philosophers wrestling with too many of the wrong problems, and his systematic intellectualizing obscured the greater achievements of Baumgarten.

Because Kant is so tremendous a presence, historians are unable to grasp that Baumgarten was probably the first man to understand the experience of art in terms of feeling having the quality of idea, and the first philosopher since Aristotle to give affect its honest due in the theory of art. In his initial treatise on aesthetic, published in 1735, Baumgarten was quite apologetic about the seriousness he awarded his subject. This is explained by the historical context. Wolff deemed the subject beneath the dignity of

---

[12]*Ibid.*, p 141. It is interesting here to note how the empirical concern for the imaginative faculty dating from Bacon, the description of the influence of the sublime that is found in Addison's essays, and Reynolds' view of a standard of taste based upon "common sense" uniformly present in the minds of men, are all themes that became central to the Kantian analysis. The broad influence of Addison, Hume, and Reynolds on the continent indicates that these themes were, in the latter half of the eighteenth century, commonplace notions literally begging for an integrating analysis achieved by Kant.

philosophy, and Baumgarten was but a precocious 21-year-old contesting the opinion of a man who then dominated German philosophy as prestigiously as Kant would just fifty years later.

The young Baumgarten naturally followed his teacher's general philosophy and came to the problem of aesthetic from the side of Wolffian psychology. He saw that the experience of art involved something more than the "confused knowledge" Wolff attributed to sense perception. To explain it, Baumgarten devised his notion of the "art of beautiful thinking." This idea contains the first explicit recognition that in the awareness of feeling associated with a work of art there is a quality of idea, which although it is nondiscursive and thus not intellectual is more than a matter of raw feeling. It is feeling with order and a unity which give the impression of a kind of knowledge and leave us with the conviction of truth. Though the character of the experience is one of feeling, Baumgarten attributed the pervasive quality of idea to a special kind of thinking, "beautiful thinking."

Descartes and Leibniz had contrasted the clear and distinct ideas of reason with the dark and confused ideas of sense, a distinction thereafter common to the tradition of German rationalism and thus central to the psychology of Christian Wolff. Baumgarten followed Wolff in practically all details of his philosophy, but in his experience of art he found reason to believe that the traditional distinction did not accurately describe the ways and nature of all knowing and knowledge. He instead suggested that out of the experience of art there comes a kind of knowing, "beautiful knowledge," that is as true and as reliable as rational knowledge. It is knowledge rooted in dark and confused ideas of the senses, made clear through "sensitive representations" that are not merely "sensual" but are connected with feeling. He proposed, in effect, another kind of knowledge: clear and confused ideas, having a sense of the clarity natural to rational knowing, yet indistinct and thus unable to be framed in the precise logical sense that rational knowings may achieve.

In his 1735 essay, *Meditationes Philosophicae de Nonullis ad Poema Pertimentibus*, Baumgarten undertook an analysis of poetry to show how the clarity of ideas made possible through art is a function of the number of clear ideas incorporated into the form of the work. Art thus achieves an "extensive clarity" that sense experience cannot obtain in nature. Indeed, he described poetry as the technique of "sensate discourse." While logic may describe the language of the intellect, "The perfect language of sense is poetry."[13] For only in the communicative vehicle of a poem are the clear but confused ideas of sense linked into a form, or structure, that allows one to achieve "sensory cognition" of truth.

---

[13]*Op. Cit.*, para 9.

What Baumgarten devised in 1735, then, was a concept of another avenue to knowledge, an avenue based upon sense perception that through the function of art led to achievement of knowledge no less certainly than did reason. A year later, in 1736, J. J. Bodmer, in his *Correspondence on The Nature of Poetical Taste*, developed a similar idea, but essentially with less innovation of thought than that of Baumgarten. Bodmer, that is, remained fully allied with the tradition of German rationalism, and depreciated the fundamental importance of feeling in the art experience. Feeling in the experience of art, according to Bodmer, is a kind of epiphenomenon of no actual import. The seat of the experience and of all the powers we call art is the faculty of imagination. His importance to this study is that he combined the notion of the imaginative basis for the art experience with the enthusiasm for man's ability to determine the nature of things by their natural laws. He devised a notion of a "logic of the imagination" separate from that of reason, a logic with its own rules or laws that lie at the root of whatever is constant or standard in the experience of art.

Baumgarten, already thrust in the direction of such a notion by his analysis of poetry, seized upon this idea of a logic of art and turned it to his own ends. Out of it came the idea of a new kind of logic, not a logic of reason or of imagination, but of the perfections of sense achieved through the function of art. For the remainder of his life his major project became the precise analysis of the terms and conditions of this new logic that he called "aesthetics." Yet, his major work, *Aesthetica*, was never completed. The work of G. F. Meier and other pupils, however, indicates that the principal features of his thought are available in the two volumes that he did finish prior to his death.

In *Aesthetica*, we find aesthetic to be neither a study of works of art nor a technique for determination of standards of taste; nor is it a psychology, as alleged by some text writers. Rather, Baumgarten saw aesthetics as a field of philosophy distinguished by an unique methodology of knowing. In such terms, aesthetic and logic were considered as companion fields, each based on its own methodology, which together comprise the science of "gnoseology," the theory of knowledge.

Aesthetic has principles of order peculiar to itself, as perceptual cognition. Aesthetics is the science through which we may understand those principles. Indeed, they are approachable only through the method of aesthetics. While logic determines the rules for clear ideas accessible through the superior part of the faculty of knowledge, intellect; aesthetics establishes the rules for the clarification of the darkest ideas approached through the inferior part of the faculty of knowledge, sensation and perception, via the function of art. Through art, sensations and perceptions, ordinarily and by nature confused, become clear (but never distinct as in intellectual cognition) and produce a kind of cognition different from but no less valid than that produced by logic.

Aesthetic experience, then, is said to have a logic of its own, and aesthetics is the study of perfections of that logic, which constitute beauty. Aesthetics determines the rules of the logic of beautiful ideas, just as classical logic deals with the rules applying to rational ideas. To know the rules is to know truth and beauty. Thus he asserted, "The goal of aesthetics is the perfection of sensory cognition as such. And this is beauty."[14]

In the philosophy of Leibniz, the property of Monads known to intellect as the perfection of ideas, or truth, is perceived by the confused method of our senses as beauty. Baumgarten carried the essence of this notion forward to achieve a true innovation of thought. He developed the idea of aesthetics as a new conception of knowing. He connected the "sensitive representations" of art not merely to the inferior faculty of sensation, the "sensual" part of knowing, but also and primarily to feelings, which in his psychology was a function of the faculty of will. [15] This remarkable achievement was little understood and was effectively lost as the Kantian analyses consigned Wolffian rationalism to the garbage heap. Baumgarten's sole lasting influence became that he made inquiry into art and aesthetics philosophically respectable. His main contribution – a basis for considering the significance of feeling in the experience of art – bore fruit only outside the mainstream of philosophy.

Thus it was that by the middle of the eighteenth century the way had been opened, principally by Addison in England and Baumgarten in Germany, for art and aesthetics to be dealt with in romantic terms related to feeling as opposed to the classical terms centered on intellect. Upon that scene appeared Immanual Kant and Gotthold E. Lessing. Kant, from his ivory tower, rendered an overwhelming analysis of aesthetic experience. Lessing, more polemicist than analyst, rubbed elbows with the world while fashioning an impact upon the arts and aesthetics no less significant than Kant's. Kant is the father of modern philosophy. Lessing is the originator of modern art criticism in general and the romantic tradition in particular. Between them they wrought a revolution in the history of philosophy, art, and public taste, a feat accomplished in the span of their lifetimes (Kant: 1724-1804; Lessing: 1729-1781). Their work became the foundation for practically all subsequent contributions to the philosophy of art and aesthetics.

---

[14]*Aesthetica*, para. 14.

[15] Tying aesthetics to feeling, and thus to the will, may have been the primary cause of Baumgarten's theories virtually to die with him. For Kant's analysis emphasized the disinterestedness of the experience, allowing separation of the principles of aesthetics from feeling and the faculty of will, letting it reside entirely in the "higher faculty of cognition," specifically as a "reflective judgment."

Lessing and Kant were born into the spiritual age of rationalism in which the Newtonian world view was becoming a powerful instrument of the human mind. Kant, a coldly calculating logical machine, worked apart from the bustle of the world. Lessing was a fiery polemicist elbowing his way through the theaters and publishing houses, ever attacking the theories of his contemporaries.

Kant found himself in the Newtonian universe and, discerning its paradoxical implications for a theory of human knowledge, set about to deduce how it is possible for men to know truth, be moral, and have aesthetic interests. Lessing found himself in a work-a-day world and took knowledge for granted. He arrived at his ideas not from axioms derived by pure reason, but from the situation of contemporary art and critical theory. Kant, for all his innovations, drew his aesthetic from the main body of his philosophy. Lessing drew his from the theater and the gallery.

From an historical point of view, Lessing was something new and different as a thinker. He had no metaphysical axe to grind, no moral point of view with which his aesthetics must conform. Here was a man examining art and aesthetic on their own terms. As such Lessing was more a revolutionary than Kant. Lessing's approach paved the way for aesthetics to divest itself of metaphysical axioms and be freed from moral imperatives. Problems of aesthetics thenceforth could be resolved in terms of the feelings men have in the experience of art instead of in terms of the classical standards of taste referenced to intellectual appeal.

In the *Laocoon*, Lessing maintained that the aim of art is pleasure. Art achieves this by serving as a catalyst for the emotions. Art produces emotional effects which are pleasing. As for the old "laws" of beauty imposed by classical criticism, "All their rules can at most produce nothing but pedantic twaddle."[16] Art is free of all rules except what is natural for art itself as a means for producing pleasure.

Such notions opened the door for the later doctrine of "art for art's sake," a theory Lessing himself did not advocate. Yet, it is but a small step beyond his own concern for art on its own terms alone, free from all others. For that insistence, Lessing's aesthetics have been accused of being "monadic,"[17] or completely divorced from all other fields of human thought. But the accusation mistakes the facts. In the *Hamburg Dramaturgy*, Lessing admits the influence of moral considerations, but only as a factor intrinsic to the nature of art and the artist. That is, both art and the artist possess an inherent moral nature. Pleasure is unattainable if that nature is violated; therefore if pleasure, the

---

[16]Lessing; H.B. Garland, p 58.
[17]Lessing's Dramatic Theory, J.G. Robertson.

goal of art, is to be achieved, an essential morality must be maintained. That is not to say that art must be morally didactic or that there are moral rules of content which must be adhered to. There is but one ultimate rule, and that is that art must produce pleasure.

The paradox of Lessing's argument is that while his fundamental position is that art must strive only to produce pleasure, the artist may be criticised not in terms of his achievement of that goal but only in terms of the manner in which he utilized his medium and subject matter. Such a position disallows criticism in terms of taste, although Lessing was reluctant to admit it. Yet taste, he believed, is a matter of feeling, and feeling is an inadequate basis for critical judgement. Feelings are simply too complex and adventitious. Feelings work together in such infinite variety that no one can say just how anything will affect us at any time. So, if we try to evaluate art in terms of feelings, we will immediately discover exceptions to every rule, leaving us with no objective and immutable standards for criticism. For that, Lessing turned away from feeling and toward the thing of art. He formulated rules of proportion and subject peculiar to the various media. Those rules, he held, are universal rules which provide the only legitimate bases for criticism.

Kant contemplated this same problem of private aesthetic taste versus objective standards for public criticism and found in it one of his famous antinomies. According to the argument producing the antinomy of taste, we do but we cannot dispute about taste. We argue because aesthetic judgement is a subjective matter. The experience of art is private. We ought not argue because the experience of art is universal and tends to be associated with the same objective things, thereby implying a universality of taste.

In resolving the antinomy, Kant did not turn to the objective artifact and explain the matter in terms of principles of being related to the object. Neither did he find the answer in our experience of the object as such; that is, sensuously. Instead, he resolved the antinomy in terms of the fundamental nature of the mind; that is, on the basis of the *a priori* forms of perception and conditions of reflection.

This orientation of Kantian thought involved a significant departure from the psychology of Baumgarten, a change in ideational direction best revealed in Kant's *First Introduction to The Critique of Judgment*.[18] There, in paragraph VIII, he defined the objective of his *Critique* as an analytical understanding of how beauty, and thus aesthetic, is not a quality of an object but rather an experience of a subject. He disengages himself from Baum-

---

[18]   The *First Introduction,* discarded by Kant as "too long," is remarkably clear and readable compared with the *Critique* itself, or even the "second introduction" that accompanies it. Scholars have long noted the many evidences of the ease and clarity of Kant's style when he chose to write for the sake of easy general access to his ideas by an intellectual audience. The

garten's position at the outset by arguing that since beauty is not the quality of an object, beauty cannot be related to sensuous knowledge. Therefore, he concludes, "Because all determinations of feeling are of purely subjective significance, there can by no scientific aesthetic of feeling [as Baumgarten insisted he had identified], as there is an aesthetic of the faculty of knowledge." This aesthetic is "transcendental" and has "the form of a science pertaining to the cognitive faculty."[19].

Divorced from both objects and sensuous knowledge, aesthetic judgments thus are a priori in nature; not conceptual, but related to a feeling brought about by the harmonious interplay of the judgment's two cognitive faculties: imagination and understanding. But while he admits that feeling of harmony in the aesthetic experience, he will not award it a place of interest to aesthetics. Equally he admits the aesthetic relevance of sensuous pleasures, but the analytical fact he establishes is that "only aesthetic judgments of reflection are. . .based on essential principles of judgment."[20] In other words, feelings have no theoretical significance to aesthetics. Aesthetic judgment, by reason of its principles, belongs to the higher faculty of cognition. It is a "reflective judgment." As such it is not based on feeling but has its roots in the a priori conditions of reflection. And with that, Kant had effectively eliminated Baumgarten's theory of aesthetic as beautiful thinking and aesthetics as the science of beautiful knowledge from further consideration by philosophy. Aesthetics literally never quite recovered from Kant, who tied it so convincingly to the conditions of reflection.

Kant argues that since all minds are regulated by the same a priori conditions, then if one person perceives a thing as beautiful, then everyone must. Obviously, they do not. Since they do not, then the aesthetic sense of some people is more obtuse than it is for others. By the same token, the feeling of beauty may be enough for us to warrant that a thing is beautiful, but the very

---

scholarly consensus has it that the labored intricacies of his *Critiques* were a product of a stylized method intending philosophical clarity. But that is a half-truth. Philosophers typically seek clarity of thought in their communication. Closer to the mark of understanding the basis for the Kantian style of philosophical writing is the idea that Kant was in effect following the instruction of Baumgarten. Kant, the pupil, admired Baumgarten. All his life, Kant taught that Baumgarten was the greatest metaphysician of his time, and used Baumgarten's texts in his own classes. Those texts, so familiar to Kant and the font of his own early philosophy and the foil of his analytical departures into a philosophy distinctively his own, possess the same ponderous formalities of structure, pompousness of style, and intricate convolutions of dialetic that characterize the Kantian *Critique*. It appears that Baumgarten, in Kant's estimation, had established the model of philosophical presentation of argument leading to clear and distinct ideas.

[19]*Op Cit.*, p 26.
[20]*Ibid.*, p 29.

subjectivity of feeling disallows that judgment so based can be proved to the satisfaction of others. Only if one person educates the taste of the other to be like his own will there be agreement, and that agreement will be practically evident as a matter of feeling. So, in the final analysis, practical taste is a subjective matter of feeling, but it has no theoretical relevance to aesthetic theory. Theoretically and ideally, taste is a reflective judgment liable to objective criticism based on universal standards.

The determination of an analytical basis for such objective standards was accomplished by a devious, complicated argument motivated by Kant's overpowering sense of duty. He found that the aesthetic sense is a "faculty for judging the sensible illustration of moral ideas." The critical fundament of aesthetic therefore was established at the heart of and connected intimately with his entire system of philosophy. That foundation for aesthetic was thus made moral and ideational, and "The true propaedeutic for the foundation of taste is the development of moral Ideas and the culture of the moral feeling; because it is only when sensibility is brought into agreement with this that genuine taste can assume a definite, invariable form."[21]

In terms of Kantian psychology, aesthetic ideas are images of the mind which cannot be symbolized and dealt with by reason. Those ideas function, none the less, in accord with the fundamental processes of mind. That is why aesthetic has the quality of idea. It has its source in the pleasures of imagination. Aesthetic ideas are moral ideas imbued with sensuous qualities by the imaginative process.

That complicated description led Bosanquet to remark that only because of the influence of Kant could later thinkers recognize that "the aesthetic consciousness is...in its positive essence...the meeting point of sense and reason."[22] Yet that exact position had been pioneered by Bacon two hundred years earlier. He, too, had located aesthetic consciousness in the imagination, which he saw as the bridge between sense and reason. His viewpoint differed radically from that of Kant, however, because of his empiricism. Bacon saw the direction of meaning proceeding from sense to reason through imagination. Kant reversed the direction. Aesthetic ideas became the ideas of reason imaginatively cast as sensuous form.

Kant deservedly won the reputation of having set the course for and defined the problems of modern philosophy. How different the history of aesthetics might have been had Kantian theory focused upon the personal, free, affective quality that he recognized in the experience one has of art. Instead, he hung that experience on one horn of a fabricated enigma called an antinomy, and developed a theory of taste which ignored that experience because of its willy-

[21]*Critique of Judgment*, p 202.
[22]*A History of Aesthetic*, p 265.

nilly unpredictability, its defiance of objective analysis, and its *a posteriori* logical relationship to the construction of moral ideas by the mind.

Under hard-eyed scrutiny, the aesthetic antinomy has the appearance of being manufactured, a logical convenience, a handy fellow of his other antinomies, a dubious rationalization of his moral hangups. Exhaustive as the Kantian analysis was, the fact remains that it was a step backward from the advance accomplished by Baumgarten. Kant simply failed to comprehend the notion of feeling possessing the character of meaningfulness in its own right. Rather, Kant retreated to a solution consistent with the traditional mood dominant since ancient times. He joined Socrates – and Heraclitus before him, for that matter – in asserting that the taste of *hoi polloi* is an unfit critical standard. Genuine taste, Kant said, is marked by cultured morality. A true aesthetic is possible only by virtue of the educated sensibilities and moral awareness achieved by the cultural aristocrat. Since feelings are essentially uneducable and common to all, then feeling is incidental to the experience, which is centered upon rational idea. Specifically, aesthetic is the product of rational idea having moral qualifications enabling one to have pleasures of the imagination.

The Kantian version of the aesthetic was published late (1790) among his ideas as he filled out his "system" of thought by an analytical adventure into moral philosophy on the basis of his earlier critiques. There is evidence, however, that the position of aesthetic in his general philosophy had been worked out in preliminary form about two decades earlier when he initially established his philosophical goals; i.e., to discern how freedom, moral responsibility, and value judgments are possible in the deterministic universe revealed by Newtonian science.

During the earlier time frame, unknown to Kant, the modern concept of aesthetic meaning took shape outside the philosophical mainstream then defined by Wolffian rationalism as most eminently interpreted by the then late A. G. Baumgarten. Bosanquet tells us that the actual invention of the idea is attributable to Goethe. He traces Goethe's inspiration in turn to the work of Winckelmann, who was passionately admired by the young Goethe. Bosanquet, however, erred because he never did understand Baumgarten or the influence of Baumgarten on Goethe.

Ernst Cassirir, in his essay on Goethe and Kant,[23] shows that Goethe was of a temperament and intellectual orientation that literally barred him not only from sympathy with the prevailing philosophical currents and Kantian philosophy in particular but also prevented Goethe from even understanding what that philosophy and its problems were all about. Bosanquet saw some-

---

[23]*Rousseau, Kant, and Goethe*, p 63.

thing of this same tendency, and exactly that tendency was probably responsible for Goethe finding something in Baumgarten that philosophers were too
blind to see. For Bosanquet (and anyone else who has studied Goethe)
recognizes that he was, in his youth, as rapt a student of Baumgarten, and in
effect followed Baumgarten in the direction rejected by Kant. Goethe's innovation, in other words, was as directly the product of his fascination with the
novel aspects of Baumgarten's aesthetics as with the rather confused
classicalism of Winckelmann's analyses of art.

Winckelman used the term "expression" with our second meaning; that is,
as a signification embodied by the activity of art in the object itself representative of human nature. This expression, however, he found to be, by nature,
"hostile" to beauty because it confuses the perfection of form that constitutes
beauty. Expression, that is, disturbs the "repose" of the pure form of beauty.
As he explained it, "Expression in art . . . is the imitation of the acting and suf-
fering condition of our soul and body, of passions as well as of actions; in the
widest sense it includes our action itself, in a narrower sense, merely the play of
feature and gesture which accompanies the action. It is hostile to beauty,
because it changes the bodily form in which beauty resides."[24] Yet, he would
not for that reason recommend the banishment of expression from the arts,
because "Beauty without expression would be characterless, expression
without beauty unpleasant."[25] In other words, Winckelmann's study of the
great art of the world had led him to conclude the classical theory of objective
beauty embodied in a kind of perfection of form appealing to the intellect was
not enough to differentiate great works of art or even that which deserved the
term of "art." Rather, he saw the need to identify the passionate character of
the experience of art, a character that stemmed from its expression of the passions of the human soul and body.

That notion of the necessary passionate *character* of the beautiful in art is
the alleged seed which bore fruit in the mind of Goethe. Bosanquet relates
how, in 1773, a small book appeared which contained a piece by Goethe on
Gothic architecture. That obscure little work, according to Bosanquet, contained "perhaps the profoundest aesthetic utterance of the eighteenth century,"[26] for it presented the initial assertion that "the excellence of art consists
in expression adequate to a meaning."[27]

According to Goethe, in a work of art— no matter what its forms or contents, "its parts will agree together, for a single feeling has created them into a
characteristic whole. . ."

---

[24]*A History of Aesthetic*, Bosanquet, p 248.
[25]*Ibid.*, p 249.
[26]*Ibid.*, p 306.
[27]*Ibid.*, p 312.

"Now this characteristic art is the only true art. When it acts on what lies around it from inward, single, individual, independent feeling, careless and even ignorant of all that is alien to it, then whether born of rude savagery or of cultivated sensibility, it is whole and living... Approach, and recognize the deepest feeling of truth and beauty in relations..."[28]

Goethe's notion of the "characteristic" gained little notice outside the immediate circle of his friends. Some of them also wrote on the subject but obtained no more attention than Goethe. So, the idea was lost in an obscure body of literature until Schelling, studying Goethe nearly thirty years later, discovered the idea and injected it into his own discussions of aesthetics. Schelling, however, treated Goethe's idea of the characteristic as if it were ideational in the Platonic sense rather than as the affective unification of the experience through its possession of an essential "feeling of truth."

The importance of Schelling in this history of an idea is that, as scholars have long recognized, Schelling influenced both the form and content of Hegelian philosophy. Most important to us is that through him Goethe's basic notion of the characteristic was transmitted to Hegel, and the idea recast into the first clear statement – in the *Phenomenology of Spirit* in 1807 – of the "characteristic" as feeling adequate to a meaning.

The nature of aesthetic experience, for Hegel, is understood in terms of his complex description of the human spirit and the intricate dialectic of his history of aesthetics. Yet, his position can be relatively simply stated. The beauty of art, he held, is essentially the beauty of spiritual idea presented in a form appealing to the senses rather than in a form suitable for addressing the intellect. In the latter form, spiritual idea would be presented as the true instead of the beautiful. The meaning in art, then, is the meaning of spiritual idea presented as feeling.

In terms of his idea of Absolute Spirit, which is the ongoing process of world and self, the whole content of Spiritual Being can be described as idea and nothing else. That being, however, must be thought of as a unity of different phases or natures. Idea, then, finds a different expression in each phase, and so it is that art appeals to the sensuous nature of the spirit. As Bosanquet explained, "Beauty is the Idea as it shows itself to sense."[29]

Although Hegel firmly and finally turned theoretical interest in the direction of the affective nature of the experience of art, his own preoccupation with the dialectical development of Spirit through historical stages tended to give credence to the classical notion that the judgement of the aristocrat is superior in all things. Based as much upon the romantic dialectic of Hegel as

---

[28]*Ibid.*, p 310 (Bosanquet's translation of the work by Goethe).
[29]*Ibid.*, p 336.

upon the moral prejudice of the Kantian analysis of aesthetic, there then developed a kind of theoretical consensus that while the crucial matter of art is expression, understood in affective terms, the objective form and content of that expression are paramount in determining matters of taste.

Perhaps no one better represented that consensus than Bernard Bosanquet. He did not deny that uncultured taste has the appearance of the true aesthetic. Feelings are unquestionably the mark of aesthetic and feelings are also experienced by those of vulgar sensibilities. If however we hold that the mere presence of feelings is enough to establish that something is beautiful, then we have devised a subjective and psychological definition of beauty which places vulgar and cultured taste on equal par, and allows no possibility of objective standards by which we might judge anything to be better or worse. For that, he absolutely rejects any psychological definition of beauty. Not that beauty does not elicit exquisite feelings in the beholder, but because feelings are simply not suited as a basis for judgement of what is truly beautiful. Any ignoramous can have feelings.

By the same token, even the most casual observer can see that the highest beauty, whether natural or artistic, is not necessarily even pleasant to the "normal" sensitivity. Further, natural beauties have no particular significance to aesthetic theory for natural beauty requires only the "average capacity of aesthetic appreciation." The beauties of the fine arts, on the other hand, are products of the perception and imagination not of the ordinary mind, but of the genius. In consequence, he asserts that the fine arts may "be accepted, for theoretical purposes, as the chief if not the sole representative of the world of beauty."[30] If so, then the true analysis of beauty therefore abandons any concern with the undeniably essential subjective feelings of the beholder and is directed toward the contents (common properties) of art accepted as beautiful by those of refined taste.

Analysis of the beautiful solely in terms of contents therefore does not reject the notion of expression in the arts. There is expression and Bosanquet describes it as a matter of feelings, or felt significance. His position is simply that there is a unity between contents and expression, and because of that connection the analysis of content provides an objective standard traceable ultimately to subjective taste — specifically to that cultivated taste which is the proper measure of beauty. In other words, expression occurs because an object of art has the objective contents that it has. Equally, the object possesses those contents only because the expression in the man placed those contents in the object. As Bosanquet phrased it, "The man, as he is when his nature is at one with himself. . .is the needed middle term between content and expression."[31]

[30]*Ibid.*, p 3.
[31]*Ibid.*, p 457.

The conditional quality of the middle term, "the man when his nature is at one with himself," implies a contingent and not a necessary connection between contents and expression. Bosanquet failed to see or thus examine that implication and therefore suggested but missed a key condition of the aesthetic. Also, he described the middle term only as it functioned in the experience of the artist. That description turned out to be a restatement in different words of the "divine madness," although no less poetic.

For the artist, the middle term is "the fulness of a man's heart," all consuming and focused in the aesthetic activity and by that achieving full freedom from all but the activity and its object. In such terms, a man's nature is indeed "at one with himself," and by "disciplined habit together with overmastering impulse," expressive contents get into the object of art through the man. This is more than "art for art's sake." It is art for the sake of expression. As such, art is a serious, vital function implicating man's highest nature (his genius of creativity) and his highest achievement as a man (the ideal considerations of beauty).

Bosanquet traced aesthetics from the first glimmerings of aesthetic consciousness through the nineteenth century approaches to understanding it. His scholarship was prodigious, just like that of the German scholars he loved to quote. Yet Bosanquet failed to see that he had fallen into the same trap as many others before him: Whenever the prejudice of the nonaesthetic – in this instance the unmitigated bias of caste – is brought to bear upon the problem of aesthetic, there is a confusion of basic issues, a foreshortening of one's viewpoint, and a resultant disregard for much of the fundamental data of aesthetic experience. The particular fault of Bosanquet was that although he recognized the kindredness of the "lesser arts" and the aesthetic qualities of vulgar feeling in the craftsman's experience, in the end he denied the legitimacy of such experiences as reference data meaningful to a definition of the "true aesthetic." Authentic aesthetic sensibility is measured by the objective contents which distinguish the art of the cultural aristocrat and nothing else.[32]

Bosanquet railed against the "new" philosophy of experience for its subjectivism. He objected strenuously to tendencies of aesthetic inquiry spawned by that philosophy and suggested by the new psychology that took shape during the latter half of the nineteenth century. Still, he was willing to admit, "in the aesthetic of the future Psychology has. . . a leading part to play. Though I do not believe in aesthetic as the analysis of expression apart from the analysis of content, it appears that to analyze the pleasurable nature of utterance or

---

[32] Benedetto Croce remarks: "Among the principal reasons which have prevented aesthetic. . .from revealing the true nature of art, its real roots in human nature, has been its separation from the general spiritual life, and have made of it a sort of special function or aristocratic club." (*Aesthetic as The Science of Expression and General Linguistic*, p 14.)

expression will be a necessary pendant to analyzing the kind of content which, in the course of evolution, comes to demand embodiment or appreciation."[33]

With such faint praise, Bosanquet practically repudiated the worth of any psychological approach to aesthetics. Yet, his words testify to his awareness that at the end of the past century man's understanding of his own behavior had advanced to where his experience of art could begin to be described in a more scientific universe of discourse. Indeed, in large part because of that new understanding, the final ten years of the nineteenth century became probably the most fruitful decade in the history of aesthetics. Virtually the first and last words now current on the subject were phrased during those ten years.

The ideas of Bosanquet, summed up in his monumental *A History of Aesthetic,* in 1892, reflect the transition out of the classical past in which his roots were buried, and point toward a future he was not quite prepared to accept. One who holds the liberal, democratic sentiments popular in our own day might regard him with some impatience, finding him as an apologist for an outmoded aristocratic viewpoint. Ironically, the self-appointed cultural aristocrats of our **day** – the liberal, double-thought intellectual democratic avante-garde – **no less** assert that their's is the only true art even if ordinary folks find little interest in it. Indeed, the "common properties" defining the art of the modern sophisticate are simply different in some respects from the contents certified by Bosanquet as necessary for any true art. True art remains no less that art which the cultural aristocrats determine to be authentic art.

That whole idea was challenged with bitter polemics in that same decade by the elderly Leo Tolstoy, whose *What is Art?* was published in 1898. That work remains the classic assertion of the universality of man's aesthetic sense and the justice of art necessarily appealing to that sense in all men. Bosanquet's ideal of an art appealing only to the cultural aristocrat was therefore soundly damned by Tolstoy, although at the same time he shared the Englishman's view that any and all psychological definitions of art are patently false. Such definitions, Tolstoy explained, are based on the premise that the goal of art is pleasure, an idea he considered absolutely scandalous.

"If we say that the aim of any activity is merely our pleasure, and define it solely by that pleasure, our definition will evidently be a false one. But this is precisely what has occurred in the efforts to define art. Now, if we consider the food question, it will not occur to anyone to affirm that the importance of food consists in the pleasure we receive when eating it... And in the same way, beauty, or that which pleases us, can in no sense serve as the basis for the definition of art; nor can a series of objects which afford us pleasure serve as a model of what art should be."[34]

[33]*A History of Aesthetic,* p 466.
[34]*What is Art?,* p 43.

Tolstoy argued that art must not be thought of simply as a source of trivial pleasures, not as a means of alleviating the ennui of a bored aristocracy. Art must be considéred rather in terms of the influences it discharges into the total context of life. Indeed, he finds it as one of the fundamental conditions of living. Art is as basic to human life as knowing and thinking, and just as important. Its primary influence is the contagious expression of emotions, an infectious communication of feelings among men. That is what we must therefore demand of art. It must serve as the language of emotion no less than ordinary language must serve as the vehicle for the transmission of scientific knowledge.

The Tolstoyan viewpoint, which fundamentally required that art be universal in both its expressions and its means of expression, and that the expressions of feeling must be significant, remains current in many quarters to this day. We find such notions reflected in such extreme positions as that of socialist realism on the one hand and in the democratic art extolled by the disillusioned aesthete, Jean Gimpel, in his *The Cult of Art*. For in this view, art for mere art's sake is scandalous. It must be art of the people, for the people, expressing only those feelings which are important to everyone, appealing to everyone.

While Europeans debated aristocratic versus democratic bases for aesthetic judgement, on the other side of the world, George Santayana, in 1896, published *The Sense of Beauty*, which must be regarded as the milestone work of modern aesthetics. In that work, for the first time, a full blown aesthetic theory was invested with the new psychology. Previous thinkers, from the English empiricists and Lessing to Bosanquet and Tolstoy, had admitted the psychological basis for art and the affective essence of taste. Their aesthetics, however, invariably turned toward the objective characteristics of the object of art for definition of taste and the fine arts. With Santayana, for the first time, there is an aesthetics which remains entirely within the subjective realm of feeling no matter that in the end he followed after Kant and discovered the essence of aesthetic in moral feeling. More, with Santayana for the first time we have an aesthetics stated in terms of psychology as a modern science.

In his achievement, Santayana's principal theoretical innovations – the first and second terms of expression – were evolved out of ideas suggested in the psychology of William James. Oddly enough, James made his summary statement of that psychology in the very same decade, presenting ideas which only now are coming back into vogue after being out of fashion in psychology for nearly a hundred years. In a subsequent chapter, as we develop the basis for a modern aesthetics, we will have occasion to dwell upon James' contributions and their reaffirmation by recent investigations.

Again, in that very same decade, Benedetto Croce was already at work on his *Aesthetic as The Science of Expression*, published in 1902. Croce, following the then still dominant Hegelian tradition, was fascinated by Hegel's notion of beauty as the sensuous nature of spiritual idea. Abandoning many of the trappings of the intricate system, Croce concentrated upon the description of the Absolute Spirit in its personal development from blind ignorance to knowing self and world. Out of his ponderings came a beautiful and provocative understanding of Spirit as an activity of feeling, forming self and world out of its affective experience. The essence of that activity is not other than aesthetic. The expression that is fine art differs from spiritual expression in general only in the way the artist meets his object; that is, the artistic object retains its essential aesthetic character as formed feeling, even though it also obtains an abstract form as a thing existing in the world as the object of art.

The ideas of Croce, Tolstoy, and Santayana, formulated originally in that remarkable decade ending the nineteenth century, continue to define the existing limits of aesthetic inquiry. Later embellishments and clarifications were certainly achieved by such men as John Dewey and Robin Collingwood, but the basic positions and understandings achieved by those men remain central to all current thought. Each of these men understood expression as a kind of felt meaningfulness. Certainly, their descriptions and interpretations of the nature of that meaningfulness were markedly different, but each followed in the modern tradition established by Hegel from Goethe's and Baumgarten's insights. Each man, that is to say, described the ideational character of an essentially affective experience.

Chapter 4

AESTHETIC AND INTELLECT

Hardly a trace is left in current aesthetic theory of the old explanation of the experience of art in terms of contemplative intellect. Aesthetic and intellect are now seen at opposite ends of the spectrum of experience. Modern theorists, whether they adhere to some theory of expression or not, explain the experience of art in terms of affect. Aesthetic experience now is generally understood as a specialized achievement of feeling.

In the typical description, aesthetic is not essentially different from feeling in general. Aesthetic differs from other feeling not in nature, but in form. In aesthetic experience, that is to say, there is a distinctive quality, not possesed by feelings generally, that originates in the form or organization that feelings come to have in the aesthetic process.

The preceding is a kind of distillation of current aesthetics. No matter how diverse modern viewpoints are, brief descriptions reduce them to statements such as those above. Just for example, compare the appearance of this theoretical consensus in the work of Walter Pater and Robin G. Collingwood. While there is practically no theoretical likeness between their descriptions of the aesthetic process, the notion of the essence of feeling, and the explanatory mechanism of the organization or form of feeling in the propagation of aesthetic, are fundamental to the ideas of both men.

Pater recognized only a sensuous basis for aesthetic, and cited the experience of the aesthete for definitive exemplification of his theory. The mark of the connoisseur, according to Pater, is his skilled orchestration of the ecstasies of sense. He is a virtuoso of feeling, able to create the form – or structure – of exquisite sensuous pleasures in his experience of life. He is an aesthete not because of his ability to feel, for that ability belongs to everyone. The reason for the aesthetic excellence of his experience is rather his ability to control and organize his pleasures of sense.

At the other theoretical extreme, Collingwood devised a theory which emphasized the aesthetic pleasures of imagination rather than those of sense. He tells us that the aesthetic comes of the primitive feelings of the psyche achieving unity in form. In that achievement, feelings obtain a meaningfulness which the maelstrom of raw feelings can never have. He explains the process in terms of imagination, poetically described as the cutting edge of the mind since imagination provides the raw material for all other mental activities or processes.

Art, for Collingwood, is imagination. Art is imagination giving form and meaning to feelings where only affective chaos existed before. Imagination, in his description, literally takes the wild, primitive feelings which are the foundation of the psyche and creates affective organization, or form. These forms become not only the images which in consciousness are the things of the world; each image also is an aspect of the fundamental sentient being a person is. The abstract thing of consciousness is but the objective measure of the concrete spiritual being of feeling.

That description applies to the formation of all things as consciousness, so in the final analysis the creativity resident in the fine arts is only one phase of imagination. The whole of the world and the whole of the self-knowing consciousness are products of the imagination, jointly formed from the blind sensitivity of the passive psyche. Out of imagination therefore comes all creativity, whether practical or aesthetic, scientific, or moral. The aesthetic is distinguishable, however, as imagination which shapes raw feelings into "feeling things," or emotions, which only incidentally happen to be physical things. Aesthetic imagination, then, seeks only to form the feelings one has, organizing them into a unified whole, an emotion. That an abstract image, or thing called an object of art, also is formed in the act is significant only because it is the outward appearance of the inner value – the formed feeling – which is the aesthetic or spiritual thing.

In such terms, Pater and Collingwood diversely represented the modern consensus that intellect and rational behaviors have no part in aesthetic because intellectual processes dealing with thoughts are obviously different from aesthetic processes which deal only with feelings – whether sensuous or imaginative or both. A student of aesthetics, however, might object that at least one modern theorist violated that consensus and recognized the influence of intellectual processes in aesthetic. That authority was George Santayana, first among the moderns to study the function of reason in art.

Santayana, like Bacon and Kant before him and Collingwood later, located the seat of aesthetic in the "airy pleasures of the imagination." These pleasures are attained through the impress of order or form upon the surges of primitive feeling. Santayana did not believe, however, that the whole matter of aesthetic was explicable on such purely affective terms. Rather he maintained that aesthetic as we experience it in art is possible only upon the intervention of reason.

Rational art, by trial and error – learning – taking account of actual skills and real material possibilities, turns blind impulse into conscious and creative action. That description, of course, fits every purposeful human action, each of them artful in remarkably different ways. Yet, one kind of action, one art, is unique among all. Only the fine or beautiful art consciously turns back upon its affective source to find both its direction and its fruition in feeling itself. Involved in that process are not only conscious habit and awareness, but also selective and creative responses which exhibit all the characteristics of rational activity. That these are responses to feeling is significant to understanding the artistic process, but that is beside the point at issue. The matter of importance here is that those responses are artistic in nature, not aesthetic. They are rationally guided shapings of things rather than an intellectual foundation for or involvement in the aesthetic process behind those shapings. Thus, Santayana also failed to escape the consensus in modern aesthetics. In no way did he think that the aesthetic process was intellectual, no matter his recognition of the rationality of the artistic activities which call out and sustain that process.

The fundamental scheme of Dewey's aesthetics closely followed the approach taken by Santayana but for one remarkable difference. Dewey ignored the role of reason in art no matter that he admitted conscious direction. Reason was granted its place in the practical arts and sciences. Because of the aesthetic process natural to the fine arts, however, Dewey saw in them but a superficial resemblance to the other, useful arts. Surely, there is craftsmanship and manipulation of materials. There is also conscious direction and processes of thought are involved. Yet, the distinguishing structural feature of aesthetic experience is that those other mental processes are fully integrated into a perceptual process finding its focus on the pleasure of the experience itself without reference to objects or values outside the moment of the experience.[1]

In the work of Dewey and Santayana, then, we find no assertion of an intellectual basis for aesthetic. They simply recognized that the artist must think to make. They recognized the controlling, selecting activity of thought, or reason, in the process of art. They further observed that in the fine arts the controlling function responds to an immediate awareness of feeling. Reason, or thought, is thus made extrinsic to the aesthetic process no matter that the processes of conscious direction are central to the possibility of art as aesthetic production.

Now, it bears noting that when we use the term "aesthetic production," "aesthetic" no longer retains its original meaning of "perception of the beautiful." Instead, "aesthetic" obtains the meaning of "a process of feeling."

---

[1] As phrased by Dewey in *Art as Experience* (p 254), "Not absence of desire and thought but their thorough incorporation into perceptual experience characterizes aesthetic experience, in its distinction from experiences that are especially 'intellectual' and 'practical.' "

This, of course, was the ultimate evolution of Dewey's description of art as experience. In these terms, art may be said to serve as the source of that process of feeling called aesthetic experience. Art, as the activity of producing that process of feeling, literally is aesthetic production. The essential feature of art as an activity thus is its creative shaping of an affective domination of consciousness, a controlled formation of feeling into what is best described as an aesthetic object.

Given the terms of this discussion, the aesthetic object can be defined only as the formed appearance of feeling as consciousness. It cannot be confused either with the art object or with the perception of the art object. Neither may one find in the terms of the discussion, therefore, legitimate grounds for taking the aesthetic object to be a symbol or for the aesthetic process to be described as one of symbolization. The aesthetic object symbolizes nothing. It is what it appears to be: a particular nexus of feeling pervaded by a unifying sense of meaningfulness.

By the same token, the art object also is no symbol in terms of its actual function in the process of aesthetic production. It is but a particular source for an exchange of energies out of which, in the beholder, aesthetic production may ensue. Art, therefore, cannot be a process of symbolization, although it certainly may utilize symbol as one of a whole artistic armory of instruments useful in aesthetic production – a subject we will dwell upon later for detailed analysis.

The old idea of aesthetic as a perceptual process, vestiges of which appear in Dewey's theory of art as experience, was well suited to the concept of beauty as the objective quality of a thing. That presumption, now mostly out of fashion, supported the notion of aesthetics as the philosophy of beauty resident in things. As modern thought turned toward the affective qualities of the experience, the consensus now current came to regard aesthetics instead as the "philosophy of taste" for beauty. Taste is personal and subjective. Aesthetics thus tended away from analysis of objective "contents" and toward the analysis of the qualities of affective appeal that characterize the experience of beauty.

That tendency is observable in Dewey's notion of the experience of art being notably one leading to what he called a fruition of feeling, in terms of which he defined art as experience. It is perhaps remarkable therefore that he should retain the central concept of perception in his description of the aesthetic process. It is explicable, however, when one observes that Dewey's psychology was fundamentally behavioristic, and perception for a behaviorist is not an experience of feeling but is an integration of sensa. In contrast, the position being developed here is that perception (understood as an integration of sensa) is taken to be a necessary condition for, rather than an essential aspect of aesthetic experience (which, the preceding discussion shows, is an idea quite alien to the thought of Dewey). That is, in terms of the affective essence of aesthetic, perception understood as an integration of sensa is a peripheral rather than a central matter in definition of the beautiful or determination of the nature of aesthetic experience. For aesthetic experience, in the terms being developed here, is in no way perceptual. Aesthetic experience is "feeling experience," specifically feeling with controlled qualities characteristic of the experience of art, as contrasted with the tumultuous appearance of "raw" feelings in general.[2]

While the concept of aesthetic as feeling organized in the process of perception places Dewey and Santayana within the modern consensus described at the outset of this chapter, we find that their emphasis upon perception tends to be both anachronistic and troublesome for theoretical development. The central difficulty comes of their attempt to explain how a process that they regard to be perceptual is able to involve a sense of meaningfulness. No matter what else they say of aesthetic experience, aesthetic understood primarily as a process of perception is an idea that appears entirely inadequate to address the sense of meaning, expression, peculiar to experience of the arts. Yet, the problem with setting up perception as the central concept for understanding the aesthetic process is perhaps difficult to appreciate from the more or less provincial point of view of aesthetics. Viewing it from the more generic standpoint of axiology sharpens the issue considerably.

Dewey described meaning as the "distilled import" of existence, a consequence of what is, with "what is" defined as a causally related process of events. By that, meaning is no mere consequence. What something (a process of events) means is what it promises or portends. The process as such, of course, simply is. The import of it all is the contribution of a human awareness.

Meaning, as the distillation of import of a process, is something consciousness contributes to its own experience. For a process to have promise, it comes to achieve a portent, an emotional quality called a sense of value. A prereflective evaluation of worth has occurred. Aesthetic meaning can be no different in essence, and this understanding places aesthetic meaning and all meaning in general within the one analytical realm of value theory. The question begged, of course, is the nature of that prereflective evaluation.

Now perception is certainly prereflective. As an integration of sensa, however, does it seem proper to speak of perception as an instrument or process of consciousness out of which meaning, or even just a nebulous sense of meaningfulness, results? It may seem just that when one considers that percep-

---

[2] Yet if one regards the process of perception as a process of feeling, perception again must be admitted into the sphere of aesthetical inquiry as an essential element, albeit on terms quite different than before. Just that approach is one of the evolutions of thought to be undertaken as we proceed in this study.

tion certainly is selective, and the traits of perceptual selectivity are demonstrably able to be modified by learning. Indeed, clinical evidence indicates that perception is not only modified by learning, but is entirely learned.[3] Yet, an odd situation results if perception is an evaluative process on any level, including the prereflective level of aesthetic judgement, the alleged product of which is aesthetic value. For if such be so, then at least some values are perceived in the same way that things are perceived. The consequence, if perception is a process that is able to produce awareness of aesthetic values as well as awareness of things, is that the axiological subjectivism that dominates modern experience philosophy results from a colossal mistake. For in such terms, values must have an objective, substantial persistence out in the world, just as things do. Goodness, truth, and beauty all then must be able to be perceived in the same way as roundness or squareness, or aesthetic experience is not essentially perceptual.

Such an argument has the flavor of antiquity. It stirs echoes of the old Platonistic philosophies. No one who speaks for prevailing trends in Western philosophy today would have much patience with it. As far as recent philosophy is concerned, the battle between theories of objective versus subjective standards for value judgements was fought to a decision a hundred years ago. (Still, in a later chapter, we will see that the scientific community in just this last decade has developed concepts that revivify the argument in terms of the character and consequences of man's genetic inheritance, alleged by some to include even percepts and concepts, while others find that it provides psychic models of experience against which actual experience gains "standard" genetic interpretation or evaluation.) Dewey and Santayana participated in the waning episodes of that conflict and no doubt were keenly aware of the kind of argument, such as we have presented, that might stem from aesthetic considered to be essentially or entirely a matter of perception. They avoided the axiological dilemma by maintaining that while aesthetic has its foundation and organizing principle in perception, the quality of meaningfulness that marks the experience is a matter of the affective repercussion that comes of the total process. Aesthetic is the consequence of our experience of the artistic act. That experience is grounded on perception while including intellectual or rational behaviors that control the act and one's perception of it. By virtue of that control, those rational behaviors also manage the development of the affective consequences of the total experience.

---

[3] Experimental evidence indicates that one must learn to perceive even the simplest forms, such as circles and squares. Thus H. J. Eysenck remarks (*Sense and Nonsense in Psychology*, p 312) that roundness and squareness are not "inherent qualities in the object, just waiting to be perceived. Rules for the perception of these qualities had to be acquired, just as we have to acquire rules for the perception of beauty."

By that description, the nature of expression in the arts is revealed as a passive but not incidental affective repercussion to other psychic events; but that notion hardly seems satisfying as a rationale for the character of meaningfulness central to that experience of feeling, for meaning as a repercussion (for that is the affective consequence) essentially appears to be a peripheral matter in terms of the process of art as experience per se.

That experience, Dewey tells us, is a process of causally related events organized on the basis of a perception. It achieves a felt consequence called expression. The consequence is described as a kind of blossoming of feeling, an affective fruition that contains a quality of meaning. It is the product not only of the perception that cements the experience through its function as the primary instrument of order, but also of the other varied mental processes which find a common focus, just for the moment, by virtue of that instrument.

Expression (as a fruition of feeling) thus is certainly the consequence of the experience. As a kind of meaning, its description is compatible with the definition of meaning as a consequence. But, we saw that Dewey considered that meaning is no mere experience, but one of portent. And that sense of meaning fails to be accommodated in the notion of expression as the affective repercussion of a process of psychic events. In other words, the affective qualities of the experience are made out to be something apart from the processes that constitute the experience. Again, while this "repercussion" of feeling satisfies the definition of meaning by being the consequence of the experience, it fails entirely to come to grips with the character of the actual experience that people have, an experience imbued with a quality of meaning in its immediate essence as feeling.

Dewey, of course, insisted upon that latter understanding, and its incompatibility with the terms of his fundamental analysis of the experience needs to be searched out. But clearly seen, his analysis would seem to lead inevitably to the notion of expression as an awareness that the felt repercussion was the meaning of the experience, an idea that has no relevance either to his own final understanding or to the actual experience people have. Rather, expression is an awareness of meaning in the experience of feeling, which is quite a different matter.

The crux of this entire matter is that we are attempting to understand the "sense of story" that men find in their experience of art, a quality that may be called "aesthetic meaning" if one chooses, or perhaps "aesthetic meaningfulness." In this attempt, it has become clear that this quality appears to have little direct connection with perception as conventionally understood, and thus it begins to appear most advantageous theoretically to separate notions of the aesthetic process from its traditional alliance with perception.

Dewey and Santayana developed their ideas such that the problem of perception is obscure, even alien, for example, to Dewey's description of the aesthetic experience as "an experience" in a sense that no other manner of experience may become. But, in the final analysis, we consider that meaning – even non-discursive meaning in aesthetic experience – implies something more essential than a repercussion of feeling called out by the process of perceptual integration of sensa, more than the psychic presence of a conglomeration of mere sensa as such, and even more than the affective residue of thoughts aroused as "echoes" out of past experience.

Meaning, as the contribution of a human awareness, implies something more than a perceptual process, no matter how selective that process may be. If there is aesthetic meaning – and the evidence of human experience throughout the ages asserts that there is a kind of meaning natural to his experience of art – then the aesthetic process may be said to be evaluative in nature and not merely selective. It implies a process where import is distilled, where meaning therefore is an active rather than a passive contribution of consciousness. Further, the evidence of experience indicates that the generation of meaning occurs as part and parcel of the aesthetic process and is not some manner of judgement made after the fact. In other words, the evaluative function is not an affective repercussion to some other extra-affective processes, because the experience is immediately imbued with meaning in the very moment of the experience.

Kant's initial perception of the aesthetic enigma was in terms not so different from these, although with an unmistakably different flavor. Given the traditional views of the German rationalists on the nature of perception, we may understand how easily Kant might turn away from the affective aspects of the experience when determining the source of that quality of meaning in the experience of art. And we can further appreciate how he could then make aesthetics subject to a reflective judgement. Further, the indubitable sense of immediacy possessed by that quality of meaning presented no problem for Kant, since the experience by the mind of its own processes is naturally immediately present to it. Indeed, the Kantian position is virtually impregnable from within, but we have already discussed our distrust of it as a proper measure of the actual experiences men have. We continue to find more favor in Baumgarten's notion of "the art of beautiful thinking." Indeed, to escape from the nest of problems hatched by modern aesthetics following after Kant, we might for a moment turn the clock back to a pre-Kantian time where we might give serious consideration to Baumgarten's theory of aesthetic as "the art of beautiful thinking." With Kantian arguments set aside, Baumgarten's theory then is appreciated against the long tradition of thought that found the meaning of art residing in the perception not of things, but of forms. Indeed, the meaning came not of a perception, but of a cognition by the contemplative intellect (as contrasted with the active intellect where the power of reason was said to reside in the old faculty psychology). In this description, the cognition of truth or meaning through art comes effortlessly as it were, as the contemplative intellect simply makes itself "open" to awarenesses of truth and knowing. The "perception" is through the mind's eye, and is concerned not with things but with the eternal forms of Plato, or perhaps in modern terminology, with the essences of Santayana.

Now let us consider that these ideas of the perception of truth and beauty by the mind's eye are not mere examples of mythological thinking. Suppose, instead, that they are poetic descriptions of man's timeless sharings of aesthetic experience, and the framing of the discussion in terms of intellectual function is accurate. If we follow this line of thinking, then the notion of aesthetic meaning implies direct involvement of intellectual functions in the experience. Reason would not merely control the activity of aesthetic production, it would be the essential element of the process, a process suddenly very aptly described by Baumgarten's "art of beautiful thinking," or Santayana's idea of rational art more radically interpreted than he intended. What this implies is that the peculiar affective quality of meaning in the arts comes of a direct connection between feeling and intellect, a connection necessary to explain the characteristic meaningfulness, expression, of a work of art.

The possibilities of that connection are intimated by other experiences than that of art. In the idiom of everyday speech, for example, people tend to make little practical distinction between saying "I think that..." and "I feel that...." Or irrationality, intellect gone wild, is blamed on the influence of feelings. "He is emotionally so upset he can't think straight."

Scholars use equally significant idiom. Emotional behavior, according to some psychologists, may be explained only as a response to rational intepretations of things and events. Educators talk about feelings blocking or facilitating processes of cognitive learning. As a philosopher, Bertrand Russell had scant interest in aesthetic matters, yet he remarked upon the aesthetic qualities of a mathematical solution. Nor is it uncommon for academics, caught up in the heat of disputation, to accuse their fellows of arguments that speak more of their feelings than of the rational development of ideas. But there is no actual awareness of the fundamental issue extant in these examples. They are incidental asides, generally ignored or treated as comic relief in the dramatic dialogue that became the history of ideas. Never-the-less, we can identify an occasional scholar who perceived and sought to elucidate something of the affective foundation on which that history unfolds. Taine's monumental history of English literature, as we will have occasion to observe in later chapters, was shaped out of just such a perception. Less known is Basil Willey's four-volume study of English intellectual development as expressed in art and religion in the seventeenth through nineteenth centuries.

Willey's work is, for us, unusually significant because of his explicit awareness of the affective dimensions of the history of ideas. He showed how, in the seventeenth century, the affective character or temperament of human experience suddenly and irrevocably changed. It suddenly made both acceptable and necessary the opening up of ways to questionings and intellectual methodologies as novel as the newly discovered feelings about self and world.

Man's search for understanding is a search for explanations. Concepts of "explanation," and of the "truth" and "reality" with which explanations deal, gain their validity from "habitual assumptions" or "doctrines felt as facts," Willey wrote. In short, the truth of an idea is a function of the affective value the idea lends to the experience of the person encountering the idea. Truth is something we feel comfortable with, or which otherwise satisfies some deep affective need.

In these terms, Willey described and analyzed the radical changes in Western thought that occurred in the seventeenth century. He identifies it as a major turning point in human thought, and traced its further development into the nineteenth century foundations of current trends of thought. In his terms, we must recognize the change to have been of the same magnitude as that which created the Greek inventive genius that Hellenized the ancient world. In a thousand years, men will speak of the Teutonic genius that Europeanized the world of our day. Then and now, one view of and approach to the world took the place of another. And it occurred in each instance because men were suddenly able to desire other kinds of explanations than those the past had taught. While Willey describes the seventeenth century, we find a likeness to that other time when he tells us that the ideas of men underwent such a wrenching change "because they no longer wished to feel as they had been taught to feel about the nature of things. To be rid of fear—fear of the unknown, fear of the gods, fear of the stars or of the devil—to be released from the necessity of reverencing what was not to be understood, these were amongst the most urgent demands of the modern as of the ancient world; and it was because it satisfied these demands that scientific explanation was received as the revelation of truth."[4]

Thus in the seventeenth century, man's explanations became matters of "how," rather than "why." "How" is a question that obtains answers in terms of mechanical, or efficient causes. It lends credence to and justifies

---

[4] *The Seventeenth Century Background,* p 5. These sentiments are worth comparing with those of Edith Hamilton in her study of the changes in Greek thought and feeling about self and world, so delightfully rendered in her *The Greek Way.* She perceived of the Greek experience something of the same affective elements and relationships that Willey sees in our own.

emotionally the fantastic integrating intellectual inventions of Newtonian science. "Why" is a question natural to the older Aristotelian science. It lends itself to explanations in terms of final causes, explanations satisfying only in another, older age.

Given Willey's perception of the connections between thought and feeling in the shaping of our age, how remarkable it is that he did not enquire into the nature of that connection. He reveals no notion of the connection being more than an operational one, where thought and feeling —separate functions of the mind — work in concert with each other. In one passage of his analysis he remarks, for example, that "in poetry thought is not pure, it is working in alliance with the feelings and the will."[5] How that echoes a faculty psychology, yet how representative it is of what passes for the best thought on the subject even to this day. But when these typical assertions — both scholarly and idiomatic — of some manner of connection between feeling and thought are recognized, how amazing it is that so little attention has been granted to the matter by scholars and scientists of any age. And to the extent that it was broached, it is clear by hind-sight how virtually impossible it has been for anyone to break away from the old ways of thinking.

Despite his erudition, it appears not to have occurred to Willey that there is an issue at stake in his discussion other than the operational consequences of the connection. Baumgarten, two hundred years earlier, had sensed that an issue was there but could not frame it properly. He could not see how it might have been possible to challenge the traditional dichotomy between affect and reason. Heir to Wolffian rationalism and its upside down psychology, he was merely puzzled by the peculiarly ideational but non-logical character of our experience of beautiful things. That experience, he observed, led to more than the "confused knowledge" attributed to sensations by Wolff. On the other hand, he noted that the experience led to less than the exact terms of knowing that intellect produces. From that, he concluded that aesthetic must involve a separate and distinct process of mind, "the art of beautiful thinking." This mental function applies itself to perfections of sensuous knowledge, perfections which when approached intellectually (logically) are that knowledge called truth.

A similar notion is preserved in Hegel's theory of beauty as the sensuous form of idea, although Hegel's ponderous system obscures his alliance with Baumgarten. Also, one must recognize the difference between them. The Hegelian description of aesthetic is a kind of Platonic union of the true and the beautiful, different therefore from the functional union of feeling and thought implicitly achieved by Baumgarten, but so little understood by Hegel or any-

---

[5]*Ibid.*, p 205.

one else. A century later, for example, Bosanquet gave cursory consideration of Baumgarten's "art of beautiful thinking," and shrugged it off as incomprehensible. The union of sensuous perfection and thought in aesthetic function was an idea simply too antithetical to everything Bosanquet believed in to be understood, much less entertained seriously in development of his own ideas. Anyone can see that sensation is one thing, reason another. As all authority has maintained for thousands of years, feelings and thoughts are entirely different and unrelated mental phenomena. To this day, the idea generally remains inconceivable that the hot, tempestuous passions have anything in common with the cold blade of logic and the orderly process of reason.

Charles Peirce was one of the few philosophers able to suspect a union, much less inquire into it. "Esthetics and logic," he remarked, "seem to belong to different universes. . . I have become persuaded that the seeming is illusory, and . . . on the contrary, logic needs the help of esthetics."[6]

Aesthetics, according to Peirce, is "the theory of the deliberate formation of . . . habits of feeling (i.e., of the ideal)."[7] Aesthetic ideals, that is to say, have their basis in excellences of feeling to which "the mind accords a certain approval in pronouncing them beautiful,"[8] because of embodied relational affinities in the aesthetic materials. In brief, aesthetic ideals are actual embodiments in nature. They are not subjective except insofar as we sense and apprehend those excellences. Beauty has an objective being and consists of the relational order within and between things.

Since logic, as Peirce understood it, was a normative science dealing with objective relations, then by definition the affinities of logical order approach or achieve not only logical ideals but aesthetic ideals as well. But, after identifying this relationship between logic and aesthetic in their objects, Peirce denied finally that logic therefore can be founded on subjective feeling.[9] The contents of the logical order, he argued, have only a virtual and not an essential aesthetic quality, if only because feelings and thoughts are entirely different matters of the mind.

Peirce's conclusion testifies more to the force of traditional understandings than to his real achievements as an innovator of ideas. His example also illustrates why neither philosophy nor science offers much explicit assistance in solving or even approaching the problem of the connection of thought and feeling. The traditional bias of the history of ideas tends to obscure the fact even that there is a problem. In consequence, at this point in the development of

---

[6]*An Introduction of Peirce's Philosophy*, Feibleman, p 388.
[7]*Ibid.*, p 392.
[8]*Ibid.*, p 393.
[9]*Ibid.*, p 390.

human knowledge, the actual connection remains mysterious to the point of enigma, and the enigma so fundamental that it is seldom even recognized as such, much less made the subject of scholarly inquiry or scientific research. That is not to say that no one ever looked into the matter before. Peirce demonstrates otherwise. What we find rather is that such inquiry is obscure to current scholarship, and was seldom undertaken in any case.

In sum, we find ourselves in the position of having an intuitive notion that there is a connection between thought and feeling, a notion which evolves from the necessity of explaining the qualities of meaningfulness we find in our experiences of the arts. In support of the notion, we find that both common and specialized languages idiomatically suggest that the connection indeed exists. We also find that as distinguished a thinker as Charles Peirce shared our suspicion of the connection, although his motivation was quite different than ours. In opposition to this, however, we have the tremendous weight of authority, which almost universally has asserted an essential difference between thought and feeling. As Socrates phrased the perennial bias of men of all ages, the intellect is that power of the psyche most noble and truly human, while affect involves only the baser powers of the soul.

In philosophy, the separation of affect and intellect has been a prime consideration in the "mind-body" problem. Even in this century, when the old mind-body problem allegedly has been laid to rest by the philosophers, Santayana and Dewey were still unable to resolve the problem of intellect because of their inability to escape vestigal theoretical hangups stemming from the age-old distinction.

Santayana and Dewey talked around the problem. They asserted the behavioral unity of the organism and its powers of being, but they never quite came to grips with the crucial problem of intellect. As a result, the passions of the body and the clear processes of reason were as different for them as for Socrates. While they saw all human behavior originating in the primitive sentience of the organism, intellect remained a superadded function using sentient materials of the psyche but standing alone and apart from the psychic maelstrom. Aesthetic, as feeling, was psychic, thus intellect could have no role in aesthetic. Certainly, intellect could exert conscious control, but only of the activity of art. Aesthetic is the affective result of the activity controlled, and not the control function as such.

Dewey was certain Santayana had gone beyond this with his notion that the basis for the second term of expression is the "association of ideas," which implies rational function. Santayana in fact denied such a notion and insisted rather upon the "aesthetic echo" of ideas, which is purely a passive affective consequence, stemming mostly not even from presently recalled ideas, but from a kind of psychic residue of past experience, nonspiritual thus nonintellectual.

An oddity of human thought throughout the recorded history of ideas, and reflected in the theories of Dewey and Santayana, is that intellect and aesthetic have always been regarded as poles apart while at the same time considered remarkably and solely human achievements. In other words, man's intellect *and* his aesthetic sense are behaviors taken to be peculiar to man alone, and thus are the primary criteria for behaviorally differentiating man from his beastial cousins. Even more odd is that both are regarded to have a common root in psychic sentience while at the same time they have been universally thought of as monadic behaviors. Certainly overtones of affect produced by intellectual behaviors have been recognized, but as activities they are regarded as essentially and functionally unrelated.

Such a position marked the limit beyond which Santayana could not proceed to a clear conception of the function of reason in art, or resolve the "problem" of the intellectual function. This conceptual constraint was evident not only in his public writings, but also in his private ponderings. In a letter to his friend, Daniel Cory, he remarked, "The spirit awakes to its [the world's] presence under the stimulus of sense. I think all consciousness is intellectual: the subintellectual flux is purely material and only potentially conscious. . .not a psychological, but a physiological reality."[10]

That remark implicitly asserts that the Realm of Spirit is coextensive with the realm of intellect, a notion antithetical to his basic writings. It also indicates that despite the conviction of his writing, Santayana was yet perplexed by the relationships between feeling and thought and dissatisfied with the answers given by himself and others. His assertion of the purely intellectual consciousness, however, was only transitional in his thought as he wrestled with the problem. Ultimately, he worked his way to an entirely different understanding, revealed years later in another letter to Cory. Then he wrote, "The knowledge we have of the world is a system of ideas; but it is not our psychological life, which is only feeling diversified. It is the function of parts of that life, in its vital alertness, to be the *signs* of existent objects and of their virtual character in terms of our own possible experience."[11]

In achieving the latter notion, Santayana was strongly influenced by the later works of Collingwood, who also understood sensa as significations of objectivity. His philosophical idealism made of it quite a different matter, of course, than did Santayana's realism. Pragmatically, however, the result is the same. Consciousness, our psychological life, is a matter of feeling. Knowledge comes of our learned objectification of feelings, whether exter-

---

[10]*Santayana - The Later Years*, Cory, p 171.
[11]*Ibid.*, p 272.

nalized as "things" or internalized as "ideas." Feelings may function as signs for things real or imagined, or as abstract instruments for conceptualization. But whether things or ideas they are affectively "embodied," in that they are made object in our awareness. Each, therefore, is as real and as objective within consciousness as the other, for both are purely mental phenomena produced of affect and so are equally real in their appearance. Ideas, then, no matter that they are considered to be "purely mental," are like things insofar as they are an appearance as consciousness. Thing and idea are both constructs of feeling and thus purely mental while they are also completely and equally objective, since each appears as an object in consciousness.

The psychological similarity of thought and feeling, thing and idea, found clear expression first in the psychology underlying the radical empiricism of William James, a dominant influence at Harvard during Santayana's tenure as student and teacher. Although Santayana rejected both radical empiricism and James as a man, James' psychology left an indelible mark on the philosophy of Santayana. Still, it was a half century between his acquaintance with James and the developments in his own psychology which stemmed from his appreciation of Collingwood, who achieved what is effectively an idealistic restatement of aspects of James' psychology.[12]

A basic tenet of James was that experience – our psychological life – is, as Santayana phrased it so many years later, "only feeling diversified." For James, the "river of life" is the "river of elementary feeling," a stream in which whirlpools and eddies of feeling coalesce into such mental facts as perceptions and conceptions. The diverse phenomena of consciousness therefore are expressions of a single unified consciousness, unified not only in its history and its immediate experience, but also in its function. All human consciousness, that is to say, functions solely as feeling.

No matter the reverence accorded to James in American philosophical and psychological history, his fundamental insight into the nature of consciousness was virtually ignored by subsequent philosophy and psychology. Much of the fault belonged to James. He tried to fight his battles in terms already dominated by his opponents. And while pounding nails into the coffin of old time

---

[12]   From the outset, Santayana was aware of James' influence and its limits. Note, for example, his *James' Psychology* (Collected in *The Idler and His Works*, p 97 ff), a review in 1892 of James' *The Principles of Psychology*, where Santayana lauded the work for exactly what it gave him, "instruction and inspiration," as well as for the openness of James' approach. Possibly the most significant inspiration was that part of the Jamesian analysis that became the antecedent of Santayana's theory of the first and second terms of expression. His principal condemnation concerned James' vaunted theory of emotions, which Santayana rejected on intuitive grounds related to his feeling for moral philosophy. In that same collection of essays, note also Santayana's repeated rejection of and philosophical distaste for the modern philosophies of experience, and the relevance of his objections to Jamesian points of view.

metaphysics, James himself became too metaphysical as he sought to frame his simple theory of consciousness into the structure of an ontology. Thus, the essence of his theory became obscured by language as he addressed an audience prepared to understand him in the terms of thought established by the British empiricists, and he fares little better even today. Consider the example of R. J. Bernstein's introduction to a recent popular edition of *Essays in Radical Empiricism and A Pluralistic Universe,* which were collected by Ralph Barton Perry as exemplary of the principal statements by James of his later thoughts on philosophy in general and his own approach in particular. While one assumes that Bernstein intended to familiarize the uninitiated with the Jamesian point of view, the work completely misses the primacy of affect in the formulation of that philosophy. He treated "affectional facts" as mere *instances* of pure experience, rather than exemplifications of its pristene character. He recognized how James' philosophy celebrated the "thickness" of living experience as opposed to the "thinness" of abstract intellectualism, but he was silent upon the nature of that "thickness" as experience.

There is no doubt that James himself, with his perambulations about the various sacred cows so long established in the field of philosophy, allows his essential point about affect to be missed quite easily by trained philosophers whose eyes are preconditioned to see and interpret more familiar ideas. Yet, at certain junctures of his argument, James cannot be misunderstood if one will but read what he says. He tells us, " 'Pure Experience' is the name which I gave to the immediate flux of life which furnishes the material to our later reflection with its conceptual categories. . . Pure experience in this state is but another name for feeling or sensation."[13] It is the stream of diverse affective undergoing, amidst which self and world take form and where "thoughts and things are absolutely homogeneous as to their material, and . . . . their opposition is only one of relation and of function."[14]

These notions had been developed long before and analyzed in detail in *The Principles of Psychology.* Yet, even there, the student of philosophy may gain a first and probably lasting impression of a theory of consciousness where percepts and concepts float down the river of feeling and appear to be mental phenomena quite different from feelings, not only functionally but essentially. And since James talked about all mental phenomena in terms of the "stream of thought," then the first impression can develop into a notion that James was talking about the stream of thought essentially as a stream of percepts and concepts, and the consequence is an understanding of his psychology and his philosophy that is quite different from that which he proposed, Indeed, in *The*

---

[13]*Op. Cit.*, p 50.
[14]*Ibid.*, p 72.

Principles of Psychology, it is necessary to read a footnote to find his only explicit assertion that the "steam of thought" is properly to be understood as the "stream of feeling," and that the terminology, "stream of thought", is used strictly for convenience of discussion.

While there is no doubt that the term is convenient relative to discussion of consciousness as an activity that subsumes a variety of functionally different mental phenomena, it is fatal to understanding in the hands of students reading "selections" and text writers garnering their ideas second hand, or perhaps from too cursory a review of the material from the point of view of their own philosophical preconceptions. Perhaps the most disasterous consequence, however, was that James may have fallen into his own "trap" of words with the usage of the term. As we shall have cause to examine later, as he proceeded into the work of analyzing the various relationships that consciousness adopts in the generation of self and world, he developed a theory of emotions that is inconsistent with his fundamental theory of consciousness as feeling. And it must be admitted that his renowned theory of emotions is another source of confusion about the nature of consciousness as the basis for his radical empiricism.

The sum of all this is that there is a general historical misconception of James' fundamental view of the psyche. Bernstein's example is the rule, not the exception. It is entirely too possible to take a full semester course in the philosophy of William James and hear only of experience as the "stream of thought" with no mention by instructor, text, or selected readings of the fundamental affective endurance James was really talking about.

The problems of philosophers and psychologists with the ideas of James are not unique. One may also be instructed in the philosophies of Croce and Collingwood, who achieved understandings similar to those of James (no matter that they are poles apart philosophically), and also gain no inkling of the fundamental principles of the mind which for them unified thought and feeling. The reason, let us emphasize this, is the bias which sees an unbridgeable gap between thought and feeling, which finds intellect and aesthetic as alien faculties of the psyche no matter that they are distinctively human powers. Furthermore, in spite of the supposed sophistication of philosophy in this day and age, the bias remains no less dominant in the thought of scholar and layman today than it was a century or even a millenium ago.

Of course, there are exceptions. Painfully few. Notable among them is Suzanne Langer, who early developed insight into the role of feeling in life. That insight ultimately led to the ideas in *Mind: An Essay on Human Feeling*, where we find lucidly asserted – for the first time since Collingwood – that "works of art are images of the forms of feeling, and . . . their expressiveness can rise to the presentation of all aspects of mind and human personality."[15]

---

[15]*Op. Cit.*, p xviii, Vol. 1.

Langer appears to be unaware that what she thought to be her own "discovery" had been clearly set forth and analyzed at depth (albeit from a different philosophical orientation) by both Croce and Collingwood before her. She did admit her debt to James, but failed unfortunately to follow him out to the conceptual boundaries that he established.[16] Still, for all that, Langer is virtually a voice crying in a wilderness, and for the first time attempted to draw from the data of the life sciences of the mid-twentieth century a consistent view of human mentality as "a vast and branching development of feeling."

Elsewhere in the wilderness, the bias persists where thought and feeling are found to be entirely different matters of the mind. There is the crux of the mind-body problem as it persists today in fact if not in name, even in the work of the most prestigious thinkers. That prejudice leads into a theoretical *cul de sac* for both psychology and philosophy, where there is no hope of real understanding of the nature of expression in the arts in particular, or of the nature of man's psychic behaviors in general.[17] Escape is possible only if we

---

[16] For her claim of "discovery," see the context of the quotation cited by the preceding reference. As to her shortfall from James, consult the opening chapter of Volume I of the work cited. Note that there she shows no apparent comprehension of his idea of "fringe" (see esp. p 29) or of the intentional character of feeling. See also her remarks at the bottom of p 22 where she shows no appreciation of the dispositional nature of feeling, lack of which was particularly debilitating to development of the theory of mind that her first two volumes of *Mind* attempted.

The root of Langer's problem in handling both problems of mind and of art in terms of her intuitive understanding of the function of affect in human mentality, is no doubt her preoccupation with her "new key" to philosophy, the notion of symbolic transformation. That is, to describe art as "the symbolic expression of an artist's knowledge of feeling," (p xv) leads her off into conceptions of art in terms of symbolization, which analytically produces quite different kinds of concepts of art and aesthetics than are developed when one finds works of art as "images of the forms of feeling." The latter phrase describes the concrete essence of art that is the proper subject of philosophy of art and aesthetics. The former terms lead inexorably back into the sterile maze of problems characteristic of the neoclassical philosophies of art, providing excellent vehicles for the essayist in the production of useless knowledge, but tending to wander far afield from the central issues of the philosophy of art or aesthetics.

The above observations may be unfair to Langer, however, since she has completed and published only two volumes, including but four of the six promised parts of her *Essay*. The first was by far the superior effort; Volume II was too much a collection of scientific knowledge that bore too heavily upon the behavioral psychologists and too little on the remarkable advances of neurology and neurochemistry, with little advance of her thesis.

[17] As we find Langer in Philosophy, we also find a few psychologists and physiologists not only willing but also able to incorporate feeling into their constructs of theory. Yet, while a few are able to approach a Jamesian point of view, thorough-going theories of consciousness as feeling

share Peirce's "persuasion" that there is some manner of connection between aesthetics and logic, a connection expressed in the apparent reciprocity of influences between the humanly distinctive behaviors of intellect and aesthetic.

Using the suggestion of the Jamesian theory, we take the position that intellect and aesthetic are not two behavioral differentiations between man and beast, but one behavior that the psyche is able to use in two different ways. Intellect and affect—and therefore thought and aesthetic—are not entirely different matters of the mind. With James and now with Langer we share the conviction that intellect and affect are unified in terms of the fundamental psychic function, which is feeling. If this notion is valid, then it is possible to hypothesize that the meaningfulness characteristic of expression in the arts has psychic roots in the same ideational sources as intellectual meaning. And that implies that there is a single elemental problem from which all other problems of consciousness derive—the problem of affect.

---

are rare birds indeed. The most common approach to integrating thought and feeling into a single theory is to make one the cause of the other. On the one hand we find, for example, H. J. Campbell, in *The Pleasure Areas,* asserting that thought is a distinctively human cause of feeling. At the other pole, Freudian psychology finds affective elements (the unconscious) to be the cause of percepts and concepts (consciousness). While that is perhaps an oversimplified statement, the fact remains that Freud held that the unconscious (notoriously apt to description in affective terms such as drives) is the cause of consciousness (which is equally apt to description in terms of perceptual and conceptual processes).

Occupying a middle ground are the ideas of Paul Schilder. He saw both the genesis of thought and its subsequent appearance as consciousness to be heavily entwined with affective phenomena. Each and every thought, he said, undergoes a preconscious development during which, particularly in the later phases, affective influences play a critical role. When those thoughts then emerge into consciousness, moreover, they remain deeply involved with affective contents. The entire process of thought development, in Schilder's terms, is a kind of turning the raw, primary processes of the psyche into forms appropriate for the secondary processes of consciousness, a notion not exactly foreign to Collingwood's theory of imagination.

An excellent summary of Schilder's theories is given by David Rapaport in *Paul Schilder's Contribution to the Theory of Thought-Processes,* which may be found in the journal identified in the List of References, or in the appendix to the edition of Schilder's *Medical Psychology* used here.

Chapter 5

THE PROBLEM OF AFFECT

The idea that the art experience has an affective essence was a revolutionary concept two hundred years ago. It was antithetical to everything that most people, artists and philosophers among them, had learned to believe or were ready to accept. Now, it is just as revolutionary, and for exactly the same reasons, to assert that the affective essence of the experience is ideational and is rooted in what the ancients chose to call the contemplative intellect. This conceptual reversal has occurred because in this century there has developed a dominant consensus that the felt aspects of aesthetic experience are the fundamental subject matter of aesthetics and the philosophy of art, and the functions of intellect have no immediate connection with that subject matter.

Earlier chapters have made clear that the current consensus is one of broad dimensions. Indeed, beyond a few central notions, it embraces radically different understandings of the nature and function of affect in our experience of art. More significant, perhaps, is a pervasive appearance of discomfort concerning the specific subject matter the consensus deems to be primary: the diverse phenomena of affect, commonly called feelings and emotions.

As the idea of the affective essence gained a kind of provisional, tentative form, we saw Winckelmann's neoclassicism virtually wrecked upon the dilemma posed by the affective elements of the experience. Reynolds almost reluctantly allowed the affective dimensions of the experience to enter into his discourses, seeming to say, "Yes, but. . . ." With Lessing, on the other hand, there was a firm, total assertion of the primacy of the affective essence of the experience. The inability to cope on the level of theoretical analysis with that essence was also at the root of Lessing's swift retreat to the neoclassical concern for the rules of art. Similar difficulties with the matters of affect led to Bosanquet's restriction of aesthetics to analysis of content. Nor was Kant any different. He also accepted the validity of the affective dimension of aesthetic experience, yet rejected it as the basis for theoretical formulation of an aesthetics. Among the moderns, Dewey and Santayana described affect as the essence of the experience, but they were unable to cope with it on any terms

58

except as a consequence of other behaviors. That turn of thought in effect undermined the very foundations of their aesthetics, where value lies.

The summary impression gained from a review of the development of the idea of expression stated in affective terms, is that philosophers do not appear to have any better idea than anyone else of just what to do with affective data. For some of them, it appeared to be enough just to assert that feelings are involved in the experience, and are central to its nature, and effectively to leave the issue moot while they went about discussing works of art and conventions of style, technique, and content. What we find at the extreme are a few philosophers, even on the current scene, who have argued that if feelings and emotions are the primary data of the aesthetic experience, and since feelings and emotions indubitably are psychological phenomena, then the appropriate solution to the problems of affect in general and aesthetics in particular is to hand them over to the purview of the psychologist.

While there is a certain dubious logic to such an argument (thought and knowing are also psychological phenomena, thus the same argument also hands over epistemology), the consequence turns out to provide no means for resolving the problem of affect in its original and essential form. Psychologists, unfortunately, appear to be no better prepared than philosophers to cope with the problem. Many psychologists even deny that there are such reference data as feelings and emotions within the boundaries of their science, because feelings and emotions defy the scientific need for direct measurement and experimental control.

One cannot deny that, from the point of view of philosophy and psychology as it is commonly taught and pursued professionally, there is the incontestable appearance of fact that feelings and emotions are notoriously unsuited for investigation using accepted methodologies for either scientific or logical analysis. Yet, despite the appearance of that methodological barrier, significant advances in understanding of the physiological foundations of human behaviors, and especially of affective behaviors, have been made recently in specialized disciplines of the life sciences. At the same time, a review of the journals and texts of philosophy and psychology reveals how remarkably little of this new knowledge has penetrated the conventional wisdom of general psychology and philosophy.

It can also be shown that the fundamental methodological criteria for approaching and dealing conceptually with the problem of affect were defined by specialists in analytical methods more than a generation ago. The work of these men, however, appears to be little appreciated and generally ignored by the philosophical community. What we seem to find is that affective phenomena, *a priori*, were not considered to be adaptable to methodological disciplines, and that virtually closed the book on the matter.

A part of the methodological difficulty arises out of language and its logic. C. G. Hempel succinctly clarified one dimension of a proper solution to the difficulty, writing, "The theoretical content of a science is to be found in propositions," and "The meaning of a proposition is established by the conditions of its verification." If these assertions are accepted as true, then it follows that "all psychological statements which are meaningful, that is to say, which are in principle verifiable, are translatable. . . . into physicalistic propositions."[1]

In such terms, affective phenomena need not be rejected from consideration, but simply to conduct one's investigation such that assertions about affective phenomena regarded as true ought in principle to be translatable into physicalistic statements.

Moritz Schlick clarifies another aspect of the problem of language applying to affective phenomena when he observed that "The adjectives 'physical' and 'mental' formulate only two representational modes by which the data of experience are ordered; they are different ways of describing reality. . . .

"The so-called 'psycho-physical problem' arises from the mixed employment of both modes of representation in one and the same sentence. Words are put side by side which, when correctly used, really belong to different languages."[2] And this mixing of universes of discourse, we will have cause to note, is a central source of theoretical confusion about affect.

But, the problems of language and logic are hardly the whole of the trouble. There is still the matter of feeling *per se*. The plain fact is that no one knows very much about how we have feelings. Consult any basic text in psychology. Find that first-rate scholarship turns halting and ambiguous when affective experience or behavior is broached. The same fault is epidemic in physiology as well, which is not unexpected when one observes that physiology supplied the foundation for and defined the practical limits of the principal achievements of psychology – whether considered as an experimental or as an analytical science. In sum, the situation of science, no less than of philosophy, is that it appears unable to cope successfully with the theoretical problems arising from the fact of feeling.

Take for example the treatment of affective phenomena by Henri Piéron in *The Sensations*, which is the summary statement of his long and meritorious career in physiological research. Let us not deny that his ideas aptly demonstrate the point at issue here; yet he is no straw man either. Anyone versed in the field recognizes him as a scientist and teacher of the front rank, but when he turned to matters of affect he stumbled as clumsily as the greenest

[1]The Logical Analysis of Psychology; in Feigl and Sellars, *Readings in Philosophical Analysis,* pp 376-378.
[2]On The Relation Between Psychological and Physical Concepts; in Feigl and Sellars, *Readings in Philosophical Analysis,* p 403.

sophomore. To read his work is to become convinced that he was baffled by affect and wanted to be held only to descriptions of the sensations which produce
tangible effects such as changes in vegetative processes, motor activities, or even
perceptions since the latter have a virtual objectivity although they are as purely
subjective as feelings. Leave out feelings and science has methods adequate to
demonstrate connections between sensations and particular receptors, nerve
bundles, and types of stimuli. That is the stuff a science is made of.

From his data, Piéron defined sensations not according to the traditional five
senses,* but in terms of nine "categories of impressions." Affect was made the
ninth and last of his categories, and it was identified as "Affect (of pleasant or
painful character)."[3]

The phrasing used for the ninth category was unique on the list. Its form
failed to parallel that used for the other eight. Each other category was described as an "apparatus," e.g., visual apparatus, auditory apparatus, etc. The
change in phraseology, of course, was necessitated by the fact that he could
discover no "affective apparatus." In that event, perhaps the truly odd thing
about his "categories of impressions" is that he added the ninth category at all.
We can almost hear him say, "Well, yes, there is affect and we cannot doubt
that it has something to do with organic sensitivity. Therefore, it must involve
sensations.** And, since I can't include affect in any other category of impressions, I must add a final extra category to account for it."

There are further indications of Piéron's puzzlement over affect. In his listing
of the categories of impression, he described the "fundamental qualities" of
each. Arriving finally at affective impressions, he wrote that affect, as impressions, is related to sensa derived from all the other categories, and are "Reduci-
ble to an undetermined number of fundamentals (the affective repercussions being more important than the sensory specificity)."[4]

In the text supporting that rather opaque pronouncement, little help is
available for understanding his exact meaning. But he did remark, without further amplification, that "The irreducible fundamental qualities it [affect] contains are very little known. This group consists of affective impressions having ill-
defined sensorial specificity adapted to the nature of the stimuli."[5] And with

---

*As Piéron remarked, the traditional "five senses" retain a practical descriptive value which
relate to modalities of behavior definable in terms of the unity of sense in, for example, the "act
of seeing."

[3]*Op. Cit.*, p 33.

**More precisely put by Piéron himself, "Sensory impressions involve affective characteristics,
agreeable or disagreeable, at the same time as perceptive information." (*Op. Cit.*, p 27) This,
however, is a statement based on introspective fact rather than data from his science, and is un-
supported in the remainder of his work.

[4]*Ibid.*, pp 32, 33.

[5]*Ibid.*, p 31.

that he dropped the subject of feelings, while going on to analyze in detail the apparatus and data pertaining to each of the other categories of impressions. Only in his summation does he return to take a parting shot at the problem of feeling.

Describing the course of excitatory disturbance from stimulation to perception, and the occurrences at the various neural "substations" along the way, Piéron says, "At the penultimate station, affective functions—which, however, are under control of the higher centres—are released. These are translated into motor and glandular manifestations, which are fairly variable, but are directed, in the appetitive or repulsive direction, by relatively diffuse propagations of certain excitations, or by very strong excitations."[6]

While that statement has the appearance of being a summing up of some preceding analysis of feeling, the fact remains that the seeming summation is more a bolt from the blue. Earlier chapters prepared the way for that summation no more than his initial description of his subject matter justified his ninth category of impressions. Indeed, his approach to matters of affect has to contain fundamental internal contradictions.

Recapitulating the scheme of his book insofar as it dealt with affective behaviors: He initially described the role of sensation as a regulatory process of several types, each related to a specific mode of physiological behavior correlated with specific kinds of physiological mechanisms. Affect played a part in only one kind of regulatory process: hormogenic regulation. Indeed, he stipulated absolutely no affective function or role in any of the other kinds of regulatory processes of sensation. Yet, just a few pages later, when he arrived at description of the various categories of impressions, he asserted that sensory impressions in general function both as sensa and affect, and that affective impressions are involved with all other kinds or categories of impressions. In the end, however, he took still another tack when he asserted that affective functions are "released" and controlled by the "higher centres," and these functions are "translated into motor and glandular manifestations" which orient one's global behavior in appetitive or aversive directions.

One might suspect that Piéron's views gain scant justice in the preceding summary. Unfortunately, that single paragraph—replete with its internal contradictions—is practically the measure of what his work revealed of affect. Yet there is also a single thread of consistency running through his three versions of affective behavior: In each instance, affective phenomena are repercussions to other psychic events.

Piéron addressed the problem of affect as a physiologist, hence he described these affective repercussions as afferent energies associated with hormonic and

---

[6]*Ibid.*, p 413.

muscular responses, or as resonances in the nervous system stemming from energies associated with other categories of impression, or as a complex of energies released and controlled by the higher centers of the nervous system. In other words, no matter how at any given time he chose to describe the fundament of affective behavior, in every instance it was the consequence of some other psychic function. Further, it is in each instance finally understood or implied to be a passive response, a repercussion. The actual physiological basis for his whole series of arguments, however, was never demonstrated. He was unable to describe any specific neural mechanism specializing in affective response as an "apparatus" of affect, or how affect in general seems to permeate the appearance of all other impressions, or how feeling can be the product of the activity of the "higher centers" of the nervous system. What his whole position ultimately reduces to is rather a lame physiological description of a psychological fact. There is feeling. It cannot be ignored or denied by any science that pretends to study the behaviors of man. Neither can it be explained in the terms of his science. The only reasonable thing to do with it, then, is to make it inconsequential to that science. Make it a purely passive consequence, a repercussion, to those other psychic behaviors which are apt to scientific experimentation and analysis.

The "repercussion theory" of affective function is generally accepted in scientific quarters. And it must be admitted that this point of view has a strong measure of support from the naive psychology of everyday life. Feelings, that is, have the appearance of psychic experiences which simply happen to us. We neither will to have them nor is there any consequence apart from the simple fact that we do have them. Certainly, we may undertake or cease some pattern of activity in order to gain or to escape specific feeling experiences, yet the feeling involved is no less an apparently passive undergoing about which we have little choice. As often as not, feelings simply appear independent of what we happen to be doing at the moment, and must be traced analytically into the labyrinth of past experience. But even in this instance, the feeling is no less a repercussion to that body of experience.

This line of thought leads in the end to the notion that since the repercussion of feeling is different from the initiator of that repercussion, then the feeling consequence is categorically different from its cause. Obviously, since feeling is the repercussion of what the body does, or senses, or what the psyche thinks or perceives, and since there is no mechanism of the body that appears to be connected other than indirectly with the experience of feeling, therefore the phenomena of feeling are purely mental. This line of thinking eventually leads to the notion of a separation between the body that senses and the mind that feels and perceives. The problem of affect, in other words, is a main source of the so-called "mind-body" problem that has plagued philosophy for so long.

Piéron, of course, would justly maintain that the "mind-body" problem of philosophy is irrelevant to his science. Yet is it, when at the foundation of his science he finds affect inexplicable and is forced to admit how little he or anyone understands the relationships between sensations and affective phenomena? He is able to assert only that there is a connection between them. With that, we have reached virtually the same impasse found earlier when seeking the connections between intellect and affect.

That we should arrive at the same predicament approaching from two different ways is remarkable. In the former instance, feelings were said to be the repercussion of thoughts. Now we find that feelings are also the repercussion of sensations and perceptions. The constant factor is that feelings are a consequence of other psychic events. They are a passive response, a repercussion, to other processes. Yet this purely passive response is in some contexts said to be the root of appetitive and aversive behaviors actively modifying the situation of the individual in his world.[7] This creates the odd notion of a passive repercussion being an active agent in behavior, which would require that feelings be more than mere repercussions to other events.

When discussing matters of affect, most theorists avoid contextual juxtapositions of ideas which tend to reveal that anomaly in prevailing theories of affective behaviors or experience. But playing hop-scotch around the problem is self-defeating. Better to take on the problem directly and see it for what it is: perhaps a problem with words, at least in part; more probably a problem of viewpoint.

Suppose, then, that the whole problem is one of looking at the matter from a faulty position; it would follow that from another point of view the difficulty might easily be resolved. Imagine, therefore, that we abandon the notion of feelings being nothing more than repercussions to other psychic events. Let us hypothesize that all mental phenomena are, in essence, affective. As such, feelings are neither more nor less passive, since they are no more or less affective than any other psychic event involving the nervous system.

Looking at this possibility from the point of view of Piéron's theories is perhaps helpful. He noted that sensory impressions in general function both as perceptual sensa and affect. They are at least said to be somehow involved with each other, for neural energies which are integrated as percepts at least

---

[7]   An extreme of this point of view is found in H. J. Campbell's *The Pleasure Areas: A New Theory of Behavior*, which makes excitation of the "pleasure areas" in the limbic brain by sensory and thought processes the root of all human behavior. While he has hardly given us a new theory of behavior (the pleasure principle, again), Campbell provided a neurological description of that principle, meanwhile sustaining the idea of the affective experience as strictly a repercussion to other kinds of neurological (mental) events.

involve energies which are experienced as feelings. The question in those terms becomes: Do feeling sensa result from perceptual sensa, or do they accompany each other, or are they the same identical psychic energy events functioning both ways? In any case, there is asserted a hidden union of perceptual sensa and affect in the subjective processes of perceptual awareness, a union which must be reflected in the objective physiological processes involved.

As remarked, we earlier described the several indications of a union between intellectual and affective processes. Now we find indications of a similar union between perceptual and affective processes. Suddenly feeling becomes pertinent to both percepts and concepts, taken subjectively, or to the processes of sensation and thought, taken physiologically.

From the physiological point of view, however, how is it possible to speak of such a union? For it to be true, then either (1) all cerebral tissues associated with perceptual integration or intellectual function have complex connections with other tissues specializing in producing affective repercussions to those processes; or (2) within the cortical network specialized cells act as affective adjuvants to associational processes; or (3) all three neurologial behaviors —perception, feeling, and thought—are functionally the same kind of activity.

Of those alternatives,[8] we may rule out (2) because all nerve cells in the brain are neurologically the same. Their differences are systematically spatial or chemically particular, and not categorical. As for (1), the peculiar function of the limbic lobe suggests the real possibility of this alternative. Some neurologists go so far as to call it the "feeling brain." But in the final analysis, the limbic brain is just another complex switching center heavily involved in the integration of feelings and emotions within the nervous system. Other centers equally involved with affect have been identified, or their presence suspected, in diverse sectors of the brain including some in the so-called higher areas. So, what we find is less an indication that specific organs of the brain specialize in affect than that the affective function of some cortical tissues cannot be operationally differentiated from associational function.

The evidences substantiating the above conclusion will be examined later. Now, the important matter is that we understand the implications of the third

---

[8]   There are certainly other possible alternatives, e.g., the processes of the brain merely parallel the functions of mind, or simply act as the agent of the mind in performing motor and sensory functions. We are no better able to cope with the transcendental or naturalistic alternatives today than a millenium ago or, for that matter, a century ago when James analyzed the issues in Chapters V and VI of his *Psychology*. Notably, James formulated his own psychology in terms of functional parallelism. This allowed the "spiritualistic reader [to] believe in the soul if he will; whilst the positivistic one. . .can continue to say that nature. . .has mixed us of clay and flame, of brain and mind, that the two things hang indubitably together and determine each other's being, but how or why, no mortal may ever know" (Vol. I, p 182).

alternative suggested above; that is, the suggestion that aesthetic, perceptual, and intellectual behaviors are neurologically and psychologically identical. Objectively they are neural energies. Subjectively they are feelings.

There should be little argument about the objective side of the equation. The physiologist is able to deal physiologically in meaningful ways with the notions of percepts, concepts, and feelings as neural energies operative in cortical tissues. From the subjective side, on the other hand, there is little or no inclination on the part of anyone to discern a similar unity among percepts, concepts, and feelings. And we cannot dispute that, subjectively, these energies have the appearance of being operationally distinct from one another. We rather proceed on to the notion that – since there is no way of identifying a neurological basis for this differentiation of neural energies as such into various kinds of psychological phenomena – there is no difference. Subjectively, in other words, these energies obtain merely the appearance of being different, while in essence they occur as feelings.

The assertion that mental phenomena other than feelings are a "mere appearance" has little practical value, and seems to fly in the face of experience itself. From the point of view of theory, however, it has the advantage of parsimony in constructing a theory of consciousness; i.e., there is only a single phenomena of consciousness to explain instead of several. And in terms of the neurological facts, as we shall see, it has certain advantages.

Suppose that we accept the third alternative as a working hypothesis. The implication it offers for the present study, which concerns the nature of expression in the arts, is that the distinctive aesthetic quality of affect said to be peculiar to the experience of man (since objective energies and subjective feelings are one and the same phenomenon taken two different ways) ought then to be a function of some development of the nervous system which is no less peculiar to man. The most notable difference is the cerebral area of the brain. While it is not unique to man, it is peculiarly human in structure and development. Indeed, there is no doubt that these tissues are the physiological basis for the humanity of the human animal, since those tissues appear to make possible the intellectual behaviors which are as remarkably human as the physiological structure itself. What is suggested here is that these same tissues make possible the equally notable human experience of aesthetic.

This is not to imply that cerebral behaviors are all there is to aesthetic. Rather, the position here is that those tissues and the functions they allow are considered essential to the emergence of both intellectual *and* aesthetic behaviors. Neither does that mean to say that intellectual and aesthetic behaviors are subjectively the same. Obviously, they are not. Instead, we assert that while the fundamental behavior of the cortex is affective, the qualities of affect are "translated" into "objective" contents (percepts and concepts) appropriate to instrumental function. Percepts and concepts, in other words, must be conceived to be translations of feelings into psychic "objects."

That in no way means to assert the existence of some new class of objects in the world. It simply describes the character of certain occurrences of feelings which exhibit a form or structure which persists during an interval, and which are experienced with other similarly persisting forms or structures of feeling. This discrimination of constructs of feeling against the background of feeling that constitutes the being of the psychic reality was the essence of consciousness described by William James a century ago. It was also the fundament of Collingwood's well known theory of imagination and held an equivalent position of importance in Croce's concept of intuition. So there is nothing new in the idea that feeling is the foundation of consciousness; there is only the appearance of novelty since the notion is virtually forgotten in recent philosophy and psychology.

That the idea today is generally forgotten may be understood as testimony to the fact that James, Collingwood, and Croce spoke on the level of speculative philosophy and psychology. Psychologists and philosophers today exhibit a general disdain for speculative approaches to their fields, and turn more to investigations based on philosophical or scientific methodology. Logical analysis, of course, tells us about the language we use to discuss the problem of affect but reveals nothing about the problem as such. Scientific method, on the other hand, as previously noted, has no way of approaching the problem. So, to allow approach to other psychological matters, science has to assert or at least presume a clear distinction between feelings and other mental phenomena.

From the point of view of a science that has one leg grounded in that kind of an assumption, the idea of translation of feeling into other psychic events is a contrived answer to the problem of affect. When examined fairly, however, is the idea of "translation" more contrived than the idea of "repercussion"? If anything, "translation" appears to be a more direct answer to the problem of affect because it asserts a single kind of psychological phenomenon companion to the one identifiable physiological phenomenon − neural excitation − that underlies psychological events. Yet it is appropriate to ask how one makes the translation of feelings into other mental events.

As this point we know little more than that "one does." Yet, that "psychological trick" of turning feelings into other mental events is no more mysterious than the processes by which feelings become the repercussion to other mental events. What we are faced with, then, is the need to choose between two presumptions on which to base a description of the psyche. The great weight of authority lies on the side of repercussions, so it is a presumption needing no explanation for legitimacy. Thus, while we can no better describe the "trick" of the translation, we need at least provide an argument in its favor —even for use of the term, "translation."

Support can be found initially in Piéron's work. In his description of the behaviors involved in sensations, he used the term "translation" as a kind of linguistic convention to describe the connection of affective events with muscular and glandular events. He described how affect is "translated" into motor and glandular manifestations, events which of course are not even neurological. In other words, he described how affective behaviors of the nervous system are translated into physiological events which are not only organically remote from the nervous centers that called out the activity, but are physiologically different in kind.

The translation of affect into percepts and concepts, in contrast, would seem to occur in the same higher areas where feelings are called out and are perceptually integrated, and thus must involve precisely the same kind of physiological events in the very same kind of tissues. It would seem that these conditions would lend a greater *prima facie* validity to the translation of feeling into percepts and concepts, but the opposite is rather the case, and for the very legitimate reason that considerably more is known about the physiological trick of turning nerve impulses into muscular or glandular functions. Yet that is hardly unexpected when one recognizes that muscular and glandular responses to nervous action are accessible to methodical observation and subject to experimental control to an extent to which the translation of nervous energies into feelings, much less feelings into percepts and concepts, possibly may never be.[9]

All that is more in the way of explaining away a need to explain instead of explaining the process of translation, and therefore it does little to justify the position taken here. Still, on the basis of Piéron's data we may argue that one translation is as reasonable to presume as the other even if physiological description of the mechanism of the affective translation remains obscure.

The translation of affect into percepts and concepts is no less mysterious when discussed in the terms conventional to current psychology. In this psychology, feelings are said to function differently from percepts and concepts. The latter are instrumental facts of consciousness. They are tools used to represent the world for purposes of control. Feelings, on the other hand, are something that happen to a person as he bangs into the world.

---

[9]   While it is true that neurology, by both clinical and experimental means, has proceeded far along the way of mapping out the general areas of the brain in which translations of nervous energy into psychological events may be said to occur, the nature of that translation remains as mysterious as ever. We shall see later, however, the growing awareness among neurologists of the role that affect plays in all psychological processes, even if feelings as such are held by them to be different from other psychological processes.

There is no need to take issue with the above description of these different kinds of mental events. It is a fair practical description of our experience of such events. By the same token, we need to recognize that a deeper analysis reveals that the so-called instrumental facts of consciousness are no less consequences of bumping into the world than are feelings, nor are they necessarily used in a different way as facts of consciousness. That is, our feelings about the world are as potent as initiators of behaviors as are our percepts and concepts of that world. In short, the distinction between percept, concept, and feeling tends to disappear the deeper one analyzes either the physiological or the psychological features of these several modes of consciousness.

While we maintain that there is no more than an apparent difference between these various mental events, we do not deny that in our experience of percept or concept the qualities that characterize feeling are largely absent. If present to consciousness at all, there is simply a kind of "residue" of feeling that adds a flavor or affective temperament to the stream of mental facts focused upon the perception or conception. This affective residue is usually ignored because of its instrumental irrelevance, and there is no practical reason why it should not be ignored in the ordinary course of events. Indeed, it must be ignored for that is what the translation of feelings into percepts and concepts is all about. It makes instrumental coping a possibility. It allows us to deal with the world as a world and as idea instead of as a symphony – or cacophony – of subjective feelings.

The translation of psychic feelings into objective matters of consciousness was said by Collingwood to be the function of imagination. Imagination, he explained, is the activity of the mind shaping its raw sentience into manageable form, a form which for practical purposes becomes an abstract thing out in the world, an object of thought. But the term "imagination" seems too limited in scope to embrace the whole concept of the "trick" mind plays with feeling, and the idealistic notion of "mind" too fraught with potential misunderstandings, no matter how sympathetic we may be with the basic ideas resident in Collingwood's philosophy. Better to say that the translation of feelings into instrumental processes of consciousness is what the brain does with feelings. It is an activity just as natural to the brain as walking is to the legs. And the analogy goes further than that. As F. J. E. Woodbridge remarked, mind, like walking, is a way a body has of getting around in the world. And we take to doing both like ducks take to water. Long before my son had any notion that he had legs, his legs straightened as I held him, reaching out for something to stand on; and when I stood him, leaning against the back of the sofa, he held his balance and stood alone, and was pleased as punch with the feeling of I'm sure he knew not what.

The translation of feelings into percept and concept is an inherited propensity. From the evidence of a whole host of human behaviors, it is a psychic potential realized by learning such that in its very appearance as behavior it has the character of automatism.* It is an instinctive behavior, like the grasping action of the hand or the sucking action of the mouth. The translation is quite literally a "trick of the mind." It is a trick the mind—as a function of the nervous system—finds itself doing instinctively, then learns to play expertly and forgets in the process that it is just playing a trick with feelings. No one remembers when or how he learned to "see" circles or squares. Few of us recollect even learning the grammatical and logical structures of the various languages (including mathematics) that allow us to conceive of circularity and squareness. But such is hardly remarkable, for we have no remembrance of how we learned to suckle or to crawl or to raise ourselves erect by holding onto something, or to let loose and walk the first few steps to something else to grasp.

As we learn to objectify our feelings as consciousness of things, the practical demands for our concentrated interest in those things (items of food, shelter, safety, play, etc.) as things ensure that we in effect ignore the feelings that the things are to our psyche. Even more than ignored, they are forgotten – or disowned, to use conventional psychological terminology. While that latter term ordinarily is applied only to pathological behaviors of consciousness, the fundamental trait so pervades experience, is so universally a "normal" behavior, that its pathological aberrations might be expected to occur. Indeed, the tendency is so pervasive within all experience that it is virtually

---

* These ideas seemed terribly radical to me as they initially took shape during this study. In the light of more recent formulations in the scientific community, however, I have the feeling of being a conservative. We regard these dispositional behaviors natural to mind as the product of propensities of the nervous system which appear only when called out, and then in forms that must be shaped by learning and perfected by reinforcement—indeed, they must be if one is to survive his human condition in the world. Others now regard the behavior as actually cast into the nervous system. For example, C. D. Laughlin, Jr., and E. G. D'Aquili, in explaining their theory of biogenetic structuralism, assert that "the brains of normally functioning adults possess a number of models of reality that are genetically preconditioned and against which sensory input is almost constantly compared... The models of reality and the channels through which they are judged for 'fit' with the world are all comprised of real neurological material, and *only* such material." (*Biogenetic Structuralism*, p 101)

Now there is no reason to doubt that the adult mind indeed has developed models of reality against which new experience is compared. But while I read Laughlin and D'Aquili sympathetically, I do not find the evidence sufficient to hold that the brain is genetically preconditioned with those models. But perhaps this makes too fine a distinction between propensity toward behavior and neurological models of reality, since in fact there is only what may be called dispositional behavior being questioned, and both may be said to be representative of such behavior. In any case, this footnote anticipates a subsequent chapter where the behaviors which may be said to be preconditioned are examined in more detail and in the light of other data and assumptions than those yet presented here or offered by Laughlin and D'Aquili.

transparent to our awareness but for its aberrations. Yet, some have called attention to this function in even the most mundane behaviors. Rolf Hassler, for example, in describing the process of perception, tells us that actual sense impressions more or less "vanish completely" while the perception, such as the recognition of an object, remains. Even more pertinent to this discussion of expression in the arts, is Hassler's observation that "In many cases, perception is restricted to extracting the meaningful from the less important details of the perceived object," and "Especially impressive is the restriction to the absorption of meaning in the process of fluent reading, in which many letters are not perceived at all."[10] In effect, we censor or ignore our awareness of detail in order to grasp the total figure, whether of thing or speech. The sense impressions are none the less present; they have simply been obscured or integrated into an affective whole that, particularly in experiences of art, dominates the poise of consciousness.

Since this "trick" of consciousness is perfected for very practical purposes, it is just as useful for a disturbed personality. A pathological phenomenon embodying this "forgetting" of feeling is the notorious ability of the disturbed psyche to disown selected feelings of traumatic significance. In this instance, the trick serves extremely practical purposes for a neurosis. In terms of our thesis, however, of greater significance was discovery that this ability to disown psychic phenomena applies to mental functions involving more than feelings as such. Pioneered by Janet a century ago, this area of study revealed that not only feelings, but things (which we understand to be objectifications of feelings) also may be censored from a perception and specific concepts banished from thought, acts that no less serve practical needs of the disturbed psyche.*

---

[10]New Aspects of Brain Functions Revealed by Brain Diseases: in *Frontiers in Brain Resarch*, J. D. French, Ed.; p 252.

* Pierre Janet's history of Lucie and similar subjects is recounted by William James in *The Principles of Psychology*, Vol. 1, p 202 ff and 385 ff. A more technical review of aspects of this area of research appears in Paul Schilder's *Medical Psychology*, II.2, e, f, and g. He describes various modes of psychic blindness, including the "so-called associative psychic blindness," and the "so-called perceptual agnosia," which he shows may have a clinical source (nerve damage) or be similar to cases of perceptual and imagined material suppression described by Freud. Particularly interesting is a case reported by Charcot, a disturbance that Schilder (p 73) attributed specifically to "dynamic-affective conditions." Harry Stack Sullivan's work on schizophrenia led him to conclusions compatible with the development of ideas we are describing. Sullivan, that is, considered that the schizophrenic thinks and acts the way he does in order to feel the way he wants to feel. His behavior is pointed toward a certain kind of experience, and indeed the various disorders of schizophrenia are but one disorder, and the disorder itself is an escape from a condition of order that, for the schizophrenic, is untenable. Thus schizophrenia is not merely a disruption of normal thought, but a total syndrome involving disordered perception, thinking, and feeling. The only difference in the position taken here is that the total syndome is but the appearance of a single disorder, and that lies at the heart of the affective poise of disorder

The translation of affective experience into such things as percepts and concepts is just as practical. That facility of the brain is the psychological fundament of all purposive and creative actions a man undertakes in the world around. It provides the raw materials for perception and thought alike. It makes the consciousness of self and world possible and controllable instead of a completely holocaustic undergoing. Our experience of art, with its creative control of the whole spectrum of feelings and material objects, can have no different basis. But how would it be possible to say such things on the level of discourse natural to physiology? On the basis of Piéron's data and the consensus in physiology, the translation would be impossible. Yet by understanding the difficulties of the physiologists, and introducing data provided by more recent neurological studies, the key may be found.

In investigation of afferent function of the nervous system, physiologists base much of their science upon the premise that nervous function, whether afferent or motor, is the same.[11] In other words, the afferent and motor nerves have a systemic and not a physical difference of function. Moreover, the basic systematic functions, such as recruitment of fibers, convergence, and divergence, are common to both and are alike in principle. Differing are the results of those systemic functions: motor versus perceptual behaviors. And, of course, we must not forget, there are also affective consequences in the afferent function. So let us turn back to those affective results to discover more of what the experts tell us about them.

In his table of categories, Piéron defined such impressions as "of pleasant or painful character" and as "affective repercussions" to sensory impressions of all categories. His remarks typify how physiologists and psychologists tend to talk only about pleasure and pain, as if such were the sum total of affective experience. Without a doubt, the subjective character of pleasure and pain is so attention-getting and particular that they have a kind of tangibility ordinarily characteristic only of perceptions. But, the first thing we must note about pleasure and pain is that they are affective extremes. Also, they may be said to have variations of quality or intensity in the vicinity of those extremes. But what of those variations away from the extremes which are less attention-getting and less particularized as subjective experiences? What of the midrange between both extremes? Little is said or written about that. But does that mean there is no midrange?

---

sought as the escape from the condition of feeling that could not be tolerated. Solomon H. Snyder, in his *Madness and The Brain*, takes a similar position when he remarks "The very fact that feelings and thoughts influence perception already suggests that underlying the disturbance in perceptual integration might be a more primary disorder of feeling or thinking" (p 158).
[11]*The Sensations*, p 336 ff.

On the contrary, in common language we find constant reference to the midrange, but language then becomes more ambiguous, more imprecise, just as the affective quality does. We say we feel *comme si, comme sa* – not good, not bad. And there is a large increase in vulgar descriptors or low vernacular. We feel "blah," or indolent; "yakish" or vertigo (low level); "sharp" or "alert." We feel "nostalgic," "anticipatory," "blue" or "rosy." None of these are pleasures or pains described, unless the intensity rises toward one of the extremes. And the above are but a narrow sample of the descriptors applying to midrange feelings. If, as Bebe-Center said, pleasure facilitates and pain inhibits learning, what do these midrange functions do? If pleasure and pain polarize behavior, what does the midrange do? No one talks about these things because no one knows quite how to talk about them or what to do with them. And the key to all that silence is that such feelings are not extremes – pleasure and pain – demanding that adequate note be given them; *plus* there is no physiological mechanism to which they may be attributed. They are affective repercussions, nothing more, so forget them.

Yet, we are left with the puzzle of affect as such in a biological system which neurologically operates according to set principles, differing systemically. And since physiologists are willing to talk about pleasure and pain, we may ask how it is possible for this same system to produce affect having two extremes. For example, the system of nerves associated with an index finger can produce tactile sensations resultant from mechanical stimulation (Piéron's category V). Also, those sensations may produce a feeling of pleasure (the touch of velvet) and a feeling of pain (the smash of a hammer), although the category V apparatus is involved in both extremes. Certainly, the mechanical stimuli operate with different intensities and modalities, and the receptors are certainly more violently involved in one instance, but the system is the same. Or is it?

The answer is: "Yes" and "no." The biological system available to stimulation does not change. The receptor neurons actually triggered in each instance, after the all or none behavior of such cells, are triggered at no higher level. Yet, the frequency of impulses does increase, the number of receptors involved is increased, greater convergence results, and other fibers are recruited into the sensory activity. This, however, describes only the results typical of any sensory intensification, an excellent description of which is given by Piéron in full detail.[12] No mention of affect is made in that description, but the actual variations of intensity are almost always discriminated in terms of affect; e.g., the difference between two weights is distinguished by how heavy they feel. The only impressions where affective awareness is not the basis for judgement are visual impressions. Piéron's data explain why.

---

[12]*Ibid.*, p 374 ff.

The visual apparatus is systemically different from the others. Its structure is such that significant recruitment of fibers is not possible, and there are marked differences in convergence-divergence effects, compared to the other categories. A further peculiarity of the optic apparatus is that the retinal receptor, responding to photodetection of visual energy by the outer segment of the receptor cell, hyperpolarizes rather than depolarizing. A. Cavaggioni, in his *Physiology of The Retina*, further notes that receptors common to a given ganglion cell in some instances hyperpolarize while others depolarize, tending to cancel out each other. He concluded that this makes possible the extraction of "spatial contrasts" from visual data. That is, the action of the retinal receptors, bipolar cells, and ganglia appear to develop precise sensory shading without need for the intensification processes typical of the other categories. In consequence, visual data is able to retain a preciseness the others cannot achieve. At the same time, visual events cannot be pleasurable or pain- ful the way a tactile or even an aural event can be.*

Piéron's analysis permits a description of differences in sensory intensity. It also implies a basis for the sensuous extremes that are pleasure and pain. That is, the variance of optical sensa from the affective qualities normative to other categories suggests that the sensations of pleasure and pain are connected with intensification processes dependent not simply upon nerves as such, but upon the dynamic systems that nerve fibers form as functional phase sequences. Piéron's data, however, do not suggest an explanation of the phenomenon of polarization (pleasure *and* pain) or the qualities or "modalities" attendant to such sensations, either as affective extremes or in the "neutral" midrange of feeling. That is, qualitatively different pleasures and pains come not only from different sensory apparatus, but also from the same apparatus. On this prob- lem, R. P. Mackay remarked, "We know utterly nothing of the neural specificities characterizing these modalities. So far as we know, all neural im-

---

* The variance of the visual apparatus has striking implications for philosophy. Man's central focus of attention – indeed, his primary dependence – upon visual data, coupled with its variance from the affective richness of the other categories of impression, establishes the ground for the perennial bias that the clear, precise consciousness focused upon consciousness organized in terms of vision, is essentially different from consciousness that arises from the other senses. Because of man's dependence upon vision and his awareness of self as *sapiens*, this bias led to the notion that the cold, clear light of reason has no common ground with the hot, dark passions. The language of vision is the language of thought. "I see," one says as he arrives at comprehen- sion, and such use of language implies that the bias is older than the language in which it is con- ceptualized. This ancient bias is the source for the tendency of thought that for modern philosophy became the mind-body problem, and which in much of modern psychology divorced the psyche from the study. The empirical validity of the ancient bias is not contested, however. Rather, physiology now clarifies its basis, and from that philosophy may draw implications far different from those that follow from the ancient prejudices.

pulses are alike, being of a single type of chemical and electrical disturbance. Yet they must differ, in order to represent separate modalities, and even shades of difference and degree in each modality...."[13]

Mackay suggests that the modalities are the product of tremendously complex differences in patterns of neural energies, but admits he has no notion of how this can happen in what is essentially a fixed system. He assumes that the differences must stem from spatial summation, frequency, and amplitude phenomena, which lead to different involvements of the biological structure. Piéron's data also suggest that systemic functions stemming from various levels of frequency and amplitude, coupled with integration phenomena particularly at higher levels of the system, are the sources of qualitative differences. These mechanisms of systemic function have only recently come to be understood to any significant extent, and then only in terms of intracellular chemistry. Of interest to us at this point, however, are the systemic functions of nervous tissues rather than the chemical foundations of those processes.

From a systemic orientation, Mackay's analysis of evidences leading to understanding the brain functions involved in the various modalities of affect are of prime significance. His data point to the primary involvement of the oldest part of the brain, the rhinencephalon or "visceral brain," and particularly to the affective functions of the hippocampus and cingulate gyrus. His summary descriptions are readable and lucid but shall not be repeated here, for our interest lies in his analytical findings.

The data available, according to Mackay, are sufficient to reveal only a "general outline" of the neural connections involved in affective response. He is candid in his admission that on the basis of such data he is speaking as a philosopher rather than a neurologist. In his work, he also appears to have no notion of nor inclination towards our thesis of the totally affective nature of psychic phenomena. His treatment of his data, however, tends to support just that hypothesis.

Mackay finds no one mechanism of the brain which may be said to provide the affective corollary or "repercussion" to other psychic phenomena, although the function of the hippocampal cortex comes closest to such a description. Instead he discovers that various structures operating centrally in complex interactions with other structures have demonstrably primary functions in specific psychic phenomena, and that in each instance the function is one of affect. These include general or psychically pervasive functions such as those involving the thalamic structures associated with what are called attention, awareness, and interest; the hippocampal cortex, which appears to provide

---

[13]R.P. Mackay, *The Neurology of Affect*, p 48.

the tonal qualities associated with attitudes responding to sensory data; and the cingulate gyrus, which appears to perform the same function relevant to cortically generated neural excitations which form the basis for affect qualified as "emotional." His data also tell of "secondary sensory areas" in the cortex of which little is known. One of those areas is in the temporal lobe. The neurological data demonstrates that this structure is essential to the phenomena of memory, and that its function is affective.

In his inquiry into the neurological basis for memory, Mackay remarks, "Correlation of subjective states with neural processes is hazardous, but without invoking more than a parallelism, or implying any form of interaction, one may safely say, I believe, that recognition as a subjective experience must correspond to the adoption of an (affective) attitude by the organism. Therefore, recognition of a set of circumstances as something familiar is in essence an affective process – a *feeling*, if you will, of familiarity."[14] In this function –which, he points out, is in effect memory –the central function of affect is not ascribed to those other structures already mentioned which have more or less global functions in affect. Instead, he points elsewhere: to the temporal lobe.

"From our knowledge of the role played by the visceral brain in affect, and the disturbances of recognition seen in pathological and experimental conditions in the temporal lobe, it would seem that in that area the neural processes occur which underlie this feeling of familiarity. Stimulation of these processes induces the feeling and the recognition– correct, if the stimulation be natural, in the process of living, spurious if the stimulation be artificial in the process of disease or experiment.

"Thus, one need not squeeze the whole of the function of memory into the temporal lobe, or even into the visceral brain, but only the affective element of recognition, which is, indeed, the indispensable feature of memory as a subjective experience."[15]

---

[14]*Ibid.*, p 52 (parentheses and italics are Mackay's).

[15]*Ibid.*, p 53. Here it is worth observing that Mackay's analysis indicates that the Kluver-Bucy syndrome (resulting from removal of temporal lobes on both sides of the monkey's brain) is a behavioral change resulting from failure of the memory function, and is not to be interpreted in terms of "pleasure seeking" as proposed by H. J. Campbell in *The Pleasure Areas* (p 99). Certainly Campbell is correct in asserting that aversive and appetitive behaviors are motivated by affective experience of pain or pleasure. There is also no doubt that excision of the temporal lobes from the limbic brain severely curtails primary aspects of affective experience. We argue only with his interpretations of these phenomena, for his theory of brain (or mind) function is oriented back towards an outdated psychology by relating all behavior to the repercussion of that behavior on the so-called pleasure areas of the limbic brain. His point of view also retains the companion assumption of the old psychology that thought and feeling are different in nature, no matter his neurological insistence upon mind as a function of the nervous system. In

Specific features of Mackay's description immediately impress us. From our point of view his acceptance of our hypothesis or not is unimportant, and not simply because he doesn't. Rather it is because his data point in the direction of our hypothesis no matter that they are much less than merely incomplete. They are sketchy. From that data, however, Mackay arrives at certain crucial positions: First, his insistence upon the fact that no structure provides the whole explanation for affect in general or for particular affective functions, but only that certain structures are central or critical to certain functions. Second, he shows how sensory data and cerebral data are both incorporated into affective experience. And finally, he holds that "affect is an essential part of all experience and behavior."[16] In the final analysis, then, Mackay is making much the same assertions as we are making, except that we proceed finally to the quite different assertion that "affect is all experience and psychic behavior," and not merely "essential."

Concerning the problem of affective modality and polarization, Mackay admits himself to be very much in the dark. As he phrases it, "Given a certain neurological mechanism for affect in general, how is the specificity achieved? . . . . In short, how is this specificity of affect accomplished in the central nervous system? For without an answer to this question we shall not have devised any satisfying concept of the neurology of our affective states."[17] Data leading the way to an answer to his questions was not available to either Piéron or Mackay at the time they wrote. A. E. Fessard and others have recently provided the clues.

Fessard, whose earlier achievements were much quoted by his countryman, Piéron, led a series of studies during the late 1960's. These studies in part followed after the work of W. F. Collins and others who, in 1960, showed that

his psychology, we still need to deal with both thoughts and feelings. The "highest mental function," thinking, interchanges cerebral energies with the pleasure areas where feeling resides. Thinking thus is not affective in nature. The thinking brain simply has connections with the "pleasure areas" that produce feeling as a repercussion. The same is true of the sensory areas of the brain. They also connect to the pleasure areas and produce affective repercussions. What we have then, according to Campbell, is a brain that has a single kind of neurological nature (electro-chemical events occurring in neurons and their connections) but at least three kinds of psychological events. As we proceed with our investigation, we will find that Campbell's interpretation is a less advantageous basis for a theory of mind than an approach which finds a psychological as well as a physiological unity in the nature of mental functions.

[16]*Ibid.*, p 56. This approach to understanding the role of affect in mental behaviors was given a more recent expression by Solomon H. Snyder in his *Madness and The Brain.* There he sums up his inquiry with the assertion (p 221) that "Every memory and every perception has an associated feeling or 'affective' component." As he understands mental function, each mental event— as in perception— is "tagged" with an associated feeling state that makes memory, and all the other diverse functions that spring from it, possible.

[17]*Ibid.*, p 56.

the recruitment of specific types or groups of fibers in the sensory process is coincident with the appearance of pain sensation.[18] Fessard reported experiments that added data quantifying the step-like recruitment process, and also provided confirming evidence that the cortex has a primary role in the integration of painful sensa. The significant point here is that the mechanism underlying pain is a recruitment phenomenon coupled with an integration function, both of which are common to all sensory processes described by Piéron. In other words, nothing new has been discovered concerning the basic principles of nervous reaction applying to afferent connector nerves and cortical function. What is discovered, instead, is but a further elaboration of systemic relationships of discrete functional elements.

Carrying our argument after the same hypothesis used by Piéron and physiology in general, and further substantiated by the work of Collins and Fessard, then although the experimental evidence to date applies only to the sensation of pain, we may assume that all phases of affect may be similarly explained if only we knew how to deal with them experimentally and identify the particular systemic elaborations involved. Furthermore, if pain results from the recruitment of specific fibers (called delta fibers) into the sensory process, and the impulses conveyed by these fibers are cortically integrated as pain, then at least some impulses are subjectively experienced as affect only, and are not mere repercussions. Thus, again following after the guiding hypothesis of the physiologists, if one such instance is demonstrated, then all sensory processes are objectively neural excitation and subjectively feeling, no matter what tricks the mind learns to play.

In such terms, the source and substance of experience is the pristine cauldron of affect. A dynamic process of raw feeling is the root of consciousness, providing the ground for our entire experience of being. Like sweet frosting on the cake, moreover, that affective ground provides the possibility of aesthetic and the motive force that is art.

Art is the creative power of the psyche turned loose on the world. It is an activity through which the psyche is able to modify its situation to obtain desired experience. Art is thus any making or shaping intended to gain the experience of some desired situational condition. By that definition, all purposeful acts are artful and, since all experience is rooted in feeling, potentially aesthetic to boot. But all arts are not necessarily aesthetic or beautiful arts, since they are subject to the fundamental distinction philosophy makes between the practical and the beautiful arts. The distinction is made primarily in terms of the activity of art and the value of its product.

Practical arts obtain their primary value from the use one gains from the product of art subsequent to the making. The value of making a chair, for example,

---

[18] *Nervous Processes Underlying Behavior and Learning*

may come when used as a seat. This split between the act of making and the achievement of value is said to characterize any practical art, and the value obtained is said therefore to be extrinsic to the activity of the art.

In art as aesthetic production, the value of the activity comes of and is found within the moment of the creative act. Certainly, a thing is also created, and it may even have practical values stemming from various uses to which that thing subsequently may be put; but that thing and its possible further uses are incidental to the immediate value of the experience and of its creation. Aesthetic value, discovered in the act itself, is thus said to be intrinsic to the activity, whether the act of aesthetic production occurs in the experience of the artist or his audience.

The critical factor in the above discussion is that the distinction between fine and practical arts is axiological, since all experience is rooted in feeling and never escapes its affective essence except as an appearance. Indeed, all of this follows after Croce's insight that sensa, feelings, and impressions are but different ways of talking about the same psychic phenomena to suit different descriptive purposes of intellectual apprehension, and that even the functions of intellect are of the same and sole family of psychic phenomena: feelings.[19]

---

[19] Croce's insight initially suggested the idea central to this book. I encountered his remark, "What gives coherence and unity to the intuition is feeling: the intuition is really such because it represents a feeling, and can only appear from and upon that." (*What Is Art?*, a selection from Croce's work appearing in *Basic Problems of Philosophy*, D. J. Bronstein, *et al.* p 460) This provocative assertion, little amplified in its context, led me back to Croce's major work, *Aesthetic as The Science of Expression and General Linguistic*. There, on page 26, I encountered, "Poetry is the language of feeling, prose of the intellect; *but since the intellect is also feeling*, in its concreteness and reality, all prose has its poetical side." The italics are added for emphasis, identifying the idea that became the force behind the present inquiry. For at that point I had long been sympathetic with the views of Santayana, and really had never considered the alternative suggested by Croce, or truly appreciated the meaning of his notion of intuition that then became very clear to me.

Chapter 6

THE NATURE OF AFFECTIVE BEHAVIOR

The preceding chapter called attention to a small, quite specialized development of neurological research that tends to provide a measure of scientific support for the Jamesian description of consciousness as a process of feeling. Such use of data drawn from experimental science to support the concept of consciousness as feeling points up an interesting feature of this or any discussion of experience or consciousness in either philosophical or psychological literature. That is, between the scienfitic underpinnings of data and the conceptual assertion of the nature of consciousness, we change our universe of discourse.

The idea of consciousness as feeling is stated most naturally in terms related to subjective experience. Experimental justification of that idea is no less naturally stated in terms related to measurable events and processes. Thus, when we appeal to scientific data for support of the concept of consciousness as feeling, we move from the language and conventions of the physiological and the objective (neural processes within a system of nerve tissues) to the psychological and subjective (feelings as the processes of consciousness).

Similar linguistic transitions are made as a matter of course throughout psychological and philosophical literature. The more naive sources even fail to realize a transition has been made. Others recognize the two ways of talking about feelings, but deny any real meaning to one way or another. Yet, there is an alternative view, adopted here, that any comprehensive discussion of affective behavior necessarily involves both kinds of discourse. In short, both are inseparably bound to any adequate description. To try to describe the nature of feeling without describing the nature of the physiological structure in which it appears, would be like trying to describe a sunset without mention of the meeting of earth and sky where the setting occurs.

That the two sides of the description cannot be divorced does not mean they ought not be differentiated. Neither should the difference be defined once, then ignored. Both ways of speaking must persist throughout any meaningful discussion of affective behaviors. The need is to keep them clearly delineated, a need that creates a special problem for aesthetics; i.e., beyond the theoretical problems peculiar to inquiry into aesthetic (or any matter of feeling), there is a semantic problem coming from the requirement to keep the two levels of discourse distinct in their differences while using both to discuss the neurological basis for feeling on the one hand and the subjective appearance of feeling on the other.

All that is by way of a preamble to the next step in this inquiry into the nature of expression in the arts. We followed the trail of clues leading away from the opposing concepts of meaning in the arts to scientific researches lending substance to the notion of consciousness as a purely affective phenomenon of the psyche. Our concept of the nature of expression in the arts thus finally hinges on the more basic concept of consciousness as feeling. If our premise is valid, then aesthetic shares its essence of feeling with all other behaviors of consciousness, no matter what their appearance. So, at this point, it is necessary to define, on the basis of current understandings and interpretations of the data of psychology and physiology, the nature of affective behaviors in general, and their relationship to the apparently different behaviors of perception and conception. Only then may we presume to construct a viable theory of aesthetic.

Now whatever else is said of it, consciousness ultimately must be described as the experience one has of being. That experience, as we understand it, is a continuum of affective experience, a dynamic process of feeling. Despite the tricks the mind learns to play with parcels of that experience, the experience of being is a duration of feeling often times ignored as feeling, other times vaguely pleasant or unpleasant, sometimes overpowering and consuming of our total awareness.

To live is to have that afferent ground of stimuli. That complex interplay of energies is the foundation for and the generative source of consciousness.[1]

---

[1] Pieron recognizes only the kinetogenic energies as the generative and sustaining source of consciousness, while only hormogenic sensations are affective - no matter his later assertion that affect is involved in all categories of impression, an assertion never justified or even clarified by his data.

In our description, all sensations participate in consciousness and all are first of all affective. They are felt. And so are the energies of cortogenic origins that are central to our description of the function of mind.

An interesting point of view located between that of Pieron and that described here is to be found in the work of Susanne Langer. She holds that the body has a multitudinous variety of physiological goings on which become psychological only when they achieve a certain intensity level. Then then play "freely across the limen of sentience," below which they form the "fabric of totally unfelt activities which Freud reified with the substantive term, 'the unconscious.' " (*Mind: An Essay on Human Feeling*, Vol. 1, p 22)

According to Langer, while the limen of conscious sensitivity fluctuates the physiological

Then, because those energies occur in patterns consistent with the structures of the organism and its formal relationships with its environment, there is the potential for consciousness to achieve consistencies and organization in its processes. In other words, because the organism has the structures that it does, and because the environment has consistent conditional characteristics to which the organic structures can relate in what are after all rather limited ways, the sensitivity of the organism to self and environment is similarly structured and limited in form, no matter the infinitely varied modalities of that sensitivity in actual nervous function and conscious experience. Given that condition of permanency of structure and functional variety, there is a basis for consistency of sensitivity instead of a wild, eternally novel and thus unknown pandemonium of feeling. This condition is the basis for the processes of order which in their higher manifestations are called mind, but which also include awareness of vegetative processes marked by such feelings as of hunger, exhaustion, or a pleasant walk in the woods.

From the lowest rung of consciousness to the highest, from the most pristine to the most sophisticated mental behaviors, the fundament of it all is a process of feeling. That ground of affective experience, constituted by the basic sensitivity of the organism to its own physiological equilibrium and exchanges of energies with its environment, differentiates into three quite different levels of affective process, levels which may be distinguished both in terms of physiological structure and affective process.

The initial level is that of the simple feelings of sentience considered apart from any organization they may achieve. Not that these feelings, as behavioral energies, are unstructured and not complex. At this level, feelings are simply the subjective appearance of the energies present in the biological structure. These are best exemplified by the feelings directly related to the sensory structures involved in the immediate exchange of energies with the environment. We are most aware of these feelings because they are easily distinguishable by virtue of their objectification as things. As objectified, of course, they have achieved an organization which involves higher levels of affect, but here we want to consider them only as the discrete feelings participating in that total organization. Indeed, there are only such feelings.

---

energies are present whether those energies rise to the limen and produce consciousness or not. Thus some neural energies are the basis for affective awareness and some are not, depending upon whether the intensity level is adequate to exceed the limen, an explanation that seems contrived and mythological. It seems based on a psychological reification of "limen," properly a term describing the tendency of consciousness to attend to some facets of consciousness and ignore others. Worse, it gives little breadth to the description of actual consciousness. The concept of "fringe" developed by James is clearly a superior concept, accommodating the fact that we are never aware of all physiological events yet the structure of consciousness and its tone are their totality at any given moment. The notion of "fringe" is preserved here in the basis of the total view of mental behavior we describe.

The latter point needs emphasis. The discrete feelings of this so-called first level are in fact the only feelings there are. They are consciousness. The simple feelings of sentience, as such, constitute affective experience. All affective contents are such discrete feelings. When we speak of three levels of affect, then, we are not talking about three different kinds of feeling, nor three different biological structures underlying feeling. There are only feelings on the one hand and neural tissues on the other. On the higher levels of affect, therefore, we do not mean that there is some new kind of feeling developing. What we do find are different ways of feeling. That is, on higher levels of affective behavior, feelings as such achieve forms or organizations significantly different from the forms which result from sheer physical structure, and these forms in effect permit quite different affective behaviors. Not that this level is in any way independent of the physical structure, for of course it cannot be. Rather, the difference in the subjective appearance of feeling is a product of a difference in the dynamic function of a fixed physical structure.

The second level of affect is the product of the inherited tendencies of the organism to feel in specific ways. This level is conventionally known in terms of those psychic propensities called dispositions and attitudes, but includes unconditioned reflexes of the higher centers, and the conditioned reflexes and habitual behaviors that build upon the unconditioned tendencies of the organism.*

---

* In *Conditioning and Psychiatry*, Thomas A. Ban presents a survey of the psychological concept of conditioning, and notes that the application of the concept of the conditioned reflex to the higher functions of the nervous system did not gain general credence until about 1870. The concept of the spinal reflex, of course, had been accepted considerably earlier, and the tendencies apparent in human behavior have been remarked since antiquity. Scientific description of those tendencies, however, was not achieved until Sechenov's *Reflexes of The Brain* was published in 1863.

"According to Sechenov," Ban tells us, "all acts of life, both physical and psychological, are basically reflex, and any voluntary, involuntary, or psychological action in the reflex act begins with a sensory stimulus-impulse related excitation and continues by means of a definite psychophysical act ending in muscular activity." (p 30) In such terms, all psychological activity necessarily reflects fixed laws of physiological behavior. It follows from that, then, that all psychological phenomena can, in principle, be explained physiologically, and that these physiological laws underlying psychological behavior are determinable by investigation.

That exact thesis was the point of departure for Pavlov, who also thought all nervous action to be reflex in nature. However, as Ban points out, Pavlov did not conceive of the process in simple stimulus-response terms – contrary to what many of the psychological text writers appear to think. Rather he saw the organism as a total energy system in which a complex system of reflexes worked to "balance the external forces acting upon it." While that system seems similar to our own, it remains two-dimensional, as D. O. Hebb pointed out, and is unable in theory to cope with the behaviors resident in dispositions and attitudes. (See Ban, p 160 ff.) Our criticism, of course, is that the direction taken by Pavlov and thereafter pursued by behaviorism, has a debilitating internal limitation. Behavioral psychology, that is, cannot approach the truly

Like the first level, dispositional sentience is pre-reflective. It is a level producing awareness and not interpretive understandings. As with feelings of the initial level, the experience is one of "thereness" or "thatness," although dispositional awareness is radically different in function and complexity compared to the first level. This higher level is best understood as a dynamic and achieved predeliction of feelings to set the energies of the organism in motion in one way and not another. A disposition may be described as a way of feeling. It "points" him in one direction and not another. It moves him with a characteristic set to his continuum of experience. It is thus the source of a man's *weltanschauung*, his view of and approach to the world.

The basic directionality of the organization of a man's feelings color and guide the totality of a man's experience of the world. This is the level on which are operative those psychic propensities which for Jung became the base for his theory of psychological types, and also for his notion of the archetypes. In his description, the primary characteristic of the archetype is feeling and it functions as feelings; second, the archetype has a "pre-existent form that seems to be part of the inherited structure of the psyche."[2] This form does not have contents, he maintains, and achieves contents only "when filled out with the material of conscious experience."

A disposition, then, is an inherited tendency of an organism to feel one way and not another. But there is no one tendency; there are many, each one called out by appropriate psychic situations, many forming a complex achieving a basic directionality, with that directionality modifying as the complex changes. Thus dispositions are not static, but are dynamic and at each moment achieved no matter that their possibility and form are inherited.

The emotions constitute the third level of affective experience. They must be regarded as a higher level since with the emotions the affective realm for the first time operates not as a simple index of the state of the organism, nor even as just a predisposer of motive direction. With emotion, we have achieved the level of meaningfulness. This achievement occurs because the higher powers of the brain enter into the total affective experience on the level of feeling itself. And, with the involvement of these powers, the potential for feeling achieves a truly new dimension. Emotions become more than passive under-

---

psychological fact, which is feeling. Indeed, it must ignore feeling to sustain its science. The position taken here, in contrast, sees human behavior as a two-sided coin insofar as understanding of it is concerned. Neither side of the coin is entirely clear by itself, and at the present state of knowledge, one side cannot be considered as but the mirror image of the other since what is clear on one side may be entirely imperceptible on the other. Yet, the greater understanding comes when the two sides are made complimentary and psychic responses are approached in terms of both the physiological energies that underlie feelings, and the subjective appearance that is feeling.
[2]*Memories, Dreams, and Reflections*, p 392.

goings. An emotion is an adaptive reaction generated within the cortex as an active response to the situation experienced. It is a response which does not, through psychomotor actions, change the environment and thus modify the sensations passively available to the organism. Rather, it is a response which psychogenically changes the affective experience of the psyche. As such, an emotion is an organization of feeling which is not a mere endurance, but one which is actively generated and selected on a wholly conscious level.

This in no way means to imply that emotions are different from other levels of feeling as feeling. All feelings are discrete psychic energies. Emotions differ only in terms of the complexity of the organization of those energies and in the singular action of the cortex as a source of affective energies modifying our experience of feelings and their dispositional organizations stemming from lower elements of the system. In psychological terms, on the level of the emotions we actively select and in part generate constellations of feelings necessary to achieve a desired psychic state of affect.

An excellent exemplification of what this means is provided to us by Jean-Paul Sartre, who developed a similar viewpoint in his *Outline of A Theory of Emotions*. In that work, he showed how it is not only possible but that there are reasons to believe that in response to an intractable situation, consciousness actively chooses an emotional response designed to obtain relief from its frustration. Grapes beyond reach become "too green anyhow." Surely the grapes do not change. The situation and its energies remain the same. There are the grapes, still beyond reach. Yet in lieu of fruitless strivings to obtain the unobtainable, relief is found by the inward choice of a new attitude of consciousness. As Sartre pointed out, the consciousness that discovers "sour grapes" has affectively modified itself. The psychic state of distress is then transcended, not by effective action which changes the energies available to the self from its receptor environment, but through an inwardly generated nexus of selected psychic energies. And those energies then dominate consciousness as a new feeling state created in place of the former state of distress.

The philosophical view of man as a chooser is ancient. In modern philosophy, it had as much significance in Hegel and James, among others, as it came to have among the existentialists. Yet, Sartre's extension of choice even into the realm of affective behavior may have been a true innovation of thought. He developed the idea of emotional selectivity as a necessary pendant to his theory of consciousness. That is, if consciousness is a single, unified whole, explainable in full by the principle of intention (choice, or selection) in all its activities, then emotional consciousness can be no less intentional than any other characteristic mode of consciousness.

The Sartrean theory of emotions appears to be the rankest speculation when considered in terms of the consensus of science, for both physiological and

psychological theories of emotion characteristically insist upon the involuntary
– and therefore, by definition, unchosen – nature of emotional behavior. Indeed, one of the paramount puzzles of psychology is that subjectively emotions
can be qualitatively so diverse, while physiologically they appear to have in-
separable connections in fixed relationships with visceral and involuntary
motor behaviors governed by the autonomic nervous system. On that basis for
understanding, little wonder the prevailing view of emotions as purely
automatic and therefore completely involuntary behaviors. Little wonder also
how tentative and unsatisfying that viewpoint becomes when analyzed.

At about the same time that Sartre was developing his theory, concepts of
emotional behavior which turn out to be essentially compatible with the Sartrean theory were developed independently by A. Luria and G. Dumas. Luria,
in *The Nature of Human Conflicts,* showed that the accepted understanding
of emotional behavior as an automatic response is completely erroneous when
one analyzes emotions in terms of the situations in which they occur. He
described how patterns of emotional behavior vary in response to the total context of a situation and in no way are fixed or structured responses to specific
stimuli. Clearly then, if emotional behavior lacks specificity as a response to
given stimuli, then it cannot be automatic or involuntary, no matter the
nature of the attendant physiological events which characterize the behavior.

Dumas, in his *Noveau Traité de Psychologie,* noted the same variability of
emotional responses and concluded that emotions are "adjustive reactions" to
the exigencies of a situation. In short, emotions are just another way the
organism has for dealing with a situation. As such, emotions are used as selectively as any other controlled behavior in coping with the stresses of living.
Emotions not only are not automatic, he assured us, but cortical control of
emotional behavior as a selected total response of the organism to a situation is
a considerable and often dominant element in human behavior in general.

The notion of cortical control of emotions – the intentional, purposive function that they serve as a behavior – is particularly difficult for general
psychology and physiology to integrate into its general body of theory. We saw
how Piéron pursued the idea with little actual success. Certainly he gave lip
service to it, yet in the final analysis he continued to insist that affective impressions are mere repercussions to other kinds of sensory impressions. As
repercussions, emotions are purely automatic and therefore uncontrollable
regulatory behaviors.

Piéron's understanding of emotions is the rule and not the exception in
scientific thinking. Following after that viewpoint, if affect is purely a consequence of other sensory events, then feeling ought to be controllable
analogously to the way one controls the sound of a drum. To get sound, beat
the drum. To get feeling, have sensations. To get feelings of a certain kind,

have the requisite sensations which call those feelings out. To feel sad, cry. To feel glad, laugh. And precisely such admonitions follow from the theories of William James and others influenced by him, even to this day. Yet, as far back as nearly a half century ago, Dumas and Luria had conclusively demonstrated that the analogy of the drum is wrong. Emotions are not tied invariably to specific sensory events. You do not necessarily feel glad just because you laugh. Then again, it has been convincingly demonstrated that you may, and this peculiar relationship between what one does and what one feels has been used with therapeutic success both in operant conditioning and in the revelatory process of psychodrama.

En fin, we seem to find ourselves on the horns of a dilemma. Theoretical development has reached an impasse. Versions of the Jamesian view remain basic to psychological science and have definite physiological justification and behavioral proofs. Yet, emotional behavior in its global aspects has been shown no less definitely to be intentional or selective. A solution is possible only if we regard the two kinds of assertions about emotional behavior as essentially different. One, that is, describes discrete physiological events which have consistent relationships within categorically similar patterns of overt behaviors associated with emotions. The other, in contrast, describes a total behavior of the organism best described in subjective terms as an affective state of consciousness.

Considered in that way, we find that the Jamesian observation that you can feel sad by crying was correct for reasons other than what he thought. That is, one feels sad not because of the automatic responses triggered by the act of crying. One feels sad because one changes his specific state of consciousness by intentionally generating feelings appropriate to that state. He could have done it without bothering to cry. The crying only helped by providing supporting sensory events which corresponded properly and thus affectively lent support to the state of mind under creation. Without the intent, however, the act of crying becomes a sham and the actual feeling state is never generated.

What we have, then, is that in the generation of emotional consciousness, one may indeed obtain supporting sensory events whether from manipulation of the environment or his own body, but the core of the experience – the feelings which dominate consciousness and give it organization and direction – are the product of consciousness itself. Or, physiologically, the energies which dominate consciousness and organize the processing of all energies of the psyche, are energies created as a function of the higher powers of the brain. That, in the final analysis, is what is meant by saying that emotion is an "adjustive reaction" as Dumas held. And if that reaction is understood as a subjective modification of the affective state of consciousness, then it is not unreasonable that the changed feeling state may be considered as the primary reaction of import to any inquiry into emotional phenomena. In other words, examined from the side of consciousness, one hardly cares what sensory or visceral events occurred or what motor activities were undertaken. These are results rather than causes, although they admittedly have feedbacks into the total affective state which aid the psyche in its guidance of the whole of its behavior.

Now let us admit that, from the point of view of conventional psychology, theoretical disputation is possible. It could be argued that there is no need at all of the alleged cortogenic influences on the level of affect, while at the same time admitting that there are cortical or intelligent influences upon affective behaviors. One can conceive that it is possible to orchestrate one's experience such that by skillful manipulations of one's body (and thereby controlling one's available environment) one can achieve the sensations, hormogenic events, and associated affective impressions necessary to produce a desired feeling state. Let us further admit that exactly this purposive kind of selection of our environment by our behaviors goes on all the time. But that is no reason to say that describes the whole basis for our experience or our behaviors. The crucial matter is that such a description fails to come to grips with the rationale for the experience of "sour grapes."

Conventional psychology simply cannot explain the change in affective state that is achieved, as Sartre put it, simply by establishing a new attitude of consciousness. No motor action occurs. Any relevent hormogenic activity is after the fact. What we have is the generation of a nonreflective feeling state which modifies our whole approach to and experience of the world. It is a state consciously selected although the selection process was nonverbal and therefor not logical in the classical sense of the logic of language.

What we postulate, then, is that an emotional state can be produced as an active response of the psyche without the prior condition of specific sensory, motor, or glandular activities. Further postulated is that these purely psychogenic states of affect are consciously selected and come to operate on the level of learned habit. Were that not true, the idea of shaping objective energies so as to achieve emotional meaningfulness would be impossible. Aesthetic trial and error could not be fortified by learning and provide the fundament for taste. Meanwhile art as a creative, purposive activity operative on the level of aesthetic production would be inconceivable.

Were emotions purely passive responses to visceral events triggered by sensory impressions, as the consensus of psychology still maintains, then aesthetic theory dependent upon any mental behavior more complicated than sheer sensuous virtuosity of response to objective energies would be completely unfounded. Meaning in the arts might therefore be admitted, but it could have no aesthetic relevance. The value of learning to enhance one's appreciation of the arts would also be severely limited. If aesthetic were strictly sensuous, the quality of the experience would little relate to or depend on any manner of learning beyond the basic skills of perceptive integration. Such a restriction seems hardly able to do justice to the traditional and demonstrably accurate notion of the educability of taste.

Indeed, one of the primary advantages of our position is that aesthetic learning—the education of taste—is made subject to the same rules as apply to learning in general. By the same token, our position is ideally congenial to current learning theory. Learning, that is, is by consensus thought to be fundamentally a process of discovering which activities produce desirable conditions of the organism (indicated by pleasurable feeling states) and which activities result in the opposite (painful feeling states). From that came the conclusion, albeit erroneous, that pleasure and pain therefore facilitate or inhibit learning. In other words, feeling was thus treated as a catalyst for rather than a part of the actual psychic events which constitute learning.

Such a conclusion overlooks the need for an answer to the obvious question: "How does a subjective experience interact with an objective event?" For since the consensus describes learning as an electrochemical change at a synapse, how does a feeling interact with such an occurrence? The problem of the psychologists obviously is that they are attempting to discuss affective phenomena on two levels at once, intermixing language drawn from both levels as if they were one universe of discourse simply because grammatical usages and structues of a common linguistic base allow it. G. G. Bebe-Center was an important source of that confusion, maintaining that pleasure and pain effectively facilitate or inhibit learning by tending to sustain or block neural patterns of energies in the learning activity.[3] Two whole generations of psychologists followed after Bebe-Center, unable to see that such an assertion was an objective tautology obscured by language. We escape the tautology and the attendant "interaction" problem simply by observing that feelings and neural activity are one and the same phenomenon described in two different ways of speaking. But the confusions in psychology generally persist, although there are notable exceptions.

R. P. Mackay, for example, recently described how memory depends upon the familiarity of affect, and built a case on the basis of experimental and clinical data which led him to conclude that "Affective states are inherent in all processes of consciousness." More specifically, "The element, therefore, which makes subjective experience coherent and continuous,

---

[3]*Pleasantness and Unpleasantness.*

which makes memory, and hence learning possible, and which is essential to the formation of personality and character, is affective. There is, it would seem, no such thing as pure intellect, divorced from affect and evaluation."[4]

Mackay's is a cogent and lucid work, yet it may be faulted for his unwillingness to take the final step suggested by the data. He retained the notion that there was intellectual process apart from affect and he concludes with two corollary behaviors instead of but one. In part that results from his puzzlement with the problem of affect as other than a repercussion of such activity.

In a more recent article, Magda B. Arnold, although avoiding the issue of neural activity and affect, took a position remarkably similar to that of Sartre, tying emotion to an interpretative evaluation of the situation of the organism, and using a notion similar to Mackay's "familiarity of affect" as the key explanatory mechanism. She writes, "A phenomenological analysis of the sequence of psychological activities from perception to emotion and action has suggested that emotion as a felt action tendency depends on the person's appraisal of the situation. Correct appraisal requires memory; and memory includes not only sensory and motor memory but the remembered positive or negative attitude to something (affective memory)."[5] The key point is that the elicitor of emotion is an appraisal, by definition an evaluative mental act. And "each appraisal produces a felt tendency to action which either leads directly to appropriate behavior, or is modified by subsequent appraisals and subsequent action tendencies."[6] The only significant difference between her position and that taken here is that we say the appraisal does not produce the felt tendency; it is the felt tendency.

Eighty years earlier, on evidence much less adequate than that available to Mackay or Arnold, William James reached conclusions which subsume the ideas of Sartre, Mackay, and Arnold, and actually extend beyond. Memory, said James, is a "sense of familiarity,"[7] and "Remembrance is like direct feeling; its object is suffused with a warmth and intimacy to which no object of mere conception ever attains."[8] Thus he also saw emotion tied to the object, no matter what he appears to say later in his theory of emotions. And, like Mackay, he also considered this feeling of remembrance – of intimacy and warmth in the familiarity of the feelings of self – to be the source of the unity of the self. It is this intimacy of feeling which spans the gap of sleep or unconsciousness, the affinity which greets and knows the new experience.

---

[4] *The Neurology of Affect*, p 47

[5] *Brain Function in Emotion: A Phenomenological Analysis;* in *Physiological Correlates of Emotion*, p 283; Ed. By Perry Black.

[6] *Ibid.*, p 271.

[7] *The Principles of Psychology*, Vol. I, p 252.

[8] *Ibid.*, Vol. I, p 239.

The further step that James took was denial of the distinction between intellect and affect – thought and feeling. "The difference between thought and feeling. . . reduces itself, in the last subjective analysis, to the presence or absence of 'fringe.' "[9] "Fringe" is the totality of feelings coming of brain processes at any moment, of which we attend to only a very small portion as the focus of awareness in subjective experience. The fringe as it were is the background or backdrop of consciousness attending to things or ideas. Thought, concerned with its object, plays a functional role against a background of indefinite feelings. Feeling is structural to the background, a part of the stream in which the thought bobs along like a cork.

From that it might appear that James is telling us that experience is a river of images (percepts and concepts) guided by attention (our interest in aspects of the stream, a kind of pervasive choice of what to attend to) and immersed in the feelings of relations and tendencies which fade into a whole bed of vaguer fringes of which we are little aware except as a kind of tonality of being. Indeed, he is telling us just that. But there is more to the matter. Concept and percept turn out to be feelings also, feelings trapped and preserved through their objectification. For him, a thought is but feeling which knows much, while "every feeling is at the same time a bit of knowledge." The crux of the matter is, then, that "knowing itself, whether of much or little, has the same essence, and is as good knowing in one case as in the other. Concept and image, thus discriminated through their objects, are cosubstantial in their inward nature, as modes of feeling."[10]

So James took the crucial step from which Mackay held back a half century and more later. Mackay was as sure as James that the unity of personality is dependent upon feeling. He further understood that feelings are a necessary condition for the occurrence of all mental processes. He held back only from the final assertion that the affective unity of personality is possible only if all mental processes are, at bottom, processes of feeling.

The consequence of the line of thought pursued by James is that feelings, and more complex affective phenomena of dispositional and emotional consciousness, are no different in kind from other mental behaviors. Whether the appearance is of thought or feeling, percept or emotion, the psychological fact behind that appearance is one of pure affect.

Of equal significance is the physiological fact underlying the psychological appearance. All mental behaviors, no matter what their psychological appearance, have not only the common affective essence; they also occur only as neurological behaviors. To say that there is feeling is to say that a neural pattern is energized. The converse is also true. Feeling and neural excitation are but two ways of talking about a single phenomenon, the psychological event.

---

[9] *Ibid.*, Vol. 1, p 478.
[10] *Ibid.*, Vol. 1, p 479.

Chapter 7

AESTHETIC AS AN AFFECTIVE POISE

Saying that all the processes of consciousness are functions of feeling does not mean that we must talk about those various processes solely in terms of feeling. Perception, for example, may be described no less meaningfully – but with a profound difference – in terms of its object-oriented appearance which serves to relate the organism to its environment. In short, the most proper way to discuss the process of perception depends on the objective of the discussion.

If we wish to discuss the nature of perception, we ought to use terms related to the affective appearance of consciousness. If we want to discuss the function of perception, we ought to use terms related to the instrumental appearance of the world as consciousness. The same is true concerning all other kinds of mental processes or events.

The various processes of feeling, as a whole, constitute the endurance of feeling called the self. The self also may be discussed in two ways, either as that continuum of feeling, or as the object-oriented person that interacts with its environment. The latter self, of course, is the self as which we lead our lives. As that self we conspire to discover America or fly to the moon, then go about doing such things. It is a self known for its acts. It is what it does. But to describe the self solely in terms of what is attained in give-and-take with the world describes only its instrumental appearance and not its nature. For that we must turn to the description of self as an ever-changing flux of feeling that is always the same persistence of feeling.

James described that persistence as principally the appearance of those vague affective presences he called fringe, a kind of background of felt nuances against which the main roles of feeling are displayed. He also noted that both in the fringe and the foreground there is a kind of internal consistency in the stream of feeling, a fundamental tendency or disposition toward certain kinds or qualities of experience. As Sartre phrased it from an object-oriented point of view, each consciousness points itself toward the world in its own distinctive way.

The persistence of self as complex tendencies of feeling pointing toward the world is but the subjective side of the description of consciousness. Feelings also provide objective form for the instrumental operations of self. These are the feelings of encounter with the world, and the further affinities between those feelings which constitute feelings of relation. In short, characteristic affinities of feeling, objectified as things encountered and as relationships between those things, provide a structure based on consistent appearances, a structure that allows instrumental behaviors of coping with the world instead of a mere flood of feeling.

The two sides of affect—feelings as self and as object—are a stream of feeling persisting as a consciousness and as a world. James called that endurance "experience," a stream of discrete affective events unified not only as the single stream that it is, but also by affinities and tendencies of feeling. That river of elementary feeling recognizes itself by the unity of the stream and knows itself by the tendencies of that stream to achieve particular flavors of feeling. Meanwhile, feeling itself gains affinities between its aspects by which one feeling knows another.

In essence, that is what James meant when he said that memory depends upon familiarity of feeling. His whole psychology was based on that single principle. The individuation of self and all the processes of mind, or consciousness, are the product of exactly that fundamental phenomenon, the affinities that feelings come to have with each other. Equally, the knowledge of the world is the product of a context of characteristically related appearances of object-oriented eddies of affect (percepts and concepts) against the ground of fringe feelings.

In such a description, consciousness appears to be a continuing flood of feelings, all intermingled, with the nature of the outpouring fully dependent upon even the last infinitesimal trickle of affect. And so it is said to be. Fortunately, that outpouring achieves tendencies which focus the stream upon some feelings rather than others, and through the affinities of those feelings in the focus, those feelings are objectified as perception and conception of self or world.

In terms of the growth of the awareness of self, James saw it as the product of a kind of warmth of remembrance with which one feeling greets another and forms a kind of cohesiveness amidst the flux. This same familiarity of feeling also provides the basic function of recognition upon which memory and all other cognitive processes of consciousness are built. This dependency upon affinities of feeling—quite literally all upon all—leads to a contextualistic concept of mind and its processes. In other words, no event, no process, no function may be separated out of the flux to be understood by itself. It may be understood only in the total context of its appearance.

Since we understand feeling as the subjective appearance of neural energies, description of consciousness in terms of affinities of feeling ought, by the same token, to be translatable into a description of consciousness in terms of neural energies. By that, the contextualistic interpretation of the subjective appearance of feeling should have an equivalent description as a contextualistic theory of neurological events. Unfortunately, such is not the general rule.

The present state of neurology provides no license to change our universe of discourse and elucidate a contextual theory of consciousness in physiological terms. While there is a growing recognition among neurologists that any event in the nervous system somehow influences the whole of the system, the description of the total response of the system to any discrete event appears quite hopeless. This difficulty of elaboration of a contextual theory has led physiological science virtually to abandon the idea. Generally in vogue are versions of the so-called "pathway" theory, which is much better suited to description of mental behaviors in physiological terms. A further and more important advantage of the pathway theory is its aptness to experimental applications. It permits the investigator to approach the nervous system in terms of identifiable parts with relatively isolable neural functions.

As studies noted by I.A. Richards a half century ago made clear,[1] while the pathway theory may be well suited to physiological descriptions and investigations, it does not fairly come to grips with the psychological facts. Richards for his part opted for and outlined what he admitted to be a quite primitive contextualist theory, "unsatisfactory and incomplete," although it contained the notion of the "stable poise," an idea of particular value to a description of consciousness.

The contextualist view suggested by Richards conceived the psyche as a complex and unified energy system that tends to assume and maintain, or seeks to restore what Richards called "stable poises." Each poise involves the total energies present in the system. Each is a kind of qualitative balancing of the diverse energies that has a particular flavor to it that marks it as different from others while being recognized as appropriate to a given kind of situation. The mark and its appropriateness to some situation is, through the fact of experience, learned. Later it may be a selected response chosen to adjust imbalances of the energies in the system resulting from external influences upon the organism. "Such a system," Richards observed, "would exhibit the phenomena of memory; but it would keep no records though appearing to do so. The appearance would be due merely to the extreme accuracy and sensitiveness of the system and the delicacy of its balances."[2] A memory event could occur when "The partial return of the

---

[1]*Principles of Literary Criticism*, p 103 ff. In that discussion, Richards was principally concerned with the function of memory. His remarks naturally have significance to the whole concept of the processes of mind.
[2]*Ibid.*, p 104.

context (of sensations) causes the system to behave as though conditions were present which are not, and this is what is essential in memory."[3]

Richards admitted that the whole matter remained quite mysterious, but the mystery comes only of describing the poise of consciousness — which is a psychological concept — in physiological terms as a system of energies. Described subjectively as the affective poise of a system of feelings, the mystery tends to abate. The poise of the system is an affective balance. That it is the subjective appearance of a system of psychic energies is not inconsequential, but this is a statement which bridges the gap of two universes of discourse and not a license to mix them into a single description.

Discussed in terms of feeling, no one can fail to understand that his own experience is often dominated by a single aspect of feeling which literally encompasses and dissipates anything inconsistent with it. The only real puzzle is how the system is able to seek to assume or to maintain a particular balance, and how the system is able to behave as if conditions were present which are not. The solution relates to the same phenomenon that allowed us to understand how the coveted grapes become "too green anyhow." The tendency of the psyche to "point" in behavioral directions is, in affective terms, a dispositional tendency toward a characteristic modality of feeling, an affective poise as it were. More is required to achieve this focusing of affective energies than the mere appearance of sensory materials that initiate the affective impulsion. More is required even than the affective tendencies that dominate this directional modification of the state of the psyche. There is a release of feelings (energies) of psychogenic (cortical) origin that tips the affective balance (the context of nervous excitation) in the appropriate direction. It is as if the psyche manufactures feelings (energies) lacking from a sought after state of affective endurance (concatenation of nervous excitation), literally recollecting the feelings (energies) formerly involved when the poise (nexus of energies) was learned as conditionally desirable (it felt good), whether by trial and error or by excitation of biologically conditioned responsiveness.

This focusing of affective energies occurs not only as rapturous transport in aesthetic, but also as the reflective intensity of intellectual concentration or any other similarly gripping experience. These intensifications of affective energies do not, however, define either the whole of consciousness or the whole of the function of memory. Memory and consciousness generally function in bit format, where energy packets exhibiting a general tendency establish a context but not a qualitative unity based on some dominant affinity. Such patterns of energy or experience do not attain the gathering power of aesthetic or intellectual concentration. Yet, the common denominator of experience remains the same as for the "important" events of intensified consciousness; that is, the afferent energies lived as feeling.

---

[3]*Ibid.*, p 105.

What is described here is no mechanistic, knee-jerk automaton impelled by its genetically inspired response to its environment. Rather, there is a self-adjusting, free-running energy system that literally learns to feel comfortable with balances appropriate to various dispositions or "conventions" of energy exchange with its environment. It is a whole system responding to the condition of the whole, a concept to be understood only in terms of dynamic balance within the context of energies (feelings) present at a given interval of the process.

While many neurologists appear to be moving in the direction of such a concept of the integrated function of the nervous system, there remains a general disquietude within the scientific community when one suggests that affect be regarded as an explanatory principle of psychic behavior rather than as a mere passive undergoing or repercussion to other psychic processes. This discontent naturally leads to new attempts to cope with the problems that plague traditional behavioral concepts of psychic behavior, while still using terms and concepts compatible with behavioral approaches. One of the more intriguing of these theoretical sallies was made recently by Karl H. Pribram, in his *Languages of The Brain*. There he described the memory function of the brain by means of an analogy with holography.

Laughlin and d'Aquili adopted Pribram's innovation and dubbed it "the holographic hypothesis" of memory. They wrote, "It is not the objective pattern, or 'picture,' of reality presented to the senses that is recorded in memory, but rather something on the order of an 'interference pattern' that is recorded."[4] Just as on a photographic plate, the bits of data recorded by holography allow the whole of the recorded image to be projected from a small segment. Pribram regards that memory of a given datum is recorded broadcast throughout the brain, totally present in each bit recorded, each bit able to restore the whole memory even when large areas of the brain have been damaged.

The persistence of memory subsequent to brain damage is of course the primary matter necessitating the development of the holographic hypothesis for support of approaches based on the pathway theory. How else could memory persist when the pathways are damaged? The holographic hypothesis effectively considers the whole brain as one great pathway for virtually anything, with practically everything being recorded "on the same plate." Only this factor, Laughlin and d'Aquili conclude, "would explain the enormous storage and retrieval capacity of our memory circuitry. . . ."[5] Perhaps so, but it also makes any analysis of that capacity, or any neurological tracing of cor-

---

[4]*Biogenetic Structuralism,* p 79.
[5]*Ibid.,* p 80.

tical functions, impossible. For the holographic hypothesis proposes that the tracks of memory lead everywhere at once, allowing one to find virtually anything he seeks anywhere he wishes to look, for what he is looking for is everywhere. It is difficult to conceive, therefore, what possible practical value this theory might have as an aid to understanding the function of the brain.

Pribram, Laughlin and d'Aquili also reveal a certain ambivalence about their interpretation of the holographic analogy as such. At moments, they concede that the holographic analogy is simply a conceptual model having no basis in actual brain function. Other times, as in the quotation referenced above, the theory is used to explain particular phenomena or conditions of brain function. It is worth the reader's time to go merely to pages 79 and 80 of the work cited to see just how prevalent that ambivalence is in fact.

Perhaps it is more meaningful to grant them their assertion that the holographic hypothesis is a modelling concept, simply an explanatory mechanism that in the final analysis has no basis in fact other than that it is a way of talking about the observed functions of the brain. Then, let us talk about what they mean by a memory event being "recorded" in the brain. How is it possible, for example, to speak of a perception of reality being wholly present in each bit recorded? We are talking about brain function, and the brain is made up of billions of interacting neurons. Any recording that is done must take place among those components. Each bit must therefore be recorded as the function of a particular neural cell chemically conditioned to respond to a particular field effect. Or is the recording mechanism something else? If so, what? If not, how is a complete memory event present in the electrochemical action of a given cell, or even of a phase sequence? In these terms, the holographic hypothesis becomes much more mysterious than the idea of a whole nervous system seeking and finding a dynamic poise of energy, or feeling.

Also interesting is the manner in which these men presume that a single kind of neural mechanism in brain function produces different kinds of consciousness. They apparently never seem to wonder how the physiological unity of brain function is not the measure of some psychological unity of consciousness. Yet, opportunities for them to question their presumption are common, as when Laughlin and d'Aquili remark, "Probably the most compelling feature of the hologram is that it provides an example of recorded and retrievable information about sensory experience that is lodged in a physical 'code'; and a code that is totally dissimilar to the nature of the experience itself."[6] No attempt is made to describe the nature of that code (something to do with neural function?), the nature of experience or even the particular sen-

---

[6]*Ibid.*, p 81.

sory experience to which they refer. Yet, since their discussion is framed in terminology and conventions of language based on presumptions characteristic
of their field, only someone who challenges those presumptions and conventions would find fault with their terms.

Finally, note that they speak of a "code" completely unlike the "nature of
experience itself," and expect their analysis to be accepted. Meanwhile, the
same audience that they address would be expected to consider that the Jamesian assertion that the whole of consciousness, no matter its discrete appearances, are made of the single "stuff" of feeling, is a speculative, unscien-
tific notion deserving only to be ignored and not challenged as a legitimate
hypothesis. But we have noted this conceptual double standard before. Here,
it is worth mentioning only because it dates not from the time of Socrates, or
even from the Kantian era, but from just yesterday.

Patching up worn-out ideas with band aid analogies drawn from the latest
technological novelties is typical of any age, and Pribram's approach is thus
hardly unexpected. But, it is a cosmetic device applied to old ideas that fundamentally have no where else to lead us. For anyone willing to look, the time
has come to go back and reevaluate our guiding presumptions and conventions of thought, back to test the fundamental viewpoints that orient both our
science and our *weltanschauung*. Something of that kind of an enterprise was
at the root of the present effort, where we seek to readjust our concepts of self
and world in terms of consciousness as a process of feeling, and then reevaluate
the traditional concepts of the nature of expression in the arts. We have
described the processes of feeling as the stuff of consciousness as such. It is no
mere repercussion to other kinds of psychological events, but is a dynamic,
creative shaping of an awareness of self and world.

The dynamic, creative process of feeling called consciousness is exemplified
most clearly by the activity of art as aesthetic production. In the artistic act we
manipulate materials to obtain specific experiences of encounter with the
world's objects, while central to that process is a quality of affective idea that
dominates the entire activity. That dominant quality is a kind of poise of feeling that establishes an aesthetic focus from which inconsistency is expelled and
a core of experience constructed toward the sought after aesthetic fruition.
And, the key elements in that core of feeling, let us emphasize, are supplied
neither from the energies initiated by encounter with the environment nor the
dispositional behaviors of the nervous system processing those energies.
Rather, it is literally a recollection of feelings stemming from psychogenic
sources that underlies not only aesthetic production, but all other behaviors
based on learning. All learning, that is to say, comes of the establishment of
affective affinities within a total system of feeling. The model of the process
sees the sytem modified by impingement of new energies upon the psyche.

Imbalance – an affective tendency away from the desired affective system – results. The crisis of feeling may be alleviated in part by changing the available energies encountered, but the central and dominant factor is the generation of affective energies by the psyche itself, energies selected to change the tendency of the psyche back toward the desired poise of the system.

The description of learning in affective terms applies not only to the processes involving the total poise of the stream of consciousness. It applies also to the discrete elements of experience which are objects to consciousness – percepts and concepts – no matter that their affective qualities are more or less ignored in their translation by the learner. Concepts are the handles we put on intellectual experience. Attending to the handles, we lose touch with their fundamental appearance as feeling. Perception is a similar translation of feelings of encounter into such things as visual images and sounds.

The objectification of feelings as things is the essential first condition of any and all perceptions of the world and self. It puts perceptual handles on our experience of things as things. As the work of psychologists such as Eysenck has shown, objectification of feelings is a dispositional tendency developed into a learned behavior. As Collingwood described it, the objectification of feelings is a skill fundamental to all learning and thus of our entire mental life. It raises the indeterminacy of feelings up to the determinacy of things.

In objectifying things out of the psychic fabric of feelings, and in the experimental manipulation of things to determine the affective changes made in self, man achieves his initial control of his feeling states *and* a method of controlling the world around him. He learns from his feeling indices which control functions exercised on things produce what feelings, while in the act of sampling the affective consequences of his interactions with the world he becomes aware of which feelings are desirable and which are not.

The critical point of the above, for learning theory, is that the process of learning is not what the tradition following after Bebe-Center thinks it is. Pleasantness and unpleasantness do not facilitate or inhibit learning in any direct sense, but are rather psychologically conditional. What they do is initiate approach or avoidance behaviors of a dispositional nature which in effect establish conditions of psychic acceptance towards persisting in an approach toward the learning of specific situational contents. That is something quite different from what Bebe-Center was talking about. Learning actually takes place in either instance, and pleasantness and unpleasantness have no facilitating or inhibiting influence upon learning as such. We have a difference only in what is learned.

In other words, learning takes place in any experience no matter its affective polarity. Take the example of specific learning objectives associated with specific situational contents. If an approach is made to the materials, they will be learned. If, for reasons of unpleasantness discovered in the experience, avoidance results, then the materials will not be learned. However, in the experience learning has indeed taken place, for the avoidance behavior has been learned. And, what we have in either instance is an adaptive response of the psyche based upon affect whether we are talking about approach-avoidance behaviors or learning of approached materials.

Such affective influences are ordinarily grouped under the term "motivation" by psychologists, who admit the importance of motivation relevant to the processes of learning. Yet, classical learning theory deals only with cognitive and psychomotor behaviors as if they were entirely independent of affective behaviors. This no doubt results from the fact that these theories were generated and proved in the laboratory situation where experimental control in effect allowed none but appropriate affective behaviors as a normative ground against which learning behaviors were measured. No wonder then that classical theory can afford to ignore the problems of affect. No wonder also the problems encountered when those theories are extended to practical application in the classroom or factory.

Some modern theorists are giving new attention to the problem of affect in learning. A. W. Staats, for example, asserts that learning of any behavior in the cognitive and psychomotor domains can be shown to be dependent upon affective behaviors, which Staats groups under a single heading: attitudes. He points out that all conditioning processes – classical conditioning, behavior therapy, operant conditioning – in the final analysis turn out to be concerned with the reshaping of the affective contents and discriminated stimuli eliciting them which originate or extinguish any behavior as a situational response. Further, he holds that any learning process, if understood at depth and not merely in terms of changes in symptomatic behaviors, is essentially a matter of classical conditioning. In that process, where for example learning is unpleasant, other affective reinforcers can be introduced into the situation to reinforce the learning behavior. This reinforcement is comprised of affectively positive contents which in effect extinguish the negative contents.

The success of classical conditioning, according to Staats, is based upon conditioning procedures related to discrimination of stimuli and reinforcements of previously conditioned shapings of unconditioned (biologically originated) behaviors springing out of the basic conditions of the organism. In other words, he would trace all affective influences back through a complex chain of conditioned reinforcing stimuli supported finally by the unconditioned responses and reinforcing conditioning already achieved.[7] The fundamental similarity of such a description to Freud's notion of the causal

---

[7] *Social Behaviorism, Motivation, and the Conditioning Therapies.*

function of the libido as the shaper of behavior is remarkable. The fault in such a view is that it ties all affect and all learning to what we call the dispositional functions of affect. The growth of self, by such a notion, is but an extrapolation of behaviors by pairings of new reinforcers with old unconditioned responses – the function of classical conditioning.

The validity of the classical conditioning process cannot be denied. Neither do we deny Staats' argument that the process in effect harnesses the forces of the biological organism – the archaic and primitive dispositional organizations of the psyche – in service of possibly quite sophisticated behaviors. Rather we hold that even there the whole story of the influence of affect upon learning has not been told.

As noted earlier, approach-avoidance behaviors may be reversed on the level of emotion by the intervention of higher functions of the brain. There is no denial of the conditioning factors which enter into the control or operation of such function. There is rather the assertion that the function is of a different order than primitive disposition no matter how radically such disposition has been conditioned in service of instrumental behaviors. What we have on the level of emotion is not merely an extension of adaptive response on the basis of undergone feelings resulting from the situational exchange of energy. Certainly, those feelings are part and parcel of emotional behavior, for feelings, and their dispositional and emotional structures, are not monadic in experience. They occur together. But, on the level of emotions, there is another affective behavior entering into the nexus of feeling: The generation of feelings by the psyche which enable the acceptance of feeling contents it otherwise might avoid.

That phenomenon of cortical psychogenic affect distinguishes emotion from other levels of affect and makes it an effective instrument of the psyche. In other words, the higher structures of the brain generate feelings which modify the affective experience adequate to allow approach to and learning of what continue to be unpleasant materials. The unpleasantness is not "extinguished," as the classical theorists maintain – and indeed the whole notion of affective "extinguishment" is a fallacy stemming from analogy with overt behaviors which we say are extinguished because they end and tend not to recur. Instead, cortogenic affect simply restores the affective poise of the system to an acceptable condition. The unpleasant feelings still are present, but in a different context dominated by other feelings.

Such a notion, of course, is unacceptable to most psychologists. The consensus is that emotions as pure affect are something that simply happen to people, rather than being in their own right effective instruments for modifying not only consciousness but the supporting organism. Contrarily, however, recent psychology also holds that overt patterns of emotional behavior are nonspecific and entirely learned, no matter that certain elements of the patterns are innate, such as laughing, crying, and certain visceral functions. The contradiction, we have seen, stems from their inability to cope with the psychological problem of affect.

A particular source of this problem of psychology, oddly enough, is the work of William James. We think it odd, that is, for while psychology lost touch with his notion of experience as pure affect, his theory of emotions was widely accepted for the simple reason that his theory permits psychology to ignore subjective affective behaviors as opposed to visceral and overt motor behaviors. Even when James' theory was conclusively repudiated, shortly before the First World War, the essence of the theory was never abandoned and remains a preconception of psychological science to this day.

James' theory, briefly, holds that the body undergoes stimuli and responds with reflex effects. These effects, both muscular and visceral, produce feelings of which we become aware. That awareness of reflex effects, made possible through feeling, constitutes emotion. In other words, emotion is a passive awareness of the body's undergoing.

The advantage of such a theory of psychology is that emotions and affective behavior in general can be ignored in terms of their subjective appearance. The theory asserts instead that only physiological behaviors are important to the science of psychology, since those latter behaviors are deemed to be the specific causes of consciousness, and they are fully accessible to the experimental instruments and methodologies of science. The difficulty of this theory is that feeling must be consistently treated as an incidental effect of other, psychologically meaningful (because they are objectively accessible) behaviors, and therefore feeling is of no scientific or behavioral consequence.

That common parlance implicitly asserts the influence of feelings and emotions upon behavior is obviously a problem for the scientist. He must deny, ignore, or explain away the apparent influences of affect. In any case the fact remains that science is unable to cope with the influences of feeling upon behavior, and attempts to eliminate the problem from practical consideration by neutralizing the effects of feeling through experimental controls. Since such control is demonstrably feasible, the notion of feeling and emotion as a passive effect rather than an active influence is fully tenable for laboratory purposes. On the basis of laboratory experience, in fact, the idea of feeling as a passive effect may be asserted as a necessary preconception for science. In the final analysis, however, that particular scientific attitude towards affect restricts the actual validity of psychological science to the events of the laboratory. The uncontrolled influences of affect in ordinary behaviors out in the real world prevent the generalization of laboratory findings to the interpretation of behaviors out in that world, a situation which has been ruefully remarked by more than a few psychologists. Yet, none of them seems to grasp that the influences of affect are at the root of the problem. Instead, the cause is laid to imperfect methodologies and controls when faced with the complicating influences of the infinite number of variables present in events of interest in the normal world.

Against that background, some doubt is raised concerning the repute of James as one of those principally responsible for laying to rest the "mind-body" problem that always has piqued philosophers, especially since the time of Descartes. No matter James' radical empiricism and his view of consciousness as the stream of thought, his theory of emotions ascribes such feeling to the repercussion in "mind" of the doings of the "body."[8] Certainly, he appears to be telling us that mind is a kind of appearance of the body, or that the body is the appearance of feelings as consciousness, which are essentially similar statements. He also asserts the relationships between neural excitations of the brain and the stream of experience (the "river of elementary feeling"). Yet, in the final denouement of his theory, James was incapable of accepting and integrating into his thought the idea of the absolute identity of nervous energies and feelings.

James himself commented on the real issue at stake: "If feeling is an inert accompaniment, then of course the brain-cell can be played upon only by other brain-cells, and the attention which we give at any time to any subject, whether in the form of sensory adaptation or of 'preperception,' is the fatally predetermined effect of exclusively material laws. If, on the other hand, the feeling which coexists with the brain-cells' activity reacts dynamically upon that activity, furthering or checking it, then the attention is in part, at least, a cause." Then he adds, "The question is...a purely speculative one, for we have no means of objectively ascertaining whether our feelings react on our nerve-processes or not."[9]

---

[8] The importance of this viewpoint of James to the science of psychology cannot be overemphasized. Psychology as a science needed a rationale for escape from the subjective. Psychology as a study of consciousness – which is subjective, inaccessible, and dominated by indefinite qualities of feeling – seemed without promise of ever gaining scientific repute. As an infant science in the past century and even to some extent now, psychology was looked upon as the bastard child of physiology and philosophy, and treated with condescension and even derision by scientists of the traditional disciplines. Little wonder, then, the defensiveness of the early psychologists concerning their science, or the ascendency of behaviorism and experimental methodologies as psychologists sought to make a "true" science of psychology. By the same token, this obsession with "science" and its trappings of experimentalism also explains the virulence of the attacks upon "speculative" psychologists such as Freud and Jung. For these latter thinkers appeared to be throwbacks into philosophy rather than innovators of a new branch of psychological science.

[9] *Psychology*, Vol. I, p 448.

From our point of view, the question is meaningless rather than speculative. Objectively, there are nervous energies. Subjectively, there are feelings. If feelings are the subjective appearance of what are objectively nervous processes, then one is the measure of the other. This view does not make feeling an "inert accompaniment" as James' own theory of emotions maintained. Rather it makes the feeling state of consciousness — its affective poise — and the system of neural energies which objectively are what subjectively is that state, not a "fatally predetermined effect of exclusively material laws," but a free-running, self-correcting system which is able to shape its energies/feelings to its own self interests, e.g., create a work of art.

The notion of such a system is not inconsistent with James' view of the stream of thought developed in Volume I of his *Psychology,* where thought and feeling are made of the same "stuff" of experience. It is inconsistent with the position he took in Volume II, where he asserted that emotion and cognition are things apart, "and cerebral processes are almost feelingless, so far as we can judge, until they summon help from parts below."[10] It is these parts, he said, that make the difference between an "object-simply-apprehended" and an "object-emotionally-felt," a notion which divorced the afferent activity of sensation from the affective process of emotion, and repudiated Volume I.

Why James had this inversion of his thought is difficult to understand, particularly since his notion of the stream of experience and his theory of emotions saw print in journal articles more than a half decade prior to publication of the *Psychology.* He, therefore, had more than enough time to reconcile the divergent views, which involve a conflict that is fundamental and not merely a matter of the discussion reaching a different level of discourse.* Volume I described consciousness as a unity, a stream of thought full of percepts and concepts understood as coagulated feelings fringed by a river of less definite affective contents. The crucial point was that thoughts are feelings which know much.

---

[10]*Ibid.,* Vol. II, p 472.

* The probable reason for this internal conflict was simply that James tired of the work (he accepted the book contract a dozen years prior to its publication) before he was well into the second volume. Then it tended to become more a compendium of his knowledge in the field than a rigorously analyzed presentation of his central psychological theories. This explantation is suggested by Santayana's implicit devaluation of the theoretical worth of the work when he lauded James' approach rather than his theoretical achievements (See *James's Psychology* in Santayana's *The Idler and his works*). This explanation is supported by Cushing Strout in *William James and the Twice-Born Sick Soul* (contained in Rustow's *Philosophers and Kings*) when he reports James' expressions of distaste for the work when finished and his assertion that he wished he had never written the book. Strout also notes James' subsequent failure to ever again write anything significant in the field of psychology.

In Volume II we are no longer able to understand thought and feeling as being essentially the same stuff of experience. There is no knowledge left in feeling, little feeling left in thought, and physiologically they are entirely different matters of the body, just as they have suddenly become quite different matters of the mind. Knowledge comes from direct perceptions of an object; emotions come from the feelings triggered by reflex "currents" in the body which, perceived and combined with direct perception, turn the experience of feeling into an emotion. That describes a functional unity of thought and feeling in behavior, but that is not the psychological unity he initially described. Even worse, his theory of emotions makes feeling a purely passive effect, a mere repercussion in no way influential upon the body's acts.

While we may puzzle at great length over the developments which led James to his positions in Volume II, the initial volume provides the actual theoretical antecedent for the more fruitful approach to mental behaviors in general, and emotion in particular, which is undertaken here in search for a deeper understanding of the aesthetic experience. Here, emotion is found as entirely an adaptive response deeply seated in dispositional tendencies of the psyche. That response is no mere passive undergoing, not an affective experience which just happens to people. Rather, the functions of the dispositional tendencies of the psyche are selectively adapted by cortical behaviors which function more as feelings than as ideas in the context of emotionally dominated global behavior. These cortogenic feelings are learned and can operate on the level of acquired habit with a potential for further selective adaptation.

En fin, in the event of emotional experience what we have is a constellation of feelings progressively and selectively integrated into a dominant poise of the psyche. This integration of affect in part results because (1) the afferent nerve fibers have the structural, systemic relationships that they do, in part because (2) of inherent tendencies of the higher structures of the nervous system to functionally organize in specific ways, and in part because (3) alternatives among those functions can be selectively shaped by introduction of other energies which do not have their origin as such in sensory processes.

Of the three aspects of emotion, the third is less different from the others than it appears at first glance. No matter that a measure of free selectivity appears operative in the third aspect, it too is the product mainly of the biological heritage of the organism. In this, and in our total view of the psyche, we follow after such thinkers as Jung, who wrote, "We shall probably get nearest to the truth if we think of the conscious and personal psyche as resting upon the broad basis of an inherited and universal psychic disposition which is as such unconscious...."[11]

---

[11]*Two Essays in Analytical Psychology,* p 144.

From this point of view, certainly emotions as such are not inherited. They are adaptive responses occurring in a particular organism at a particular time in response to a particular situational context. Yet, the possibility is inherited, first of having feelings or emotions at all; then that affective energies shall organize or function in specific constellations and not others; and, finally, that in their learned affinities they initiate not only dispositional functions, but also specific modifications of feeling itself based upon conscious selection of dispositional tendencies of cortical behavior.

These tendencies toward feeling, seeming to operate at all affective levels as if always ready to be realized in response to particular contexts of environmental contents, must be regarded as the base which makes the spiritual discovery of the aesthetic possible at all. The consequent species-characteristic behaviors must also be the ground for art as the language of emotion. Without this innate basis for interpersonal consistency in organization of feeling, there would be no possibility that art could be the vehicle for the communication of feeling. By the same token, just because the aesthetic tendency is innate, there is no reason why it must be realized. It must be discovered and nurtured as an acquired skill.

Understand the matter this way. Just as man learned to attach meaning to the organizations of feelings made possible by his vocal cords, he also learned to attach meanings to the organizations of feelings – emotions – made possible by his inherited reaction patterns of feeling, patterns which are just as much a part of his biological heritage as his vocal cords. Just as vocal cords made speech possible as an instrumental language, feeling patterns make art possible as the language of emotion. Just as we must learn to form words by controlling sound, we must learn to form emotions – and thus to shape the fruition of the aesthetic experience – by controlling feeling. And both are learned by experience.

For us, the most significant part of this controlled achievement of a selected poise of the psyche is that a part of the synthesis of feelings originated not in the objective manipulations of energies or in the primitive undergoings of the organism. Part came from the function of the cortex, which is able to exert its influence over the total nexus of feeling such that the objective and psychical energies which called it into being are no longer adequate bases for explanation of the achieved synthesis, or poise, of feeling. With the introduction of this function into consideration when examining the aesthetic, we have moved beyond the notion of aesthetic as a mere titillation of the senses; we have found the basis for meaningfulness in feeling, and thus of expression in the arts, and paved the way for all other kinds of meaning in various aspects of conscious experience.

This basis of the meaningfulness of aesthetic in cortical function has direct relationship to the intellectual processes of that very same organ. The first giant step of sentient being that made consciousness possible at all was the objectification of feelings into things. The second great step that produced the human consciousness was the objectification of feelings in symbols and signs. Initially, they probably stood for things, later for relationships, then for control functions and finally for any conceivable conceptual relationship a man's imagination might produce. When that final step is reached, man is operative on the level of his intellect. Still, it is functionally and objectively the same level as before. There are neural energies subjectively appearing as feelings. The difference is that operating intellectively, consciousness with more or less completeness ignores or disowns the sentient facticity of feelings and attends to the appearance of the object or idea objectified.

We cannot deny the Kantian flavor of this whole discussion. In the sense of that discussion we are also able to find some agreement with Collingwood's assertion that objective reality is an error of the mind and real only because it is asserted as real. Yet, with Santayana, we reassert our animal faith in being. Justified by logic or not, it has the support of the experience of a life proceeding from one day to the next, as if the perceptions, intuitions, and thoughts by which we reveal, understand, and control our relationships with the world have essential and not just virtual objectivity.[12]

---

[12] The "essential" objectivity of perceptual knowledge, challenged by philosophers since Plato's parable of the cave, recently found significant support from scientific quarters. P. K. Anokhin, the noted Russian neuro-physiologist, approaching mental phenomena in terms of the physiology of the nervous system, advanced the idea that consciousness necessarily has an effective correspondence with the existing universe in which we live. That universe is not one of abstract points and places, but of space-time. And consciousness is not an awareness of abstract perceptions or discrete events, but of overlapping appearances of neurological events originating not only in the environment but in the conditioned electrochemical processes of the brain cells themselves. These processes are not accidental, but are the product of a million years of physiological adaptation; they are not random, but are integrative shapings of sense data that perceptually project the real world of space-time in which the organism lives. As he puts it in his *Chemical Continuum of Brain as A Mechanism of Reflection of Reality* (p 8), "The absolute and universal law of the inorganic world — the progression of phenomena in a space-time continuum — over the course of evolution has lead to the animal brain, as a special organ of reflection and adaptation, acquiring the property of continuous flow of its processes in full correspondence with the components of this continuum in space and in time."

Chapter 8

AESTHETIC AND THE ARCHAIC PSYCHE

Nearly a century has elapsed since William James attempted his initial description of mind as a process of feeling. He was inspired more by intuitive brilliance than by scientific fact. Now, in just the past decade, data have become available through neurology and neurochemistry which tend to warrant that description. The key discovery was that some sensa are integrated *as feelings*.

In explaining the function of nervous behaviors, physiologists find that the behavior of nerve tissue, whether afferent or efferent, is in principle the same. The principles applying to the function of one nerve are thus held to be the same as those applying to all nerves. There are particular differences in chemistry and connection, but to understand the principles underlying the function of one nerve is to understand all. Equally, to understand the functional principles of a given phase sequence or more complex organization of nerves is to understand principles applicable to all functions of the nervous system.

What underlies the preceding description of the physiologist's approach to understanding the operation of the nervous system is a principle of the generalizability of data. With billions of neurons in the system having perhaps trillions of connections, the operation of the system must be deduced from data applying to but a few neurons and a few distinguishable phase sequences. More, since the principles are indeed found to apply when the investigator probes into new parts of the nervous system, there seems little basis for doubting the validity of generalized principles of understanding concerning the various functions of the nervous system. By the same token, there is no reason why this principle of generalization should apply only in some instances to the defined functions of the nervous system. Therefore, if the nervous system integrates some sensa as feelings, the same principle tells us that what is characteristic of the processes involving some sensa are characteristic of all. If so, then the integrative processes involving all sensa are affective in nature. In short, all sensa are integrated as feelings.

Obviously, the above discussion involves two levels of discourse. The involvement, however, was initiated by the original experimentors in describing the findings of their studies. We need only clarify what they were doing. That is, they were describing the objective behaviors of nerve cells in terms of the subjective behaviors of consciousness. Sensory impulses processed in the nervous system, they said, are in some identifiable instances integrated as feelings. If so, using the same principles of generalization as before, it follows that feelings and neural energies—not only in some instances but all—are identical events in the organism.

The essential issue is whether the principle of generalization is valid or not. If it is, then the data provided by science warrant the description of mind as a process of feeling and the equation of feeling and neural function. If not, physiology would be left with much data but no science. Rather than repudiate a science it appears better to accept its principles. So, we reach the conclusion that if the data developed by such men as Collins and Fessard are genuine, and their interpretations valid in terms of the principles of science, then "feeling" and "nervous energy" are terms appropriate to two different ways of talking about, or describing, a single kind of psychic event; and speaking subjectively, as James maintained, all consciousness is affective. Objectively, on the other hand, all those behaviors of the organism grouped under the concept of consciousness, or mind, are integrative processes of the nervous system. Feeling is the subjective appearance of those energies. Feeling is no repercussion to the energies present in the nervous system; it is the occurrence of those energies as lived experience.

In such terms as the preceding, when we say that there is a unity of consciousness we can mean either that there is a unity of feeling or a unity of nervous function, with both meaning practically the same thing. There are samenesses of quality or connection between feelings, samenesses which provide a kind of psychological architecture, a structure of affective experience with consistent features which define both self and world. There are samenesses of function and interaction between nerve tissues, operating together as nervous processes which specialize in some instances to control and define the functions of the organism and in others to define the presence of the world to the organism. The subjective likenesses of feeling, therefore, may also be described as objective likenesses of nervous processes.

Considered in terms of nervous processes, the likenesses which characterize consciousness may be discriminated as three different kinds. There are likenesses derived first from the normative features of the world as a source of receptor energies. Then, there are likenesses stemming from the inherited and species-characteristic biological structure of the organism in which those energies are processed. Finally, there are the innate tendencies of that structure to channel and selectively shape the constellation of energies available in the system at a given instant.

None of those three factors working toward likenesses of our experience is in any sense to be thought of as belonging solely to humanity. We share the same world with all other living things. Other animals also share with us the nervous structures which make affective processes possible for us. There can be little doubt, therefore, that many other animals possessing such structures as our own also have an equivalent sharing of our affective psychological events and states. These sharings appear to include such fundamental traits of consciousness as the objectification of feelings as things (perception) and the dispositional integration (affective tendency) of discrete feelings into global states of affect such as fear and the other "basic" emotions.

Psychology has long observed the similarities between certain types of emotional behavior in man and other animals. Neurology has more recently shown that similar neural structures are responsible for the overt similarities. For example, neurological investigations have convincingly demonstrated that fear in man or any higher animal is a dispositional behavior attributable to specific structures in the "old" or "visceral" brain shared by man and other animals. Again, psychological studies have shown that the basic emotions—again, such as fear—are essentially irrational and not necessarily contingent even in man upon prior or coincidental awareness of meaning. Such fundamental emotional experiences must then be understood in dispositional terms. They are tendencies of feeling literally harnessed to the structures of the body. Where a particular structure appears, a correlative behavior can be elicited in the presence of appropriate situational complexes of stimuli.

Men do not share with other beings the complex structures of the enlarged cerebral cortex. Neither, therefore, ought we share — except with other men —the equally complex tendencies of feeling employed in the behaviors of aesthetic and intellect. Nevertheless there is incontrovertible evidence that we do share something in the way of aesthetic and intellect with other animals. No one may doubt, for example, that both men and animals indulge in play. If we give any credence to the well-known "play theory" of art, then we also cannot doubt that a whole host of animals share the aesthetic sense with us.

In support of the play theory, note that play has the character of aesthetic production. It is creative of affective experiences. It has no goal but pleasure, achieved within the moment of the experience. Play, therefore, possesses intrinsic or aesthetic value. On the other hand, whether the play be that of men on the squash court or puppies gamboling on a lawn, play lacks the quality of meaning essential to true aesthetic. Therefore, in the final analysis, animals do not share the aesthetic sense as it occurs in human experience, and the essential difference between play and art reduces to a matter of aesthetic meaningfulness.

Besides the pseudo-aesthetic experience of play, we also appear to share at least a measure of intellect with the higher primates and many other animals. Intellect, defined behaviorally, is the ability to meet new situations successfully by behavioral adjustments specifically adapted and *selected* to meet changed situations. A classic demonstration of such sharing was provided more than 50 years ago by Eugene Marais in his study of the chacma baboon.[1] There, he showed that the behavior of the chacma, like that of man, is not dominated by phyletic memory (instinct and other dispositional behaviors), but by causal memory (the memory of learned cause and effect), in large part transmitted by tradition.

The sum of the matter is that while we do not share with other animals the particular flowering of intellect and aesthetic that marks human experience, we do share the processes of affect which among higher animals underlie the behaviors of play and intentional adaptation to changed situations. Indeed, the various degrees of sharings we have with other animals —whether of cortical structures of affective processes — probably reflect something of our own past progress along the evolutionary path which led to the evolutionary derivation of aesthetic and intellect as we know them.

In a similar vein, Jung long ago commented on the physiological similarity of man and his beastial cousins and suggested a corresponding likeness of psychological makeup. "Just as the human body represents a whole museum of organs, each with a long evolutionary history behind it, so we should expect to find that the mind is organized in a similar way. It can no more be a product without history than is the body in which it exists. By 'history' I . . . . . am referring to the biological, prehistoric, and unconscious development of the mind in archaic man, whose psyche was still close to that of the animal.

"This immensely old psyche forms the basis of our mind, just as much as the structure of our body is based on the general anatomical pattern of the mammal. The trained eye of the anatomist or the biologist finds many traces of this original pattern in our bodies. The experienced investigator of the mind can similarly see the analogies between the dream pictures of modern man and the products of the primitive mind. . . .[2]

---

[1] *The Soul of The Ape*, p 77 ff. For reports of similar data, consult B. G. Campbell's *Human Evolution*, p 287 ff. For a comprehensive philosophical evaluation of such data, consult T. A. Goudge's *The Ascent of Life*, p 144 ff.

[2] *Approaching The Unconscious*: in *Man and His Symbols*, p 57. Continued scientific research has given this viewpoint much more substance today. A good summary introduction is B. G. Campbell's *Human Evolution*, interesting because various facets of biological evolution are correlated with the anthropological development of a peculiarly human adaptation to the living experience. He remarks (p 362), "It is probable that consciousness, like any other human

While we share with Jung a version of his concept of the historical un-conscious, there is little apparent similarity between our concept of con-sciousness as a unity complete at every moment with nothing left out, and the description worked out by Freud and Jung decades ago. Jung held that the un-conscious and consciousness are separate and apart. Freud, however, shared our notion of the psychic unity, although in contrast to us he held that all mental processes are essentially unconscious. Processes of which we are con-scious, he held, are merely isolated acts and parts of the whole psychic entity.[3] There is, then, but a single, unified psychic process in which consciousness is that nexus of psychic events to which we are at any time attending.

Despite that apparent theoretical difference between the ideas of Freud and Jung, their descriptions of psychic reality invariably express the notion of an unconscious that is the substratum on which consciousness rests, always there, going along its own way virtually unheeding of and separate from the processes of consciousness. In a manner of speaking, such a description is true enough, but hazardous. The peril comes in how easily the unconscious and con-sciousness thus described may achieve theoretical distinction as separate psychic entities. The truth comes of the fact that the psychic reality, the con-sciousness that one is to himself, is a largely undifferentiated appearance of feelings, the organization (and thus the appearance) of which depends upon given and achieved structures of the organism.

Now, let us admit that this concept of consciousness is no more warranted by conclusive demonstration than are the concepts of Freud and Jung, or the concepts of other competing schools of psychology. On the other hand, the theory developed here has the advantage of incorporating the facts of affective behavior into a theory encompassing all psychological behaviors. Also, it has the further advantage of being more parsimonious.

Although psychology long since escaped the old "faculty" description of the mind, it still uses a pseudo-faculty approach to speculative and even scientific description of mental behaviors. Psychologists still speak of perceptions *and* emotions *and* conceptions *and* attitudes *and* dispositions *and* intellection *and* motivation *and* feelings *and* so on as if they were entirely different matters of the mind. If different, each requires its own explanatory mechanism. And since in the operations of the psyche they all operate together, then one need

---

character, evolved slowly, and it may indeed appear in its most simple form at much lower levels of life than has been supposed." He also identifies both perceptual and conceptual behaviors in animals other than man, relating the growth of those powers to corresponding evolution of the central nervous system. See also Laughlin and d'Aquili, *Biogenetic Structuralism*, Chapter 3, "Cerebral Adaptation and Homonid Evolution," for a more conventional, and very intensive study of the physiological developments underlying human consciousness.

[3] *A General Introduction to Psychoanalysis*, p 25.

explain the connections between one and all the others, and their relationships to the supporting neural structure. Each, in other words, presents an
intricate enigma of its own.

If the approach taken here has nothing else in its favor, it resolves all the
problems of psychology into one enigma: How is it possible for processes of
neural electro-chemical excitation to appear as affective consciousness?
While we have described the systemic correlations between neural energies
and affective events, one doubts at this time that the detailed description of
all mental behaviors in exact affective and neurological terms will ever be
possible. The functional interrelations of the structures and elements of the
nervous system are simply too complex. On the other hand, discovery of
some fantastic new technique could open the door to just such a detailed
understanding and the tremendous detail made manageable by electronic
data processing techniques.

Nevertheless, many general understandings of the structural functions
underlying the process of consciousness have been revealed, and a conceptual
overview of the nervous system and its behavior as an affective unity is consistent with the facts of that structure. The dominant opinion in current
neurology, for example, holds that there is an integrative response of the entire
nervous system to even the simplest excitatory events. That and the continuous
ground of excitation alleged to be the basis for consciousness appears to point
ever more convincingly toward a contextualist theory not only of memory but
of all consciousness. Consciousness is the subjective awareness of a system of
energy functioning as an integrated whole, such that any and all changes in
the level and processes of that energy result in an equivalent modification of
consciousness. Better to say the change in energy is a change in consciousness.

Sources of change are: (1) the energies of the environment acting upon the
receptors of the organism; (2) the internal conditions of the organism acting
upon proprioceptors of the organism; and (3) changes in the elements of the
nervous system available for integration of those energies. The physical
changes in the nervous system may be constructive, as during the maturation
of the organism when the associational structures obtain greater complexity;
destructive, as in impairment by injury or disease; or adaptive, as in learning.
The last, of course, is the only change not involving a modification of the
biological structure, although an actual physical change is now known to occur and is the basis for a change in the functional structure.

The adaptive selectivity of neural transmission of energy has long been
recognized, but only recently begun to be understood. A brief review of current understandings is pertinent here, not only as a base for fuller understanding of the nervous processes which are affect, but also because they suggest the mechanism underlying dispositional behavior.

Three levels of affect have been described. Physically and subjectively, they are basically identical. Objectively, on each level, there are neural energies while subjectively there are feelings. The first level is comprised of feelings or energies per se. Where there are energies in the system there are feelings.

The second level relates to that kind of behavior which is termed dispositional. On this level, the feelings or energies involve specific coordinated functions of elements of the system, as if the functional structures were preprogrammed to accept the energies of neural events in a specific way. With learning, we saw that these functional systems could be modified or even inhibited and replaced by others. With modification or substitution of other functional complexes of neural elements, radically different complexes of affect result. Further, the more complex the parts recruited into the system, the more dominant or gripping the affective experience in consciousness.

The third level of affect is that of emotion, derived from cerebral functions which in part are dispositional to the cerebral cortex, in part learned habit, and in part freely associational or selective. These functions in effect produce feelings or energies which may be said to have a cortogenic origin rather than a receptor origin. While the ultimate source of these cortical energies is principally in the affective ground volleyed into the cortex from such structures as the reticular formation, these volleys are mostly pervasive and tonal in effect. These energies further serve as the fuel for cerebral function selectively responsive to volleys of sensory data mediated in large part by the hippocampal cortex. The cerebral function, as it were, selectively provides its own affective modalities chosen to maintain the affective poise of the system as it is upset by the receptor energies. This function may be powerful enough to subdue or even submerge the affective qualities of receptor origin. The importance of this function in learning has already been noted.

From the side of physiology, as opposed to psychology, the base for describing each level of affect lies in discrete pulses of energy occurring as electrochemical events within and between neurons, each having a fixed physical position in a system containing billions of such elements, each having a potential functional relationship with several adjacent elements. Behavioral differentiations of the system are dependent upon fixed physical relationships and also upon what realizations of potential functional relationships actually occur with a given neural event. The perplexing question is why some potential relationships are actualized and others are not with a given event, why some relationships are actualized from the first instance of an event (and form the basis, along with physical structure, for instinctive and dispositional behavior), why others have to be conditionally adapted in response to many instances (forming the basis for learning), and why some possibly never are actualized at all.

Neurochemistry has begun to supply some of the answers. Research indicates that genetic activity responsive to chemical changes resultant from electrical field effects are at the base of neural function and its adaptive processes. Simply stated, the genes control the functions of the cell, with the actual genetic response conditional upon the chemistry of the cell at the time of a given electrical event. That chemistry, however, is itself a product of genetic function. A part of that chemistry includes the composition of the vesicular "messengers" on the axon endings. With cell conduction, the "messengers" are released at the synapse to act upon the membrane of the adjacent cell. The chemistry of the latter cell will be such that it will accept or reject the "message," by depolarizing (firing) or not.

While ionization phenomena and enzymic action are both important and complex in neural function, the production and consumption of protein substances are central to the genetic control function. Protein is rapidly consumed in cell function. Continuous capacity of the cell to respond to electrical events at all or at relatively similar thresholds requires continuous synthesis of protein adequate for maintenance of a given distribution of protein within the cell. A model for the function starts with the firing of the cell, with resultant rapid consumption of protein and change in cellular chemistry. The change overcomes the influence of substances suppressing the function of deoxyribonucleic acid (DNA), which releases genetic synthesis of ribonucleic acid (RNA), which in turn releases the synthesis of protein.

The actual response of the genes is conditional upon the chemistry of the cell at the time of a given electrical event. The genetic response may result in more or less or different synthesis of RNA, which in turn results in manufacture of more or less or different protein. Some protein will replace that consumed, restoring the cell for further conduction. Other protein, however, may react with RNA and form a suppressor which slows down or practically inhibits RNA synthesis, with a similar result upon synthesis of protein necessary for cellular firing. Most simply stated, high synthesis of some types of RNA result in fast synthesis of proteins which restore the cell to a state of peak readiness to accept electrical excitation. Other protein, however, may react with DNA and act as a suppressor which slows down or practically inhibits RNA synthesis, prevents protein synthesis, and reduces the readiness of the cell to accept excitation.

Little is understood concerning why a cell responds to excitation with one kind of a chemical adaptation rather than another, yet this process is the basis for learning. In that adaptive process, the RNA-protein synthesis phenomena under genetic control take on a distinctive pattern producing a characteristic chemistry of the cell relative to the electrical effects that it sees. Those effects are not all of receptor origin, as impulses from the brain influence transmission along sensory pathways as a kind of feedback process. Little is known of this feedback function, yet we may speculate that it serves to secure systemic control of the behavior of the afferent elements. The effect is to make the part serve the function of the whole, by adapting the function of specific cells.

The complex phenomena of cellular adaptation not only provide the basis for learning. They also suggest an explanation for the neural functions underlying dispositional behavior. It would seem that the dispositional function results from a preset chemistry of physically related cells which facilitates chained responses of neurons in what is called a phase sequence. The phenomenon is as if the genetic message passed to the RNA of these cells is specific for establishing a chemistry for each cell adequate for excitation of a preset phase sequence, in response to an electrical event particular to (and thus characteristic of) specific exchanges of energy with the environment. It is as if the cell "always knew and was ready for" the event to occur.[4]

The inherent, automatic function of neural tissues long has been understood as the basis for the function of the peripheral nervous system, including operations of the autonomic system which in fact turn out to be extremely complex when fully analyzed. Lately, this trend of thought has led to similar understandings of the central nervous system by some investigators. This development effectively completes the avenue of inquiry begun with the work of Sechenov on the reflexes of the brain more than a century ago. The myth of the *tabula rasa* no doubt was the chief cause of the slow development and acceptance of the notion of the "reflexes" of the brain as a meaningful concept for understanding the general operations of the central nervous system. Now, the myth has been so soundly debunked that we find writers who insist not only that our ability to perceive is bound into the structure of the nervous system, but so are perceptions as such, and concepts too, for that matter.

Typical of this new understanding of the genetic sources of psychological behaviors and capacities is T. G. Bower's provocative notion that multi-sense perceptual integration is genetically cast into the nervous system. He writes, "We can only conclude that in man there is a primitive unity of the senses, with visual variables specifying tactile consequences, and that this primitive unity is built into the structure of the human nervous system."[5] But this perceptual capacity can

---

[4] Neurochemical functions in terms of gross behaviors of the organism are described with particular wisdom and clarity by H. Hyden. Particularly see his *Biochemistry of CNS Cells During Learning*. Equally excellent, and better suited for the lay reader or philosopher is *The Code of Life*, by Ernest Borek. More specialized is the excellent summary presented by John Gaito in his *Implications of Nucleic Acid Research for Behavioral Events*. Refer also to Francis Schmitt's *Dynamism in Neuroscience*, which describes how the new understandings of neural action have been used to construct concepts of the nervous system that tend to make an anachronism of the behavioral psychology still taught in our schools and colleges.
[5]*The Object in the World of the Infant*, p 32.

hardly be peculiar to man, and represents but a single facet of the character of the nervous sytem cast millions of years before man appeared on this earth. Similar traits of pristine consciousness revealed in both perceptual and complex motor behaviors by men and animals are described by Eugene Marais in *The Soul of The Ape.* [6] His conclusions anticipated by a half century the concepts of the genetic influences on behavior that the neurosciences only lately have begun to describe. Where Bower now is able to cite the "built-in unity" of the senses as being the basis for biologically conditioned discriminatory functions that once were confused with intelligence (learned behavior), Marais, fifty years ago, wrote, "An instinct is sometimes so complex and its beneficial reaction dependent upon such a long chain of causes and effects that the essential difference between 'instinct' and 'intelligence' is easily missed." [7]

Perhaps the most startling advancement of this line of thinking may be found in the ideas of R. F. Thompson. He asserts that there is not only an inherited tendency for certain overt behaviors to be manifested, but there is also a phylogenetic inheritance of specific percepts and concepts. In effect, he has made a neurological restatement of Jung's theory of archetypal consciousness when he writes, "Learning to 'see' percepts and concepts by young and adult organisms does not involve learning of 'perceptual organization,' it only involves learning to respond to the appropriate stimulus configuration." [8]

When we examine Jung's theories in the next chapter, we will see that Thompson has achieved a considerably more daring assertion than Jung attempted. For Jung insisted only upon the inheritance of tendencies toward ideational behaviors in response to particular experiences. Thompson, on the other hand, maintains that the behaviors as such are built into the organism with their full contents. We need learn only the appropriate occasions to exercise them.

Assuming the role of devil's advocate vis a vis Thompson's theories, A. E. Fischer makes the telling point that theoretical emphasis upon "preorganized" systems (such as Thompson's, or for that matter, Jung's) gains its primary value because such systems are simpler to approach and to organize for understanding. He suggests that such theory may be the product more of *a priori* axiom than interpretation drawn from fact. None-the-less, Fischer is sympathetic to the movement toward phylogenetic explanatory mechanisms having a neurological basis. He finds it a stimulating contrast to the "random connection" theory of neurological behavior, perhaps best formulated by

---

[6] *Op. cit.*, pp 90ff; refer particularly to the summary beginning on p 101.
[7] *Ibid.*, p 174.
[8] Neurophysiology and Thought: The Neural Substrates of Thinking; in Voss, *Approaches to Thought*, p 64.

D. O. Hebb, that has dominated the field for so long. Yet he finally opts for neither side. "The truth will no doubt lie somewhere on the middle ground," he says,[9] which is a politic position suited to the available data.

A summary interpretation of that data leads conclusively to a neurological basis for dispositional behavior. That basis is the inherited tendencies that mark cellular function, coupled with patterns of feedback energies emanating from the higher centers of the nervous system. While this feedback is fundamentally structural and dispositional, the energies in significant part are cortogenic and lie at the core of the aesthetic or other higher-level experiences. But, here we are interested primarily in the fundament of inherited tendencies. These neurological tendencies grossly function such that they have the behavioral appearance of dispositions. Literally, they dispose us to typical behaviors. Our common genetic inheritance is such that we tend to have common responses to like conditions of our environment. The selective shaping of that environment is able therefore to obtain conditions that a genetically similar population is able to perceive as having like qualities of value. In the activity of art for but one example, one is thus able to elicit similar aesthetic responses in the experiences of different people.

If the commonality of our experience of art lies primarily in our dispositional gifts, then since expression is at least an element of that experience, we are led to infer that the nature of expression in the arts is rooted in the dispositional behaviors of the nervous system. Remembering that these dispositions have a neurological basis, then the nature of expression in the arts appears to have a biological basis. Indeed, aesthetic tendencies understood on such terms as these must be regarded as little different from the human tendency to rise up and to walk on two legs. By the same token, the analogy suggests that aesthetic tendencies must be realized and shaped by learning no less than it is necessary for each of us to learn to walk on two legs. And so we now turn to an investigation of the role of dispositional behavior and the influence of learning upon it, in establishing the nature of expression in the arts.

---

[9]Problems in The Analysis of Complex Neural Function; *Ibid.*, p 76.

Chapter 9

THE ROLE OF DISPOSITION IN AESTHETIC

Earlier, we noted that Freud and Jung linked their concepts of the psychic reality to the physiological structure that supports it. As they expanded the scope of their science into what became analytical psychology, that fundamental connection between psyche and physical structure became a more or less obscure presumption underlying their theories. Given that initial linkage, an oddity of analytical psychology today is that it may be practised as if there is no connection between psyche and bodily structure. The obscure presumption of the masters generally is ignored by their latter day disciples.

Speculating about the origins of this condition of contemporary analytical psychology, no doubt part of it comes from what Francis Bacon called an Idol of The Theater — outdated ideas, now persisting as mere plays on words, remain vogue as expressions of the bias men have concerning the existence of a psychological entity, a conscious or psychic self, considered as independent in its being insofar as the supporting structure of the body is concerned. Another causal factor must be the sheer complexity of the science as such. The abstruse, "double-think" character of many of the theoretical evolutions of the practical science of psychoanalysis are several times removed from the fundamental axioms pioneered by the masters. And, in the process, the conceptual materials of the science have become as many times removed from the biological structure in which the psyche resides and as which it subsists.

Given the conceptual materials natural to the science as it is contemporarily practised, the loss of the connection between psyche and bodily structure goes virtually unnoticed. Workers in the field are so dazzled by the intricacies of discovered analytical relationships and the complexities of terminology invented to express them that the lost connections with the roots of the psyche are ignored. But this is a situation typical of modern science in general and not just of analytical psychology. R. F. Thompson commented, "Most (psychological) texts on thinking make little or no mention of neurophysiological processes. This is only fair; neurophysiology texts do not discuss thinking. Such mutual disregard simply reflects our considerable ignorance of the neurophysiological bases of many behavior phenomena, including such fundamental areas as learning and motivation as well as higher mental processes."[1]

Given the complexities and specialized bodies of knowledges of the various branches of modern science, then, it appears that there is a kind of institutionalized blindness built into each of the respective disciplines. Indeed, F. O. Schmitt tells us that it occurs even within the single branch of neuroscience. Even that limited field, he said, has fragmented into so many levels from the molecular to the systemic that specialists in one phase hardly are able to keep abreast of developments in others. As for the relationships between neuroscience and psychology, Schmitt noted the implications of the discovery by neuroscience of the dynamism of the brain cells individually and as a system, and observed, "Stimulus-response, reflexological research strategies and concepts—i.e., that the brain reacts only when acted on — missed essential aspects of brain dynamics."[2] Yet, various forms of behavioral psychology, in which the S-R chain is the central explanatory mechanism, prevail in psychology today. Certainly, that psychology recognizes the presence of a functioning system of afferent and motor neurons located operationally between stimulus and response, yet its dynamic shaping of the process is effectively ignored in the study of actual behaviors, held to be insignificant to the science that deals only with the measurable aspects of the S-R relationships. But, what kind of a *psychological* science is that?

The situation in analytical psychology, then, is not atypical of the times. Not that these specialized bodies of knowledge should be cast aside and a general return made to fundamentals; rather there needs to be a conscious effort by workers in all fields to sustain themselves by constant touch with the roots of their science while they soar into areas of high specialization. Without that connection, the specialized field loses touch with the validity resident in the real world of fact. And, this is exactly what has happened to much of both behavioral and analytical psychology in recent decades. Consider just the fundamental concept of the unconscious. The idea of the unconscious begins to make sense instead of myth only when it is understood in terms of the innate tendencies or dispositions of the physiological structure.

Jung's formulation of the notion of the collective unconscious rested on just such an understanding. It may also have led him to his theoretical distinction between and separation of the unconscious and consciousness. He saw conscious contents as primarily the product of the personal ego constructed in the historical process of the individual's experience, while the unconscious wells out of the phyletic roots of the species. We find that distinction to be more analytical than real, with no real basis in the physiological system that sustains

---

[1]Neurophysiology and Thought: The Neural Substrates of Thinking; in Voss, *Approaches to Thought,* p 40.
[2]Dynamism in Neuroscience, in Landis and Tauber, *In the Name of Life,* p 113.

the psychic processes. The personal ego resides in the same system as the collective unconscious. It is that underlying system to the extent that it is shaped by learning and given functional focus by its affective affinities.

Consciousness, then, does not exist separately any more than the unconscious does. Neither does the unconscious exist as a substratum for consciousness as Freudian theorists maintain, "always there" as an unconscious mentality distinct from conscious mentality. Consciousness and the unconscious are the subjective appearance of physiological functions, and therefore do not exist as such. Both appear in exactly the same way: subjectively as affective experience, objectively as nervous energies. While both consciousness and the unconscious appear as they do because of genetic tendencies of the system modified by learning, they do not exist therefore as such. They are pure potential, realized through the interaction of the organism with its environment and the affective endurance by the organism of its own dynamic functions.

The essential point of this discussion cannot be stressed enough. Neither consciousness nor the unconscious properly may be considered as a psychological entity, or even different in kind from each other. Consciousness and the unconscious are each but a purely subjective appearance. Each is the lived experience of nervous processes. In terms of that appearance, what is called the unconscious is but that part of the gross systemic response to which we do not attend within the focus of attention. Meanwhile, consciousness is that core of feelings having affinities to the particular global poise or tendency of the psyche, which defines the focus of attention.

The distinction between consciousness and the unconscious, then, is properly made in terms of affective affinity. That is not to say that the full detail of the distinction is made on such terms. Those terms are peculiar to a psychological description of the subjective appearance of the contrasting phenomena of experience. In a previous paragraph, using terms appropriate to a physiological description of the processes underlying those appearances, the distinction was made quite differently. Then, we spoke of biological conditioning or genetic tendencies of the nervous system. And, it is against both of these descriptions, each valid in its own universe of discourse, that the nature of consciousness and the unconscious is to be properly understood.

Analytical psychology tends to discuss the unconscious as a kind of psychic presence or shadow self that grasps control of our "real self" and forces it to do what ordinarily it would not. Or, the unconscious is alleged to lie quietly in the background, imperceptibly steering consciousness in ways not of conscious choosing. Indeed, there is no doubt that something of this sort of occurrence can be identified in our behaviors. Our terms, however, specify this "taking control" as the consequence of dispositional behaviors triggered by some facet of our encounter with the world. Where one moment the poise of consciousness thrusts in one direction, suddenly some incongruous tendency is released and turns us aside, or perhaps just throws the whole set of consciousness into confusion.

In sum, then, the dispositional tendencies of the psyche are the basis for the idea of the unconscious. Because those tendencies are genetically cast into the system, ever ready to be released into action, the unconscious is "always there." By the same token, the system is always active, thus there is always a subjective appearance and a poise of consciousness, no matter that one is not always conscious. So, while the unconscious and consciousness subsist as pure potential, as long as there is that system, they are realized. The unconscious is called out at the same time as consciousness. They appear together as a unity of experience, an integrated response of the entire system.

In the fundamental sense of the dispositional psyche, then, the Freudian axiom is true that the unconscious is the cause of consciousness. But, there is another part of that axiom left unstated; it is also true in exactly the same sense that the dispositional psyche that "causes" the behaviors called consciousness, is equally the "cause" of those behaviors that are said to identify the unconscious. There is no denying, of course, that this notion is antithetical to Freudian folklore as used in analytical psychology today. Indeed, it is also foreign to Freud's own work to the extent that he proceeded beyond his fundamental perceptions of the psyche and sought to extrapolate them into the body of knowledge and techniques that we know today as analytical psychology. We find a kinship with Freud, then, at the roots of his theory. This kindred spirit latent in Freudian psychology may be illustrated, for example, in Freud's analysis of the causal source of dreams.

Freud cited experiments that showed how dreams, marked by the character of the unconscious in terms of the ideational structures and images of their appearances, were in fact stimulated by sensory data. From his evidence he assumed that all dreams have a similar origin, whether external or internal stimuli are involved. From this, he concluded that dreams (as unconscious behavior) and their appearance (as unconscious contents) are not "there" in the unconscious ready to surface into dream consciousness. Rather, the psyche dispositionally elaborates upon sensory data with full poetic license. He further showed that dreams tend to appear with conscious contents of the preceding day utilized as the materials organized by the dreamwork. So what we find in dreams are consequences of both biological and individual conditioning unified in the single experience or behavior. In other words, the psyche, or mind, has the appearance of a unified process and not of being partite. We have what Marais called causal memories exercising the phyletic memories that exist as genetically cast structures of consciousness, structures that appear both as the dreamwork and as the form of the materials hung on the dreamwork.

The poetic license of dreams is but one example of the role of psychic disposition in the elaboration of consciousness out of the discrete energies of sensation. The "archaic remnants" of primordial experience, as Freud described the visual imagery of dreams and the mentality of dreamwork, persist throughout the entirety of a man's experience, no matter how subtly. Both Freud and Jung noted the particular relevance of these "constitutional predispositions" (as Freud termed what to Jung were the "collective unconscious") to the activity of aesthetic production. So, it is appropriate now to turn to the insights offered by the masters of analytical psychology as we inquire into the role of disposition in man's aesthetic sense.

From our point of view, Jung offers us more than Freud. The teacher became fixated upon the principle of wish gratification in dream interpretation and foreshortened his understanding of the operations of the psyche. Then, too, he was too much a clinician and too little a scholar. Jung, on the other hand, was thoroughly versed in history and literature, a student of philosophy before he turned to medicine, fascinated enough by comparative anatomy to plunge into paleontology, and though steeped in science and its methods of proof he was blessed by a poetic nature that enabled him to delve freely into alchemy and the mysticism of East and West.

Against that broad experience, Jung early recognized something too forced in using the Freudian axiom in approaching the dreamwork. Jung instead saw a primitive mind speaking a primitive language. He found that mind and its pristine language not only in his own rich experience and in the psychic realities manifested by his analysands. He found them also in artifactual evidence such as the body of mystical literature, in mandala and alchemical symbols, and in the art of all ages. The concept of the collective unconscious thus originated in materials which all have notably affective contents. They are affect spun into artifact, as in world literature. There from ancient times to this day, universal and recurrent affective contents persist. These contents, or motifs, persist through eras and across geographical and cultural boundaries, across artistic traditions and styles. And, they appear not only in the art of all civilizations, they appear in the dreams and fantasies of everyone whether reported in the Vision of Er by Plato, the Babylonian epics, or the patient on the couch of a Park Avenue psychiatrist.

Against that description of the inspirational sources of Jungian theories of consciousness, which are heavily entwined with aesthetical materials, we may find strange the remark by Susanne Langer that "The chief reason for our general hesitancy to undertake a serious study of psychological data themselves is that there seems to be no instrument to negotiate it; few people realize how excellent a presentation of such data is to be found in the arts... But no one, as yet, has pursued the revelation to the point of finding problematical facts never presented before, or recognizing vital patterns in pure art which may be keys to essential relations in the life of feeling."*

That assertion by Langer deserves to be forcefully contradicted, since Carl Jung clearly recognized those "vital patterns in pure art" and understood them in the general concept of the "archetype," which he saw spanning ages and cultures. From the materials of art, Jung identified a whole panoply of problematical facts and integrated them into his total concept of the psyche. He has been followed in this by his disciples, and perhaps most emminently of late by Erich Neumann. See, for example, Neumann's four essays collected in *Art and The Creative Unconscious,* particularly *Art and Time,* although each piece contains broad interpretations as well as specific psychological data that are brilliantly analyzed from an aesthetical orientation.

From such evidence, the collective unconscious was conceived as "an inherited and universal psychic disposition" evidenced by instinct and archetype, and distinct from the personal unconscious rooted in memory of one's own history (a distinction, as we discussed in the preceding paragraphs, that we believe to be unfounded.) While aesthetic trades on both instinct and archetype, the archetypes are the most significant for aesthetics. Although archetypal function is similar to that of instinct, they are manifested in different modes of behavior. Instincts have the appearance of acts. Archetypes have the appearance of ideas, no matter that the same neurological principles are responsible.

Mind: An Essay on Human Feeling, Vol. 1, p 69. While the point at issue here is a rather trivial detail concerning the history of psychology and its theoretical interfaces with aesthetics, the value of her fundamental insight is so great that it behooves us to understand the weaknesses in the way she worked out that insight as a philosophy. One needs to recognize, for his own enlightenment, that many of her supposed "key" discoveries were earlier described and generally better worked out by others such as Croce, Jung, James and Collingwood. Her apparent lack of appreciation of the achievements of those men led to irreparable flaws in her own work. Yet there is no need to contest her, minor point by peripheral issue, for her basic premise is accurate: Feeling is the basis of the human mentality. She ought to be read and appreciated for much of what she tells us is tremendously instructive, and she proceeds to a whole host of sources relevant to what we are attempting here but often ignored in preference to other sources. More, she has constructed a broad and exhaustively detailed philosophy of art and mind.

We have commented in earlier chapters on shortcomings in her overall concept of mind. In her philosophy of art and aesthetics, her fundamental error comes of making her entire analysis turn too closely on the premises of her philsosphy "in a new key," which directed her into byways that led back into old ways of philosophizing and thinking, where she may be found talking about the "picture of feeling" and not "the feeling" without realizing the transition of thought that has taken place in doing so. True, symbols are forms of feelings. So are sticks and stones also feelings in exactly the same sense, as particular things encountered. The idea of a symbol, however, is "symbol" used as an explanatory principle. Then, it is also a feeling, but not in the same sense that sticks and stones are feelings. The philosophical as well as the psychological differences between those two affective appearances of "symbol" are profound. In one instance, symbol may be described as "the feeling" and in the other it has a very different description as "the picture of feeling."

The ideational content of the archetype has its source in the personal psyche. The content merely fills out an inherited "form" which as such is dispositional. That form is not to be thought of as a mental box for ideas to be put in. It is simply the naturally facilitated neurological structure of the body that functions as primordial consciousness. Because it is the structure that it is, it has psychically formal functions, one category of which are archetypes. It is the structure that is inherited, a structure which is genetically preset to permit the appearance of typical ideas. Jung emphasized, "I do not by any means assert the inheritance of such (archetypal) ideas, but only the possibility of such ideas, which is something very different."[1]

Primitive as they are, archetypes function more as feelings than as thoughts, despite their ideational appearance in experience. Their psychic dynamics are dispositional and are best thought of, Jung says, as recurrent impressions occurring as *subjective reactions*. They operate as psychic centers of power, often autonomically. The archetype "seizes hold of the psyche with a kind of primeval force and compels it to transgress the bounds of humanity."[2] And what is that but a restatement of the ancient notion of the divine madness of art. Here, the artist, there his audience, both swept up and transported beyond the bounds of humanity to some level of divine experience. But, instead of possession by the muse, we are in the grip of an archetypal force, an inherited dispositional form with the power to take the whole of consciousness under its domination, using personal materials to fill out a form cast perhaps millions of years ago. Yet, there is even more of aesthetic significance in Jung's description of the archetypes.

The archetypes are multitudinous, often opposing (e.g., the anima and the animus), and function as subjective reactions. That leads one to question why at a given time we should experience one archetype and not its opposite. The answer comes from Jung's inquiries into the pathology of psychic disturbance. There, he observed that the dynamics of the disturbance are such that the subject appears to be the chooser of his own infirmity. His choice is manifested as

---

[1] *Two Essays in Analytical Psychology,* p 64. Compare this with the aforementioned extension of this inheritance from mere possibility to actuality, in the work of R. F. Thompson, who included even perceptual and conceptual contents. For a slightly more conservative viewpoint, consult Laughlin and D'Aquili's *Biogenetic Structuralism,* where they describe "genetically preconditioned" perceptual and conceptual models of reality against which actual experience is "judged for fit." For myself, I favor the Jungian position, and consider the more extreme viewpoints as theoretical overcompensations for the conceptual strait-jacket of the *tabula rasa* that we have so long endured. Not that the Jungian interpretation cannot be amplified, of course, and we have seen a number of expansions of that trend of thought described here, such as Anokhin's concept of neurological events being conditioned by adaptation such that we may presume that the world of experience is, for all practical purposes, the real world that exists in space-time.
[2] *Ibid.,* P 70.

the formation of a complex which, Jung tells us, has its foundation in a constellation of archetypal forms. The effect then is as if the archetypal forms were chosen as an adaptive response, and function as a selected disposition of consciousness vis a vis the world.

The complex is demonstrably subject to both spontaneous and therapeutic modification. In therapy, the realization of change is understood to be a process of learning, and it has long been recognized to be specifically a process of learning feeling. Noting that in therapeutic modification of the complex there is necessarily involved a change in the architecture of the component archetypes, and that learning allows adaptive responses which are intentional (selective) in nature, then we have a clinical basis for the traditional notion of the educability of taste, and a better concept of its mechanism. That is, there is a shaping of dispositional contents in the educative process leading to the appreciation of specific archetypal contents in the creations of aesthetic art.

Beyond that, if the consistent choice expressed by the complex is admitted, then the basic dispositional "pointing" towards the world is given a larger explanation. That is, the conditional selection of a pattern of affectively coherent dispositional contents, and the suppression of the function of others, in effect imprints the behavior of the psyche with an affective character which gives an intrinsic bias to any and all of our day to day subjective responses to the exigencies of being. The relevance of this description to Sartre's notion of the "original choice" is startling. With that description, we have also approached some of the basic psychological theories of H. J. Eysenck and Jung's theory of psychological types. For, implicit in those theories are the notions that there are common "types" of behavior, and that these "types" are rooted in inherited but opposing tendencies of affective experience.

Sociological research, turning only recently to ethology and the biological foundations for explanations of human group behavior, has begun to provide further substantiating data concerning the role of genetically inherited dispositional behaviors described by Jung. One of the best known recent studies is *Men in Groups*. In that work, Lionel Tiger hypothesizes that "The behavior of men in groups in part reflects an underlying biologically transmitted 'propensity' with roots in human evolutionary history (or phylogeny)."[3] Another work which attracted recent notice is Robert Ardrey's *The Social Contract: A Personal Inquiry into The Evolutionary Sources of Order and Disorder*. In that work, Ardrey also sought explanations of human social behavior in genetically programmed tendencies, although his

[3]*Op Cit.*, p xiii.

"personal" approach made his work more readable but less significant than Tiger's.

While the conclusions reached by Tiger and Ardrey are philosophically incompatible, and neither has a notion of what is being worked out here, they offer a virtual mine of supporting data taken from sources entirely different from those used here. The work of Tiger is most stimulating, partly because he is more scientifically disciplined as he separates out what he would like his data to show and what he finds they show. We also discover him approaching some of Jung's insights although he appears to have little familiarity with Jung's work.

Tiger remarks on the vitality of affect associated with primitive archetypal behaviors, and holds that the level of vitality is a function of biological age of the behaviors in our history as a species.[4] This adds a further dimension to the interpretation of the divine madness as an archetypal function, leading to the notion that the strength of the "seizure" is proportional to the antiquity of the central, or the majority, of the contents of the dispositional complex formed in the experience.

Considering that the dispositional character of the collective unconscious for Jung is no thing other than the body's own structure, a turn toward data provided by the other life sciences is suggested. Certainly, no one has ever doubted that a man's aesthetic sense is something achieved only with a measure of growth and maturation, but it has been long and often argued that such growth is spiritual in nature, the consequence of a long process of learning and experience. But, here we have been noting evidences of a direct connection between aesthetic potential and the physical character of the individual. If the connection is valid, then aesthetic development of the individual must have an equally direct connection with the individual's physical development.

The classic confirmation of the broad scope of correlations between physical and psychological development was provided by the celebrated Iowa studies of child development. Maturation was shown to involve more than mere learning; there is an actual development, or appearance, of higher psychic potentials as the biological organism develops. More recent studies have described the neurological capacity for and the appearance of consciousness in the fetus, and shown that the capacity of the brain to exercise its greatest powers of intelligence is not achieved until quite late in adolescence.

Recognition of patterns of physiological development led originally to the biologically formulated theory of recapitulation. That theory long since has been extended to include "mental" recapitulation. Marais observed long ago, for example, "It is known that the development, both embryonic and post-

---

[4]*Ibid.*, p 152.

natal, of the organism is to a certain extent a recapitulation of the evolution of the species. To this general rule mental evolution affords no exception."[5] If this point of view is accepted, then we might expect that since aesthetic experience is a mental phenomenon, the aesthetic development of the individual, if we understood it, is in its general outline a recapitulation of the development of the aesthetic sense of mankind. Whether it does or not, however, has no great bearing on the fundamental matter at issue here. The fact remains simply that correlation of individual development with development of the human species is now a common presumption underlying interpretative accounts of human behavioral development. We note Teilhard de Chardin, in his fascinating study of the "within" of things, describing the ascent of consciousness from "obscure primordial psychism" to the "explosion of reflection," and asserting[6] that the development of the child follows the development of the species, from single cell to intelligent being. Leonard Carmichael traced the evolution of mental processes from the amoeba to man and from the fetus to the adult.[7] And Tiger cited Yehudi Cohen's conclusion that "universal physical changes in the human body at certain stages of development are accompanied by universal psychological changes."[8]

Given that background, it would be amazing indeed if a man's aesthetic sense were not a development kindred to those. And so we arrive at the idea of the physiological maturation of genetic propensities forming the ground for a developing aesthetic potential or disposition realized in concert with available cultural materials and opportunities. Aesthetic tendency is inborn, yet it is fully invested through maturation and variously exercised dependent upon the situation of each individual. Tiger shows how a similar propensity toward male bonding practises appears in the transition into boyhood (as contrasted with babyhood), yet varying in myriad ways as experience fills out (as Jung would say) the dispositional forms. And, just as in aesthetics, there are certain consistent characteristics. Tiger finds a common denominator among the many expressions of male bonding practises: male alliance into what in effect is a small-scale community with a definite but flexible hierarchial structure formed for aggressive expression. His discussion[9] of the fantastic experience of the boys who participated in the filming of The Lord of The Flies is an inspired demonstration of his theory. The mere acting out of the novel, released behaviors genetically cast in the dawn of time, yet lingering in the collective unconscious awaiting the appropriate instance to come welling out to dominate and control behavior.

[5]The Soul of the Ape, p 102.
[6]The Phenomenon of Man, p 171.
[7]The Making of the Modern Mind.
[8]The Transition from Childhood to Adolescence, p 12.
[9]Men in Groups, p 160.

Fortunately, more than the beast lies asleep within us. The collective unconscious may be thought of as preprogrammed stepping stones that indelibly mark the *tabula rasa* of consciousness with aesthetic potential. As Carmichael showed, not all the stones are placed until far along in the development of each individual. Aesthetic consciousness is an achievement, even as mere potential, of each man's maturation process.

At birth, one is a physiological functioning marked by a pandemonium of feelings having little relevance to the cosy pre-natal experience. In only days we see instinct modified by learning and differentiation of affective chaos into distinct patterns. The cry of discomfort later becomes that of different discomforts: wet pants, hunger, boredom. Feelings now have become more than mere impulses. They have become impulsions in the sense defined by Dewey. Impulsive directionality is achieved and objectified. Food becomes something to the lips. Mother is motion. Both are undifferentiated from the sensa of one's own organism, simply present and pleasant, or absent and painful. Directionality at the outset is pointed towards the warm motion of lip-greeting, belly-pleasing mother, who only later is recognized as an object among objects and adaptable to symbolization and control from a distance, or as an archetypal idea elicited by a work of art.

Studies of infant behavior have demonstrated often and clearly that there is no aesthetic sense in the infant. Yet from the pioneering of such men as Jung and Marais, and from the venerable Iowa studies, and now from ethology and the neurosciences, we can see that sense as a potential that literally forms in one's bones and is cast in its predominant character by childhood shapings of affective tendency. The differences in potential may only be guessed. The differences in development are observable and fascinating in their variety among a society, or even in a family. In my daughter, for instance, I noted little interest in or response to music until, toward the end of her second year, I began telling her the stories of the ballets accompanied by the music. Now, in her late teens, she is somewhat of a balletomane, with her interest pointed toward the visual-auditory spectacle as story, rather than from critical understanding of either music or the dance. In contrast, my son spontaneously danced to the sound of music virtually from the time he was able to walk. We have been careful to neither encourage nor discourage, nor to "teach" him movements, so as to observe his own inclinations and development. There is no development now in several months. Recall an African tribal dance in an old Frank Buck movie; a phalanx of warriors, holding spears and shields, stand in position and weave and bend slightly at knees and waist in tempo with the rhythm; that is his dance. He appears to have no concept of why he does it, or any sense of meaning. Neither is it a game, or play. It appears to be something he does much as he nursed at the breast or crawled or walked.

In spite of such behaviors surfacing out of our collective unconscious, it bears emphasizing that our capacity to respond aesthetically to art is nothing we are born with. Even the potential cannot be said truly to be present, for aesthetic potential is a gradual flowering of genetic propensities that differentiate and organize such that the activities and feelings characteristic of aesthetic are possible. And even when a mature aesthetic sense has been achieved, the sense itself remains pure potential. First of all, then, each of us must learn to realize that capacity for aesthetic experience, and then every time we must actively achieve it, for there is no necessity that the potential be actualized at every opportunity.

All of us realize our potential in one way or another, and the process of the maturation of the dispositional characteristics underlying aesthetic appears to take a very similar course in most of us. Response to rhythm appears very early. Sensitivity to harmonies of color comes very late, often not until the threshold of the teens. An authentic aesthetic sense, however, seems to appear at about age five or slightly thereafter. That appearance is marked by creative imagination responding to meaningfulness, in contrast to earlier behaviors involving only a play with feelings, or the archetypal immersion of consciousness in feelings (as typified by the dance described in the preceding discussion).

The aesthetic of childhood differs from that of the mature adult. In the child, the potential is yet but partly formed (while in the immature adult that same potential may be blocked), depriving him of the breadth and scope of experience of which the mature organism is capable. As sheer feeling, however, the experience of the child tends to be much greater in intensity, much more vivid in character, since he has not yet achieved the emotional control of the adult. It is as if the experience bursts the bounds of consciousness in a way that for an adult might be described as cathartic rather than aesthetic. Indeed, the archetypal components of art can provoke just that kind of experience even in an adult in a situation of psychic vulnerability. And, persons with a history of mental disturbance are notoriously vulnerable to such effects.

In the normal maturational process, there is more than achievement of greater emotional control. There is also a change in the character of affective experience reflected in emotional behaviors. This change arises in part from the maturation of the biological organism, characteristic of which is a modification of dispositions to suit the changing states of the body's needs. These changing states of physiological needs give birth to revisions of psychological aspirations vis a vis the world as awareness expands and more complex and different relationships are felt, perceived, and grasped. Neatly summed, emotional behavior "changes with increasing age and experience and, in general, takes forms which are socially more acceptable and practically more effective in accomplishing the design of the individual."[10]

With maturation, then, emotion – as an adaptive response – becomes better controlled and thus more useful in service of the needs of the individual. Since the situations and needs of varied individuals also vary more or less, obviously quite different emotional responses may be required to serve particular individual needs. Yet, because of our dispositional inheritance, there are greater or lesser likenesses of needs, affective process, and emotional response.

The characteristic likenesses in human behavior led, early in this century, to a number of studies of what came to be called "psychological types." These investigations revealed what must be regarded as categories of aesthetic, or taste, directly correlated with other behaviors which characterize general psychological types. While Jung described such typical behaviors on the basis of his analytical studies, typical differences were later confirmed experimentally by the work of such men as Cyril Burt, H. J. Eysenck, G. S. Welsch, and Frank Barron. Their work revealed that specific differences in aesthetic preferences correspond consistently with specific differences in basic attitudes towards the world.

Burt differentiated so-called introverts and extroverts into sub-groups of each type on the basis of their regard for the world in stable or unstable terms. Eysenck sought to extend this approach to determine correlations between personality traits and taste. He found that extroverted, radical personalities preferred the artistically complex, unsymmetrical, unstable, and disordered; while the introverted, conservative personality preferred the simple, ordered, stable, and symmetrical. Viewing his findings in sum, Eysenck concluded that what he had found was that these typical perceptual preferences reflected a "choice of what to attend to" in the world.

Welsch and Barron[11] confirmed the dual and contrasting types of aesthetic preference, but showed that neither type ever appears to exist in its pure form. Rather there are dominant preferences which are differentiated consistently in terms of figures, paintings, and even self-descriptive adjectives. They also demonstrated that artists are predominantly distributed in one type. That type is marked by a pattern of rebellion against authority, a preference for the asymmetrical, and a basic disposition of instability. They preferred the informal, sensual, modern, radically experimental, and primitive – and women whose sexual role is emphasized. They rejected religious themes, aristocrats, "cold" women, the traditional, and the emotionally controlled.

In the final analysis, there is little new in such a description except that it was produced through experimental procedures. The artist in his role of social protest

---

[10]*Emotion and The Educative Process*, Prescott, p. 74.
[11]*Personality and Perceptual Choice.*

has been an archetype in the literature of the ages. He and his art exist quite literally outside the pale of conventional society. If he is fortunate, he is not so far out of the normal stream of things that he may not find a following at least among the so-called avant garde. However, as Welsch and Barron's studies showed, the description of the "artistic type" did not necessarily describe all artists, nor did their findings indicate that there is art and aesthetic for only the one type. Instead, they demonstrated that there are artists (although proportionately fewer) and an authentic aesthetic sense (albeit demonstrably different) in the conservative group as well.

Meditating upon such information, one is led to the idea that the smaller number of artists serving the conservative group must each obtain a larger following, generally speaking, than their radical fellows. Such speculation is supported historically by the perennial— but by the avant garde much disparaged— success of the "traditionalist" schools of art. On the other hand, we cannot overlook the fact that yesterday's radicalism may be traditionalist today. Historical evidence clearly reveals the gradual acceptance of the avant garde within the fold of conventional taste. Since we may assume that basic ways of viewing the world have not changed, this latter fact of art history appears quite inexplicable in terms of the principle of psychological types.

One explanation may be a change in the radicalism of the artist himself as a consequence of his own maturation. Significant measures of maturity, according to L. J. Saul,[12] are the degree of socialization and domestication of emotions, and a reduced degree of emotional vulnerability coupled with an increase in emotional control. With maturation, in other words, the dispositions of taste change. For the artist, we would expect new expressions to appear, expressions more compatible with a conservative, mature audience. He may be still a radical and a rebel, but his expressions, now more socialized and domesticated, are suddenly available and meaningful to his more conservative fellows. Indeed, the rebelliousness of the avant garde is a trait of youth which tends to wear itself out and lets radicalism wear another face.

Another significant factor also appears to be at work in the gradual acceptance of the radical within the scope of the traditional. Acceptance comes in this instance not because the radical has changed so much, but because it has been around long enough for the conservative to learn, or develop a taste for it. Involved in this development is, undoubtedly, the influence of the art critic, or expert in matters of taste, whose authority leads a conservative audience to more adventuresome experiences of art. In effect, the conservative learns to express himself through the work of the radical, a learning made possible by the acceptance of the radical as an established tradition respected by "authority."

---

[12]*Emotional Maturity.*

The influence of authority is a well-known fact of art criticism. It has also been the subject of a number of experiments. One, for example, showed[13] that in response to commentary by an adult "expert" on works of art, children's preferences for abstract versus conventional art increased from 7.2 to 34 percent of the group.[14]

The susceptibility of the aesthetic sense to modification by learning, and the influence of authority on such change, is a condition for the appreciation of the "fine arts" lauded by Bosanquet and damned by Tolstoy. What the elite of any society say is art *is* art for everyone, made so simply by virtue of their prestige and the consequent psychological force of their demand, or expectation, that everyone accept the standards of taste of the cultural aristocrat as the only measure of art. If others less culturally favored do not at first share those standards of taste, then they are expected to acquire the requisite aesthetic responsiveness by educating their sensibilities to the higher level of aesthetic sensitivity.

Now, considering all we have discovered concerning the nature of aesthetic, it is clear that essential to the possibility of a change in aesthetic preference so as to achieve a common ground of aesthetic experience—indeed, a language of art—is the function of emotion as an adaptive response dynamically variable in accord with dispositional influences. While the innate dispositional elements provide the base for art as the language of emotion, the language as such must be culturally developed and individually learned. Furthermore, what we know of individual development clearly demonstrates that the acquired skill and ability in using the language of art broadens in both scope and fluency as a person matures and gains more diversified experience. Aesthetic preference, or taste, then must be understood as a malleable predisposition dynamically responsive to both learning and maturation processes, with learning ultimately acquiring relatively more importance as the organism achieves its mature form.

The influence of learning upon aesthetic preference has long been appreciated. Generally, however, it has been understood as a matter of learning knowledges and skills related to artistic forms and contents, and not as a matter of learning to feel; that is, learning to integrate particular affective data into the unified experience that constitutes the aesthetic. Tolstoy, for example,

---

[13] *Prestige Suggestions in Children's Art Preferences*, D. P. Ausubel *et al.*
[14] These findings are fully consistent with a whole host of experimental data related to the influence of "authority." Carl Hovland and others showed that the "credibility" of the speaker, a function of prestige, is centrally involved in any opinion (and, we assume, preference) change; also, his work showed that when the opinion (or preference) expressed by the speaker has large variance from that of the hearer, the credibility of the speaker diminishes.

made a paramount moral issue of the learning prerequisite to making the formal intricacies of aristocratic art available to the masses – and soundly condemned the need. Bosanquet, on the other hand, found the need for learning to be concerned primarily with the contents of art, and regarded the learning process as highly desirable since it was an integral part of the growth process that shapes the refined sensibility of the cultural aristocrat.

Such theoretical focus upon aesthetic elicitors, i.e., form and content in art, is philosophically misleading. In terms of what we know today, it is better to consider the aesthetic learning process not in terms of elicitors, but in terms of their related expressions. When Tolstoy speaks of complex forms and Bosanquet of proper contents, we may look on the opposite side of the coin and see that the primary aesthetic consequence of the overall process of the learning and refinement that shapes the cultural aristocrat is his learned ability to integrate a whole panoply of feelings that are unavailable to the untrained or immature sensibility.

Now, when we compare the behaviors of child with adult, or the vulgar crowd with cultured sophisticate, a primary distinguishing feature in both instances is this: The passions of the adult and the sophisticate are relatively more domesticated. The experiences are passions no less, but they are less violent, more directed and contained instead of simply let loose on the world. The dominant behavior tends to be subtle mental behavior rather than gross physical behavior.

Generalizing that assessment to aesthetic, we then have little occasion to wonder why the aesthetic responses of the cultural aristocrat involve subtleties having no meaning to the vulgar masses. Equally understandable is how the gross emotions of vulgar aesthetic offer little appeal, and often are downright repulsive, to the sophisticate. Difference of aesthetic experience, however, does not imply a lack of aesthetic authenticity for either extreme. Indeed, the unforgivable fault of such thinkers as Tolstoy and Bosanquet is that they deny the legitimacy of the aesthetic sense and the art of one side or the other.

Tolstoy correctly noted that art is universal as an activity and that an aesthetic sense is natural to the makeup of every man. Considered in the light of that fundamental truth, differences in taste are matters of fact and not matters for reproach. The art of one group may not be the art of another, but the art of each side is nevertheless and indisputably art. What we have is simply that the aesthetic sense on the respective sides – that is, their dispositional tendencies for aesthetic integration of felt awareness –has matured differently in response to the influences of different life experiences.

In the maturation of a man's aesthetic sense, then, there are two primary factors at work. One is dispositional, stemming from physiological maturation –an evolving and enlarging potential for integration of feeling. The other stems from learning, including such pervasive effects as the achieved directionality that characterizes a personality. It consists also of less pervasive, acquired behaviors associated with discrete aesthetic elicitors; that is, with the signals and techniques the human organism must learn before socially available objects can be experienced by him as art. The operation of these latter factors also must be appreciated to obtain a complete grasp of the nature of expression in the arts.

The object of art, as pure object apart from our experience of it, has prima facie neutrality. It is not art. It is simply a part of the furniture of the universe which is apt to be encountered in the experience of someone. We have to learn to call it an object of art and not merely see it as an undifferentiated thing among things. We learn to do this by learning the signs and signals – the cues – which identify a work of art. The artist, we find, creates his work such that it presents the observer with conventional cues so that when the object is encountered among the other furniture the observer will in effect say, "Ha! Here is a work of art!"

A child, unfamiliar with the cues, might take a Rembrandt and toss it on a fire to enhance his play at cowboys and indians. A pygmy transported suddenly from his forest village to the Metropolitan Museum in dead of winter might do the same to keep himself warm. His art is signalled by different cues. For him the work of Rembrandt is just worthless furniture.

Pressed for time amid the events of life, we ourselves may enounter the same Rembrandt, recognize it as an object of art, but fail to experience it aesthetically. The painting then remains a thing among things. If in our way, we move it or go around it. If not, we ignore it. We are not ready to deal with it as art. In other words, we are not prepared to relate ourselves to the object as art.

Discussion of the significance of learned cues, we see, appropriately ends in discussion of responses. But, so far, we have treated cues and responses only in the broad sense of those general cues and responses necessary for us to address ourselves to an object as art. In the body of the experience and the work of art there are also certain cues and responses of a more subtle nature. These were analyzed, specifically in terms of the response portion of the overall functional relationship, by I. A. Richards in *Practical Criticism*. Responses, of course, imply stimuli. In the context of this discussion, such stimuli function as cues.

Richards held that "stock responses" are the key to efficient life experience. Provided with specific cues, we tend to use stock responses. We do not have to solve the same response problem over and over. This tendency toward habitual response naturally enters into our experience of art, which in Richards' description is made possible by and trades heavily upon utilization of stock responses – but with a penalty exacted.

Stock responses, according to Richards, tend to become standardized and imprecise, uninteresting, and often ill used because of their imprecision. These effects of the stock response, he said, define the fundamental difference between run of the school artistry and great art.

Great art is marked by novel responses that enlarge the experience of a man, no matter that such art also trades heavily upon the background of stock responses. But, the task of obtaining novel responses from one's public is a treacherous business indeed, ending in failure more often than not. In consequence, he concluded, most artists play safe. They remain close to what is easily accepted and generally understood. Most art therefore is built upon an inventory of stock responses. But, that is not necessarily bad for art. As Richards explained, such "stock" works of art "come home to a majority of readers with a minimum of trouble, for no new outlook, no new direction of feeling, is required."[15]

While we do not agree with his interpretation of the underlying phenomena of the art experience that he chooses to call "stock responses," Richards' notion of the stock response provides an interesting way of describing the mechanisms of the educability of taste and the dispositional basis for art as an instrument of communication. We quarrel mainly with his notion of the "novelty" of great art, a notion which we believe to be a kind of cliche of art theory that has come down to us from long ago and gone too long uncontested. We would rather note that if there is art at all, there is invention, and invention is by definition something novel. Aside from the technical excellence with which that invention is framed, however, what makes one invention greater than another is the success with which it harnesses the dispositional powers into the affective form that dominates the poise of the psyche.

In such terms as those, we can then agree with the position taken by Richards. Embodied in art is a convention of cues that elicit stock responses. Art makes use of learned cues and stock responses thereto which "have long been parts of our intellectual and emotional repertory." They come from our general life experience, including our experience of art (from, therefore, what Jung calls our personal unconscious) and also from those eons of experience indelibly imprinted upon our psychic mechanism (Jung's collective unconscious).

The ideas of Richards and Jung, pioneering as they were of the awarenesses we are just now coming to have of the physiological basis for traits of human consciousness and behavior in general and aesthetic in particular, yet were anticipated by Taine a century ago. And, Taine himself traced his inspiration to the ideas of Stendhal who, Taine remarked, "treated sentiments as they should be treated, – in the manner of the naturalist."[16] The varieties of these senti-

---

[15]*Practical Criticism*, Richards, p 245.
[16]*History of English Literature*, Vol. 1, p 34.

ments – feelings, if you will – were for Taine the discriminating characteristics of the varieties of literatures, characteristics that he tied directly to the racially and nationally varied natures of men. Thus, as he developed his description of the theoretical basis for his approach to his classic *History of English Literature*, he explained, "What we call the race are the innate and hereditary dispositions which man brings with him into the world, and which, as a rule, are united with the marked differences in the temperament and structure of the body."[17]

Taine's fundamental approach remains ultra-modern to this day. He based his aesthetical theories on an understanding of human nature that gained scientific stature only in the middle of the Twentieth Century with the conception of the science of ethology. Yet, he was not entirely alone, and how much like Jung he sounds to us when we read, "There is, then, a system in human sentiments and ideas: and this system has for its motive power certain general traits, certain characteristics of the intellect and heart common to men of one race, age, or country."[18] These characteristics, like Jung's archetypal reactions, are the bases for what Richards called "stock" responses. To create an art in a time and place among a race of men such that it embodies cues that elicit stock responses is by that very act to harness the dispositional powers of the psyche – the divine madness – in service of aesthetic goals.

As should be clear from the foregoing, of course, the functions of the primitive elicitors of the "divine madness" are insufficient to explain all the facts of art, particularly as the language of emotions. Art does not speak the same to all men. There are also culturally specific elicitors peculiar to a man's time and place, and these constitute a particular dialect of the language of emotions. Like the dialect of his tongue, a man's language of art is, in its fine nuances of detail, a product of his time and place. Also like the dialect of his tongue, his language of art springs from deep-seated tendencies and is shaped by the temperaments and dispositions of his genetic inheritance, mirrored in the nature of his culture.

The cultural specificity of aesthetic response is the root of Bosanquet's insistence upon the "common properties" he alleged to mark a work of art. Without those familiar contents, Bosanquet was lost. He had no stock response. A work lacking such contents was not art for it did not embody the characteristics of a language he understood. For the same reason, the *avant garde* of a new tradition waste away in their attics, possibly not discovered until long after they are dead. Their cues demanded responses foreign to the repertoire of their audience. They spoke only to later generations who had

---

[17]*Ibid.*, p 17.
[18]*Ibid.*, p 13.

time to learn the new dialect and catch up to the novel perceptions of self and world that the old language could not communicate.

Given the function of stock responses and the artful embodiment of cues appropriate to elicit them, we can see that the assertion common to experience philosophy that the object of art is axiologically neutral, is only half true. The object is indeed neutral insofar as it simply exists, but as an object in experience it presents real possibilities and real limitations for interactions – exchanges of energy – with the organism. Any object, that is to say, offers a limited and intractable potential for us to experience it, and thus no object is axiologically neutral since it provides a more or less fixed base for the discovery of value in experience. This is true not only for the discovery of aesthetic value, but also for truth, utility, and morality.

No matter that truth, utility, morality, and beauty are subjective judgments of experience, the potential of things to interact in particular ways as experience provides an objective basis for all value. That basis is particularly evident for objects of art, which are manufactured for no other purpose than to embody the energies which in experience produce aesthetic value. That structure of energies immediately connected with the object is what Santayana called the first term of expression.

The first requisite of an object of art, then, is that it be an embodiment which offers potential exchanges of energy, structured in a way that aesthetic integration of those energies can be achieved by the organism. The embodiment need not be sensuously pleasing, although sensuous qualities that please are more often than not sought in the embodiment. Neither must the organization of energies be characterized as objectively beautiful form. Many works of art trade on "ugly" incongruities and disorder for their actual sought expression. The object of art need only be the organization of sheerly available energies that it is, embodied such that in the exchange of energies the structure of psychic energies reflecting the structure of the material energies will tend to be accepted and processed in dispositional forms which achieve the affective focus of felt significance.

The objective structure of available energies acceptable to particular psychic structures obviously is not enough to explain the aesthetic phenomenon. As Santayana remarked, all things natural and artificial are potentially beautiful simply because they exist. They require only that someone be able to discover them as beautiful. That some things called works of art are specifically made to be beautiful is irrelevant to the issue at stake here. Were it not, we would find things which are beautiful to us are always beautiful to us. But they are not. Therefore, we say that experience of the embodied potential for beauty is not enough. What is also required is that we enter into a particular kind of psychic relationship with the objective energies that constitute the object.

Aesthetic potential lies in both the organization of objective energies and the psychic structures which accept them; but realization of that potential is a matter of our attitude toward the energies offered. We must be dispositionally set, or ready to become so set to permit the aesthetic process to occur. We must be ready to relate ourselves to the object as art instead of as some other thing toward which we tend to have a different kind of relationship. The stone figure becomes a work of art and not a doorstop or an idol. So, in the final analysis, the fundamental distinction between the object of art and things in general, and between aesthetic experience and experience in general, is a chosen relationship to a thing.

Our readiness to encounter things as art, no matter its dispositional basis, is something learned no less than our readiness to use an automobile for transportation. When this readiness comes to operate as acquired habit, it has become a stock response to specific learned cues. Such cues are perceptual and are both gross and subtle. A diagram on the sidewalk may be taken as the idle doodle of a child. The same diagram on canvas hung in a museum is called art. The grossest cue is that the canvas is hung in a museum. It is encountered in a situation where one has learned that works of art are encountered.

A full catalog of cues learned by some person– and there is no reason to believe that everyone responds to precisely the same cues – would probably comprise a good-sized volume if listed and described with reference to all the artistic media. The importance of these cues, however, must be remembered to be for the function they serve in calling out or triggering, first of all, our aesthetic sense, and then the course of the experience of aesthetic production.

The aesthetic sense, as Tolstoy saw, is a universal tendency among men. Its source is in the roots of the psyche, springing from the nature of man as a parasitic organism enduring a hostile world. As Santayana taught, the tendency comes from the basic need of a man for felt harmony of soul, a harmony difficult enough to achieve when confronted by the perils of his environment, but always available through the aesthetic relationship to things of art. But, that is a poetic truth beneath which other kinds of knowings have been found to reside. The aesthetic sense, like intellect, is just another trick the psyche has learned to play with feeling.

To call aesthetic and intellect "tricks" the psyche learns to play with feeling fails perhaps to be a seeming recognition of the astonishing fact of either behavior. More rightly, we ought to be filled with awe in contemplation of the evolutionary process through which they developed over eons of time. But, in the final analysis, that process led to more and more complex developments of organic sensitivity which led to the dispositional potential, in each of us, to behave as if the feelings which to each of us constitute that sensitivity were not in fact our feelings, but were other things. And that, no matter how practical and necessary the realization of that potential by each of us, resolves to a matter of playing tricks with feelings.

Beauty, as pleasure objectified for its own sake, is often regarded as the crowning achievement of human consciousness, the ultimate trick of tricks. In such terms, anything is beautiful which awards pleasure, and this we reject for the same reason that we rejected the play theory of art. The true aesthetic which defines the nature of expression in the arts is a pleasure no less, and indeed it is objectified in the work of art. Yet, its essence is meaning, an essence therefore connected to the same psychic potential which makes intellect possible. Art, as aesthetic production, thus achieves a difference in behavior quite apart from all other human activities. The core of the experience is in feeling, and thus it returns consciousness to its most pristine behaviors. Yet, its instrument is in those structures of feeling where meaning resides, therefore making the aesthetic the most advanced and novel of all human behaviors, no matter, as Dewey remarked, that it is hatched in the same nest with all the others.

As for art – the purposeful, creative doing of an act – it obviously serves practical and moral functions as well as aesthetic. The aesthetic, as feeling, is also no less part and parcel to any and all activities of a man, and thus of all his arts. The art of aesthetic production is distinguished by being the product of a man assuming a particular kind of relationship to the world or some object in it. Other arts are marked by other relationships producing other values. Just as a man needs and chooses to relate himself to his world as aesthetic object, he has similar needs and makes like choices to establish other kinds of relationships. That is why the moral, the useful, and the "true" can never as such become the bases for aesthetic judgments. By the same token, morality flavors the aesthetic through expression and, as Santayana pointed out so well, the moral is carried upon the scene by the useful. Truth, beauty, and goodness are separate sprouts from the single root of the practical life, for it is the practical life that feels a need and recognizes its satisfaction.

As Santayana described with great poetic charm, no ideal long escapes the exigencies of the practical requirements of life. But once the practical requirements of living are satisfied, there is opportunity for the aesthetic ideals to flower. These ideals – the sheer pleasures of being as such – also have a reciprocal influence upon the practical aspects of life. They tend to refine and embellish practical affairs with qualities of the aesthetic. The cutting tool of the artisan is not only a tool shaped to work; it has an extra fineness the work does not need. Life is shot through with these little "extras" that make our work-a-day world a better place for working. Each of these extras serves no useful end as such. They serve that disposition of self which would find ideal harmonies simply in the immediate context of experience. It is not enough to merely survive the day. We must find small pleasures in the furniture of the universe, pleasures which serve no purpose but pleasure itself. And, when those pleasures come to achieve that fuller quality that meaningfulness lends, then we are on the level of the fine arts.

Chapter 10

EXPRESSION AND ART CRITICISM

While the issues of criticism are outside the scope of our inquiry into the nature of expression in the arts, our findings concerning expression have primary relevance to the issues of criticism. Thus, it seems appropriate to examine the process of art criticism against the background established by our inquiry. Considering the complexities of the pathway we have followed, however, perhaps we ought briefly to review the essential features of the aesthetic experience as analyzed in the preceding chapters.

Expression, understood in modern terms as affective meaningfulness, is achieved when a disposition of psychic readiness to accept experience aesthetically, allows objects or events to function as cues leading to responses that are dispositionally organized such that cortical centers of ideation generate constellations of feelings establishing an affective poise marked by an awareness of felt significance. In such terms, the possibility of expression hinges on a number of interacting factors.

First of all, there must be an object of art providing an objective source of energies suitable for and adequate to initiation of the aestheic process. Sans adequate cues there cannot be an expressive response.

Given proper cues, but lacking maturational development and educative shaping of dispositional responsiveness, the affective response fails the aesthetic integration, that is to the extent where aesthetic poise is completed by the function of the higher centers. In other words, the psychic structure must be physiologically mature enough, and educatively conditioned to accept and process the whole panoply of objective energies such that psychic integration of those energies is adequate to expression.

Finally, without dispositional readiness there is no aesthetic experience. The psychic mood or situation in which the objective energies are presented must be such that the psyche enables its dispositional readiness to accept the energies aesthetically.

Given differences in psychic situations, dispositional "outlooks," educational influences, and physiological development, all interacting at once in any experience of art, there is little wonder at the markedly different aesthetic responses men have to art as such, or to different artistic media, or to particular works of art. The differences are natural and a fact. As such, aesthetic differences are quite exempt from the lashing pen of the critic who would disparage taste other than his own, or deny its justification.

To the good fortune of artists and women, tastes for the aesthetic and the amorous are of wide variety. Neither love nor beauty accepts judgment and requires no justification. To disparage the aesthetic preference of an uneducated swineherd is as ridiculous as to criticize him for finding no appeal in the frail artificialities of a lady of high society. The man of the earth revels in the smell of new-mown hay and the pure sweat of the strong-backed woman who shares his labors in the field. By the same token, the "aesthete" is beyond criticism if his taste turns toward the fragrances of hothouse roses or toiletry imported from France to obscure the sour sweat of his lady's idleness.

If beauty intrinsically accepts no judgment, if it requires no justification, if the taste of no man who finds beauty may be praised or censured, if the object in which beauty is objectified is art by the very fact of that objectification by someone, if the sole matter of interest is whether there is expression achieved or not by someone, and if art is easily identified by the fact of the aesthetic experience, the role of the art critic apparently has no possible defense. We are left in aesthetic anarchy where no man has the right to legislate or criticize the taste of another. As Sartre liked to say, "Every man for himself!" Nevertheless, people do criticize the taste of others and art critics do continue to go about doing what they have always been doing.

The function of art criticism seems to be as old as art itself, and as much accepted as that of the artist although seldom as honored. No matter that taste requires no justification and accepts no judgment intrinsically, there is also a basis for criticism which cannot be denied. As Santayana pointed out, for a man or a society there are actual scales of value which result in some aesthetic experiences and some tastes being judged better than others. However, since men and societies differ, the aesthetic judgments men have are as different as their experiences of aesthetic – and for essentially the same reasons.

Since beauty, as feeling objectified, is a fact of experience and intrinsically accepts no judgment, then art criticism is a function having no immediate connection with expression as the aesthetic response to art. It is a further response outside the moment of the aesthetic experience. As to what it properly entails, a look at what critics are doing reveals that their sphere of interest includes both the works of art which elicit the aesthetic response, and the response itself – expression. Criticism thus involves application of value criteria for construction of judgments having to do with both art (in its function as a cue) and aesthetic (in its function as a response).

Not all critics necessarily agree that art and expression are the proper objects of their critical judgment. According to Sainte-Beuve, for example, "Unless one has faced a certain number of questions about the author, and until one has answered them . . . one cannot be sure of capturing him completely, even though these questions seem completely unrelated to the character of his writings. What did he think religiously? How was he affected by the sight of nature? How did he act so far as women are concerned? . . . . None of the answers to these questions is unimportant in judging the author of a book – and of the book itself."[1]

What utter nonsense. To judge a book by its author is as inane as to judge it by its cover. That is not to deny that knowledge of the author may contribute qualities of the second term of expression to our experience of a work. So do our varied knowledges of his subject matter. The point is, to enjoy an historical novel – or a painting of an historical event – there is poorly expressive art if expression depends necessarily upon knowledge of either the author or his subject, or both. Yet, there is a branch of "criticism" still prevalent which holds to versions of Sainte-Beuve's notion. Such criticism more correctly should be regarded as a branch of psychology (the psychology of the artist) or of history (the history of artists).

Taine's historical approach to criticism appears to preserve Sainte-Beuve's error. Taine, however, was attempting something quite different. Knowledge of the man was but a first step. After that, he sought intelligence of the "underworld" of socio-cultural experience that produced the thought, feelings, and words of the writer. For Taine believed that in literature alone is the feeling of life in an age revealed. What Taine was really doing, then, was writing a kind of literary history even though in the end he brought critical judgment to bear upon the content of literature beneath his history.

Taine saw his method as the key to criticism, holding that his approach was the only way to determine the characteristic nature of a work of art. Each great work, he tells us, is an ideal of a type, the perfect essence of a socio-historical period of art and history. Any work may be judged in terms of that ideal. That is, the value of a work is measured by the extent to which the work expresses the social experience of the time and, therefore, has social significance. "The proper office of literature is to make sentiments visible. The more a book represents important sentiments, the higher its place in literature; for it is by representing the mode of being of a whole nation and a whole age that a writer rallies round him the sympathies of an entire age and of an entire nation."[2]

---

[1]Sainte-Beuve on His Own Method; From "Chateaubriand," *Noveaux Lundis;* (July 22, 1862) in *Criticism: The Major Texts,* Bate, p 499. Tr. by Bate.
[2]*History of English Literature,* Vol. I, p 35.

By that, the mission of the critic is to research an era, determine the sentiments important to the time and, where they are found in the art of the period, he must praise that art. Yet, art cannot be criticized as nothing but a mirror of a society, however much that art is a construct of some artist's possessions and rejections of socially available materials. What of the work itself? The mere presence of such sentiments cannot be the key to criticism, for they are also found in the babblings of an idiot.

What Sainte-Beuve and Taine asked in their respective ways was, "What makes one book better than another?" One thought that knowing about the author was essential to an answer. The other believed that a proper answer could be derived only from exhaustive knowledge of the author's milieu. But their question really asks something about a book and nothing else.

Pertinent and refreshing in such company is E. M. Forster's comment that the only way to criticize a book is to read it and find out what a writer has accomplished as an artist. Forster tells us that in terms of the question at issue, criticism is irrelevant in terms of authors, history, literary classification schemes or anything else except books. His point may be extended beyond literature to criticism of all the arts. His pet personal peeve was saved for the classifiers. Forster cited one critic who "classified novels by their dates, their length, their locality, their sex, their point of view, till no more seemed possible. But, he still had the weather up his sleeve, and when be brought it out it had nine heads." But, in the end, the critic was dissatisified and added, "Yes, of course, there was one more thing, and that was genius; it was useless for a novelist to know that there are nine sorts of weather, unless he has genius also."[3]

Forster's approach to criticism is refreshing because it points right to the center of things. The question of criticism is posed: "What has the writer (or painter, or sculptor, etc.) accomplished as an artist?" Relating this to the generic question, "What does art accomplish?" the problem of the critic related to any work of art is closely tied to the basic nature of art itself and nothing else, and his answer bound to the terms meaningful to the fundamental question; that is, in terms of aesthetic experience. This understanding allows us to restate the question posed by the critic: "Has the artist created a vehicle through which other people may achieve aesthetic experience?"

Sainte-Beuve's method is irrelevant to such a question. Taine's is not since we see him engaged in two functions pertinent to the question. In one instance, he was forming judgments based upon audience response to the work of a given author. In the other, he was analyzing the artistic cues and cultural stock responses which made one work "better" than another. "Better," in his

---

[3]*Aspects of the Novel*, pp 26-27.

context, was defined by the larger scope of the audience won. Certainly, he made other kinds of critical assertions concerning sentiments and their morality, but the essence of his method had to do with whether or not a work "captured an age," both in terms of sentiments and audience.

Since art is a form of communication between men, the capture of an age by any work certainly implies that it is better as communication, and thus as art, than some other work which captures little else but bookworms. But, recognition of such a "capture" is hardly the end of criticism. There is also the question, "Why?" Taine answers that the key to the capture is the expression of sentiments which have special significance, or meaning to an age. Thus, his critical method turns out to be based upon the clarity and vitality or importance of expression in a work of art as experienced by the author's contemporaries.

Using such a critical method, the critic therefore must be sensitive to the dominant sentiments – feelings about self and world – of his time. And where these are discovered expressed in art, he will know that here is art which may capture an age. Yet our original objection still stands. Any idiot may express sentiments, and the literary marketplace is overflowing with sentimental trash. Art therefore cannot be judged solely upon its contents, or the "what" of expression. It must also be judged on "how." And this is but a restatement of the fact of criticism pointed out before. Criticism must point itself in two directions, although one or the other may predominate and thus tend to produce quite different critical roles.

Criticism pointed in the direction of the object of art is fundamentally concerned with the "how" of expression, with techniques and utilizations of materials, with subject matter and its stylistic handling, all of which together constitute the nexus of cues which successfully or unsuccessfully conspire to elicit the experience of felt significance from the beholder. Criticism pointed in the direction of expression, on the other hand, is concerned with the fact of expression, the response obtained from the cues presented. Such criticism is ordinarily preoccupied with the quality of the expression; that is, its clarity and vitality, its relevance to human interests upon the contemporary scene of life, and thus its inherent value as expression. Such a critic may take it upon himself to discover and learn to recognize the responses which characterize the experience of works of art so that he may identify other works that will achieve the infectiousness of communication which in effect will capture an age. The former critic is more interested in elucidating the mechanism of aesthetic production which makes the expression, and thus the capture, possible.

Each critical role is thus quite different although neither appears in its pure form. Response criticism is more popular, exemplified by the work found in the literary magazines and the news media. Of them their audience questions:

Will I find expression in the work? Is it an especially well wrought expression? Is it the kind of an expression which has particular appeal to me? In framing their criticism such critics may enter into the analytical realm of cue criticism to some usually lesser degree. But, their skill is not and ought not be one of technical analysis, for the excellence of their function stems from their sensitivity in anticipating the response of their audience.

Along the way, such a critic may also perform the "prestige" function of educating the taste of his audience such that they are ready to accept and eventually achieve expression through cues once alien to their experience and preference. This, too, must be regarded as a real and legitimate critical function. By it, some people will be able to achieve a broader experience of the arts. But, it is a service with dangerous pitfalls. Ineptly handled, it may alienate the critic from the audience he would serve. When that happens, the fault usually is that his critical ego led him to believe that he will be followed by virtue of his lead alone. Unfortunately, the educative process he attempts is a stair with many steps.

Analytical or cue criticism is much sterner stuff. While often it may appear "literary," it is set in a technical jargon peculiar to the arts or to a discipline appropriate to the analytical base used. Analytical criticism therefore rarely appeals to the general public and often only to the "expert." It may serve artist or critic, or both. It may serve only the historian.

The analytical critic also has potential problems with his egocentric regard for his expert knowledge. He may become enthralled with the technical beauty or excellence of some work which, despite its technical quality, lacks expressive quality adequate to engage the aesthetic interest of its audience. When his praise goes disregarded, such a critic may then castigate his lay fellows for their aesthetic obtuseness. Conversely, there is the example of the novel, *Love Story*, which obtained a high place on the popular best-seller lists early in 1971, yet was regarded as trash by the critics. But, while *Love Story* was, without apology, grossly sentimental, as Taine would say, its sentiments captured its time for the moment. So, no matter the alleged technical deficiencies of the work, they were demonstrably adequate to be vehicle for an expression which established it successfully in popular literature.

The moral of the matter is simply that neither content of expression nor technical excellence is enough for aesthetic production. There must, as Dewey maintained, be adequation of form to matter and matter to form, sufficient for successful expression. Both may be powerful, one may be weak, but together cue and sentiment must find fruition in felt significance.

Relevant to the critical imbroglio involving *Love Story*, the point is well made that "Critical theory fulfills its purpose only if it is fully aware as possible of the aim and character of what it subserves."[4] Art criticism, obviously, is of art, and the character of art is this: Art is expressive. The aim of art is this: Art aims to infect other people with felt significance, or expression. Certainly, the artist may not have had that aim, but we are not criticizing the artist any more than we are criticizing the book-binder or frame-maker. We are setting about to criticize the product of the artist's work. That work, whether the artist intended it or not, is art to the measure of its emotional infectiousness.

Art is a construct of cues; expression is our response. Criticism has to do with both, and no critic ought be so enthusiastic in his technical knowledge that he loses sight of the immediate aesthetic value, expression. As Forster remarked so aptly, "The final test of a novel will be our affection for it, as it is the test of our friends, and of anything else which we cannot define."[5]

Of the two branches of criticism, response criticism deals most directly with the aim of art, i.e., the infectious communication of felt meaningfulness. This branch has also been the source of by far the most influential critical theory for more than two millenia, for it is in this side of criticism that the moralistic and metaphysical approaches reside. In an earlier chapter, we reviewed the underlying characteristics of such criticism, finding that the moralistic deals with the influences art has upon human experience in general, while the metaphysical deals with the validity, or truth inherent in the expression which comes of the art experience.

We cannot deny that such criticism is undertaken, nor even that there is some legitimate basis for it, since art and expression are not monadic in our experience of self and world. Somehow, there is a proper moral sense to our judgment of art, and it has something to do with the truth inherent in the expression that comes of it.

Lessing, arguing for the freedom of art to serve its proper goal of pleasure, assured us that to find pleasure in art we will also find in it an inherent morality. Santayana and Dewey were equally insistent upon substantially that same point. There is no beauty of expression without psychic harmony, no harmony if the objective energies obtain conflicts in the second term of expression. And, it is there that, aesthetically, moral conflicts may change potential beauty to ugliness, where credibility is found lacking and the form of beauty destroyed on the pillory of truth.

Art finds expression of all phases of life although art itself is but one phase. Expression is *of* human nature in all its minutest detail and broadest scope, having its source in the totality of human interests, desires, and needs. Art endures in the same world as man the scientist, man the philosopher, man the dreamer of a better world, man of everyday practice, man who believes or dis-

---

[4]*Criticism: The Major Texts*, Bate, p xi.
[5]*Aspects of the Novel*, p 42.

believes in God, soul, and immortality. All of these "men" are expressed in the aesthetic activity. If there is truth in the expression of art, it is the affective truth of what it means to be such a man and to believe and know and do what he does in the world.

The affective truth of expression has no equivalence to logical truth, such as the assertion of a connection between propositions A and B. Art may only be used to express the felt significance of what it means to a man to have B follow from A. Neither does art assert any moral truths. Art instead is the vehicle for expressing the emotional meaning of a man's moral sense, which is an aesthetic truth. This does not make art, as Kant held, an activity of illustrating moral ideas, and not only because man's aesthetic sense is not what Kant thought it was, i.e., a faculty for judging the sensible illustration of moral ideas. Rather, the Kantian view is repudiated because the flavors of aesthetic partake of the whole man, in whose experience the moral phase is not only varied but partial.

Furthermore, art as the illustration of moral ideas would be didactic. It would be a vehicle for moral instruction serving some extrinsic moral good, rather than a vehicle for expression. That is not to say that art is not an instrument of learning, for it is. Through the activity of art a man learns the expression of feelings which otherwise might be denied to his experience of life. Art provides additions and alternatives of feeling. Through art, a man may learn how it feels to be a man in various human situations other than his own. Paradoxically, then, a man may learn through art what it feels like to have a morality other than his own and, motivated by a learned preference for that feeling, revise his own moral sense. And, exactly that potential influence of art, discharged into man's total behavior, is the root of moralistic criticism of the arts.

Art, then, is not didactic although we cannot deny its efficacy when used as a tool for moral instruction. Yet, as art, it is nothing but an aesthetically expressive activity obtaining only aesthetic goods. And, unless art achieves its aesthetic goal, it has no vitality as a tool used for other purposes. On such terms, moralistic criticism of the arts is extrinsic to the authentic role of the art critic. The latter may indeed recognize the moral sentiments characterized by the expression, but his critical function applies to the quality of the expression as affective communication and the excellence of the structure of cues as the communicative instrument. To do more is to be a moralist rather than a critic of the arts.

Chapter 11

FOOTNOTES TO THE FAIRYTALE

Some undertakings alleged to be fine art have more in common with a workout at the gym than with art as aesthetic production. They may be quite striking to the senses, but they remain only delightful exercises in color and form, or perhaps words or motion. My cat playing with a length of twine appears to enjoy himself no differently and no less. If athletic grace and charm of movement are the sole criteria of aesthetic excellence, my cat also is as great an artist as Rudolf Nureyev.

Such exercises in artistry represent that side of the aesthetic experience that Santayana called the first term of expression. It is the simple beauty of impression, the beauty resident in the raw feelings and dispositional forms of affect stemming from sensory projection and perceptual integration. Yet, while such affective response is indeed the product of our engagement in art, it is not the measure of the experience of fine art. There is beautiful, or fine art only when there is aesthetic production, and there is aesthetic production only when there is expression in both terms of Santayana's definition. That is, there is expression only when the constellation of feelings associated with the experience of a work of art achieves a focus dominated by cerebral affect. Only then does the activity obtain an awareness of meaningfulness within the moment of feeling itself.

That description of the source and function of expression is both a clarification and a restatement of Santayana's dual-term theory presented in his *Sense of Beauty* in 1896. It is a description fundamental to any valid conception of the nature of expression in the arts. The preceding chapters have developed that line of thought along more modern lines, using data unavailable to Santayana's time, and thus allowing theoretical thrusts beyond the limits of his work, no matter that the basic foundation of an aesthetics as created by him remains valid to this day. On the other hand, there are other paths of argument leading to understandings of aesthetic quite alien to those presented here. Some people maintain even that expression as we understand it is as much a myth as the divine madness of the ancients. A less contrary view, held by the purists, allows that there is expression but its quality of meaning originates entirely in the beauty of impression.

The extreme beyond purism is admirably argued in the theories of Walter Pater, who deserves to be remembered as an aesthete's aesthete. For him, aesthetics was more than a philosophy of beauty. It was a philosophy of life.

Life, according to Pater, is but a series of moments between birth and death. The problem of life is simply to find a way to make the most of every moment. The clue leading to the best solution of the problem was provided by the richness of his experience of the arts.

For Pater, man's aesthetic sense is entirely perceptual, dealing with sense impressions. Aesthetic experience is a precise ecstasy occurring in an intensified instant of sense impression. It is no accidental achievement. It is learned and perfected by experience. Aesthetic, in short, is based on an act of enlightened, consistent, discriminative sensuous judgment developed by refinement of sense perception.

If such enhancement of our experience of art is possible, then all of our experience – every living moment – may no less be enriched by sharpening our perceptual skills. Thus, he believed that the aesthete, the disciplined connoisseur, is best able to solve the problem of life, sampling each moment for its ultimate nectar of pleasure by virtue of his cultivated sense of taste. Only through the aesthetic approach to life may we find the exquisite moments that make it really worthwhile.

Pater's perceptual approach to aesthetic made art entirely sensuous in its appeal. It may have meaning at times, but only by accident. In any case, meaning has no aesthetic relevance, since the refinement of taste achieved by the aesthete is purely perceptual and in no way connected with intelligence or intellect. Art is sensuous inventiveness, an exquisite blending of form and substance serving only the rapturous designs of sense.

The point of view represented by Pater remains fresh and current to this day. It has also found scientific corroboration, notably in the work of H. J. Eysenck. An earlier chapter called attention to Eysenck's experiments revealing correlations between preferences for artistic styles and specific personality types. In a later series of experiments, Eysenck and others demonstrated that "good taste" in art can be discriminated on the basis of perceptual factors such as color, and that "good taste" in perception of color and color combinations correlates with "good taste" in perception of achromatic form. In short, Eysenck appears to have experimentally confirmed Pater's contention that the taste of the connoisseur has a strictly sensuous basis.

The experimental discrimination of "good taste" in terms of perceptual preferences, initially achieved by means of the simple materials of color and form, was proved to be demonstrated consistently in further tests employing more complex materials. These included "portraits, landscape paintings, book-bindings, silverware, statues, landscape photographs, and many more."[1]

For the experiments, the experimental standards of "good taste" related to any of the materials were at the outset established by determining the preferences of recognized "experts" in art. Only materials on which the experts exhibited virtually unanimous agreement were used in the experiments. One of the further results of the experiments was that the standards derived from the expert consensus could also be used to predict the eventual career success or failure of new art students with "considerable accuracy." Certainly, the stylistic tendencies of the individual students could not be predicted (because of the experimental design which eliminated the effects of artistic style upon preferences of the subjects), but the agreement or disagreement of the student's preferences with those of the "expert" consensus was found to be a highly reliable predictor of the success or failure of the student to become recognized as an artist by the experts.

As a result of these experimental findings, Eysenck concluded that artistic potential and achievement can be experimentally discriminated on the basis of perceptual preference alone. From that finding, he was led to postulate that aesthetic sensitivity is purely a perceptual trait, the quality or excellence of which is determined biologically – that is, by the inherited physiological characteristics of the body. As he put it, "there exists some property of the central nervous system which determines aesthetic judgments, a property which is biologically derived, and which covers the whole field of visual art."[2] He cited other data showing that the hypothesis generalizes to include auditory art, but admitted that prose literature cannot be encompassed by his approach since the immediate stimuli of literature – printed words – are perceptually neutral aesthetically.

What Eysenck postulated, then, is that neural responses of some bodies are aesthetically better than the responses of other bodies. Certainly everybody has to learn to perceptually integrate sensuous experiences of materials and form, and other experiments show that practice and familiarity tend to enhance aesthetic appreciation. However, not the mere fact of perception, nor learned skills of perception, nor familiarity with the perceived, but the sensuous qualities intrinsic to the experience of perception are the distinctive measures of aesthetic excellence. The superior potential of the connoisseur to obtain exquisite sensuous pleasures thus is biologically given rather than shaped by learning as Pater held, although the enhancement value of learning is not denied.

---

[1]*Sense and Nonsense in Psychology*, p 320.
[2]*Ibid.*, p 319.

Eysenck's experimental evidence and conclusions supporting Pater's argument for a strictly sensuous basis for aesthetic appear damaging to our thesis, particularly when Eysenck cited further data showing that intelligence has little bearing upon good taste. We hold that intellectual function is essential to the aesthetic sense, while Eysenck's experimental findings are that "Intelligence correlates only slightly with 'good taste'; certainly the correlation is much too low to account for the findings."[3] If there is no marked correlation, then our attempt to tie the essence of aesthetic to the same mental functions as those responsible for intelligence, appears to be fully and finally thwarted.

Another characteristic of the approach to aesthetic taken by Pater and Eysenck is also tremendously appealing compared to our own. Their approach is attractive for its relative simplicity as a theoretical basis for a philosophy of art and aesthetics. Favor ought always be given to theoretical simplicity—but only if the facts are explained. In this instance, the theories of Pater and Eysenck fail to save the sense of meaningfulness men find in their experiences of art.

Such failure is hardly unexpected, however, given the orientation of their approach. Each finds aesthetic only in what we understand to be the first term of expression; that is, in sense impression gained from the mere perception of materials and form. Meaning is thus both accidental and unnecessary to the experience, and those factors which involve the "second term" have no relevance to or part in the generation of aesthetic. As Eysenck put it, such influences are "non-aesthetic in nature, being mainly based on associations with particular events which have brought happiness or pain to the individual concerned."[4]

The real issue at stake here is why Eysenck is able to be so certain that the factors of the second term are "non-aesthetic." He admits that those factors do impact upon aesthetic, for he complained about their effect upon aesthetic judgment, noting that such allegedly non-aesthetic influences (e.g., the sexual interest aroused by bosomy actresses) conspire to make aesthetically inferior works more popular than superior works (e.g., Irving Berlin won greater popularity than Mozart). If such factors have this admitted influence upon aesthetic experience and its evaluation, then on what grounds can they be declared non-aesthetic?

To say that one work is more popular than another is to say that more people prefer that work than another. Since we are talking about art preferences, we are obviously talking about such preferences as the consequences of aesthetic experience. To say that the second term is not truly aesthetic is thus beside the point, which is that effects of the second term influence aesthetic experience

---

[3] *Ibid.*, p 320.
[4] *Ibid.*, p 34.

such that they produce equivalent effects upon aesthetic judgments. There can be only one reason why Eysenck will not grant the aesthetic nature of that influence; effects of the second term were not approached by his experiments. Since such factors as operate in the second term are not as identifiable and isolable as objective energies (colors and forms), and so are unsuited for experimental control, they obviously could not figure in either his experiments or in his theoretical conclusions concerning the nature of aesthetic and the aesthetic preferences people have. What we find, then, is that his data really warrant Eysenck to say only that there is an experimentally demonstrated basis for discriminating and explaining taste on the basis of the first term of expression.

That recognized "experts" have basically excellent and consistent preferences for perceptual values despite their stylistic differences is not unexpected. After all, they belong to the club that set the official rules of excellence. Neither is it unexpected, therefore, that those whose tastes conform to the club standards are also awarded the status of "fellow expert."

We find that the most significant result of Eysenck's work for aesthetic theory is that he provided experimental data implying the biological and inherited source of the "good taste" that marks the perception of the expert. Since his data are concerned solely with the perceptual basis for aesthetic—the first term of expression as we understand it—then there is no reason for anyone to be surprised that his work found little correlation between intelligence and strictly perceptual criteria of taste. By the same token, those findings offer no particular argumentive weight for or against our position that the second term of expression owes its character to those cerebral behaviors underlying intelligence.

Far from being damaging to our thesis, then, Eysenck's data tend to substantiate our description of aesthetic in terms of the biological system, and enlarge our understanding of aesthetic qualities of the first term. His failure to appreciate the aesthetic nature of other than perceptual factors in the aesthetic experience, and his failure to respect popular taste because of its common divergence from the "good taste" typical of the "experts," together tend to discredit his theories as a viable foundation for a philosophy of art and aesthetics.

The approach taken by Pater and Eysenck also may be challenged on terms internal to their theories. The crucial point is that the sensuous ecstasies they hold to be aesthetic experience cannot be differentiated from any other kind of sensuous ecstasy that the organism may undergo. Certainly, the eliciting energies may be differentiated, but then only in terms of classes of objects; i.e., the thing perceived is discriminated as a statue and not a door stop.

Such perceptual discrimination is the product of an intellectual judgment concerning the function of the object perceived. There is still only one object.

The energies available to an encounter with it are perceptually the same. In terms of the object or the energies available from it, then, there is no basis for differentiation of the experience as aesthetic or not, one class of object or another. In other words, the approach taken by Pater and Eysenck cannot explain how the common perceptual basis for an experience – the actual energies of a perception of a thing – can for one person produce perception of a statue (an aesthetic object) and for someone else produce perception of a door stop (a practical object). Our criticism becomes even more telling, however, when we consider the matter in terms of the feelings objectified (but not translated into object) in an experience. Then, we see that the essence of the issue is that from their point of view one cannot differentiate aesthetic (pleasing sensuous experience of a painting) from any other kind of enjoyable experience (such as the pleasing sensuous experience of a hot bath) any more than they can explain how the same sensuous materials may be discovered to be aesthetic (a statue) by one person and non-aesthetic (a door stop) by another.

This inability to define a difference between aesthetic and other experience is really the central factor in the failure of Pater and Eysenck to develop an acceptable aesthetics. They describe a strictly sensuous basis for aesthetic, an ecstasy of perceptual pleasure. We can only assume that if such ecstasy is all there is to aesthetic experience, then an aesthetic experience is of the order of being tickled. No doubt the pleasure of art is sensuously more refined and appeals otherwise to the senses, but the effect described is close kin to that of being tickled.

To be tickled can be an exquisite sensuous experience, one able to grip our entire consciousness. The same is true of stunting in an aeroplane or the first plunge on a rollercoaster. Such experiences are usually categorized as thrills, wherein the psyche is overwhelmed in sensuous energies. And this, in essence, is what Pater is alleging of the experience of art. Such art becomes but another avenue of thrill seeking. Not that thrills are excluded from the legitimate effects of art. Not at all. The facilitating influence of thrilling effects upon the aesthetic consciousness was noted by Aristotle, and more ignored rather than disputed by modern theorists, although the vitalizing effects of sensuous enrichment noted by both Santayana and Dewey are not unrelated to the observations of Aristotle.

That Aristotle was describing more than purely sensuous thrills is beside the point, which is that there are experiences of art which are thrilling. But, there is not art if there is merely thrill without meaning, and that also has been understood since Aristotle analyzed the dramatic art of tragedy. This was made eminently clear in his discussion of the use and abuse of spectacle by the tragic dramatists.

Artistotle gave due recognition to the thrilling effects of spectacle in the arousal of the affective consequences – described as pity and fear – of tragic poetry. But, he saw spectacle as an artistically inferior source of aesthetic effects, often used by inferior poets for thrilling effects alone. Such poets, he remarks, "who make use of the Spectacle to put before us that which is merely monstrous and not productive of fear, are wholly out of touch with tragedy."[5]

The spectacle was but one of many devices which the dramatist might use to stir up feelings in his audience. But, merely cooking up a pot of feelings is not all there is to the art of tragedy. Aristotle emphatically drove home that thrills and sensuous tittilations come to nothing sans aesthetic meaning. The verse may be sensuously pleasing, the spectacle thrilling, but the heart of tragedy lies in the story told. The story contains the meanings necessary to evoke pity and fear. Meaning, however, does not reside in the mechanics of the story; that is, not in the plot or its devices (discovery, peripety, etc.). Meaning has its source in what Artistotle called "universal statements," which he saw as the essence of the story. These "statements" may be embodied in both words and action, and they express what is universal in the human situation. Universal, they have meaning to every man. Without such meaning, thrills and sensuous ecstasies are much ado about nothing.

In the fragment of his work remaining, Aristotle unfortunately tells us far less than we would wish to know of his "universal statements." His notion is suggestive, however, of the understandings of aesthetic found in the considerable literature produced by Jung and his followers. The Jungians reside at a pole opposite from Pater and Eysenck, and have scant regard for the sensuous element of the aesthetic experience. Instead, they find that the distinctive feelings characteristic of our experience of art have their source in the archetypal behaviors stemming from the collective unconscious.

The archetypes, as understood by the Jungians, are indeed a kind of "universal statement" asserted through the imagery of language, form, or action. We understand such behaviors as forming the dispositional ground beneath art as the vehicle for aesthetic communication. They are essential to the repertoire of "stock responses" that permit ease and clarity of expression while rendering the devices of the artistic vehicle transparent. They are, moreover, the basis for the experience of the divine madness, that feeling of possession or of being beside oneself which marks our experience as we are swept up in the work of art.

Where we find archetypal behaviors as but a higher-order dispositional function (higher because archetypes are imbued with the qualities of idea through the involvement of the higher-order functions of the nervous system) in a family of inherited behavioral tendencies, both called out and enriched by sensuous qualities of the total experience, the Jungians are generally much

---

[5]de Poetics; Basic Works of Aristotle, p 1468.

more parochial in their views. With their enthusiasm over the notion of the collective unconscious, they tend to speak as if no other factors were operant in aesthetic. Worse, they often seem to have no notion of the fundamental naturalism in Jung's own thought. While that naturalism kept his feet on solid theoretical ground, his followers tend to pervert his naturalism into a poetic mythology, and his phenomenological interpretation of the psychic reality is made over into a metaphysical psychology.

That practicing Jungians are therapists rather than scientists, and their skill an art and not a science, no doubt explains what they have done with Jungian psychology. In therapy, of course, there is no real harm done. Myth and metaphysical viewpoints can be useful tools of the work. Yet, one wonders if the fables and viewpoints of a thoroughgoing naturalism might be even more efficacious tools permitting a faster and fuller adjustment to a world full of sticks and stones, where myths do indeed reside although they may be as validly translated into fables of fact.

No matter, the fact remains that Jungian literature, understood on the terms made clear by the master, provides a broad and worthy reservoir of knowledge concerning the workings of the archetypes in human consciousness and behavior. Erich Neumann, for example, writes beautifully and cogently about the archetypal function in aesthetic production, a summary description of which is contained in his essay, *Art and Time*. He writes:

"The archetypes of the collective unconscious are intrinsically formless psychic structures which become visible in art. The archetypes are varied by the media through which they pass – that is, their form changes according to the time, the place, and the psychological constellation of the individual in whom they are manifested. Thus, for example, the mother archetype, as a dynamic entity in the psychic substratum, always retains its identity, but it takes on different styles – different aspects or emotional color – depending on whether it is manifested in Egypt, Mexico, Spain, or in ancient, medieval, or modern times. The paradoxical multiplicity of its eternal presence, which makes possible an infinite variety of forms of expression, is crystallized in its realization by man in time; its archetypal eternity enters into a unique synthesis with a specific historical situation."[6]

We quarrel only with his choice of words (an archetype as a "dynamic entity in the psychic substratum"?) to convey his meaning. Perhaps to escape some of the unfortunate verbiage of Jungian interpretations, it might be best to eschew the use of "archetypes" altogether and speak of the phenomena of the collective unconscious only as dispositional consciousness. No matter the name, however, the function is the same. The aesthetic impact of the imagery

---

[6]*Op Cit.*, in *Art and the Creative Unconscious*, p 82.

of the language of art—whether word or action, the gesture of a mime or the frozen hand of creation on the Sistine ceiling—is rooted in inherited dispositional behaviors.

The universal contents of such imagery are the archetypes. "Archetypes" are but a way of talking about inherited traits of consciousness that permit the "universal statements" of art to pass from man to man. Archetypes are no more "dynamic entities in the psychic substratum" than are instincts. Archetypes are a way of talking about ideational images that have the appearance of being innate. Instincts are a way of talking about overt behaviors that have a similar appearance. They and the archetypes are "built-in" tendencies of the psyche to respond consistently to specific kinds of cues. Out of these tendencies, and out of them alone, comes the seemingly eternal kernel of truth or meaning—the universal understanding peculiar to aesthetic experience—that persists as a bond between your consciousness and that of all men back beyond the dawn of history.

Implicit in the preceding discussion is a functional distinction between the universal statement and the archetype. They may be differentiated respectively as cue and response, with the universal statement resident in art and acting as the elicitor of the archetypal image in consciousness. This distinction appears valid although Aristotle spoke at times of the universal statement in terms of the meaning achieved in human consciousness as a response to word and action, while Neumann told of the archetypes passing through various media in several styles. Seen against the entire exposition of their ideas, however, these instances appear as difficulties in employment of language for communication, and do not belie the actual distinction, which we believe adds a further dimension to our grasp of the idea of the universal statement and the archetype, particularly as they function in aesthetic experience.

In brief, Jung introduced us to the notion of the archetype as a genetic disposition toward the appearance of a typical idea or mode or episode of consciousness heavily charged with feeling. It is a response to encounters with the world shared by people of all times and places. In contrast to that, Aristotle described the universal statement as the embodiment in words or action of meanings significant to the situation called life that all men share. These words or actions served as cues that elicited the tragic depths of feeling possible only upon the grasp of meaning. That relationship between cue and response identifies the heart of the perennial notion of art as the language of emotion. Further, it ties the language of art directly and intimately to the nature of language in general.

Just as aesthetic meaning is the product of the action of art, a man's action out in the world, as such, lies at the root of language. Perhaps the clearest exposition of this idea was presented by Jean Piaget in his *Genetic Epistemology*.

There, he explained that knowledge is not a passive copy of reality, but a product of one's action upon it. Knowing thus deals both with objects and our actions upon them, and the latter is shown to be of most importance for knowing. Further, he shows a fundamental correlation between the logical and rational organization of knowledge and the development of psychological processes that make such organization possible, then identifies the psychological ground for all logical and mathematical structures in action first of all, independent of and appearing prior to the development of language.

In Chapter 2 of the work cited, Piaget described the growth of logical thought, or reasoning, in children from the prelinguistic stage of infant and toddler, to the pre-teen. "It is very striking," he remarked, "that language does not appear in children until the sensory-motor intelligence is more or less achieved."[7] In that prelinguistic intelligence he further shows the appearance of a practical logic of action that effectively uses the logic of inclusion, of ordering, and of correspondence – a logic that provides the foundation for the subsequent construct of languages of all kinds into their various logical and mathematical forms.

When one observes that language is not only based upon action but is itself a form of action, then it appears that Aristotle's description of the universal statement as word or action is essentially redundant. That is, the universal statement has its roots entirely in action, as does any kind of language. Equally, the archetypal response of ideational imagery loaded with felt meaningfulness is a developmental product of emerging psychological processes, yet it has an immediate connection with action in the world insofar as the potential of those processes is realized as archetypal experience.

None of this is meant to obscure the fact that the languages of both instrumental and aesthetic consciousness have particular formal structures and logical intricacies that go beyond the origin of language in action and feeling. Man has a psychological capacity for rationality and aesthetic; the original structure for that capacity comes out of the genetic tendencies of the nervous system acted upon and given initial order by the organism's encounter with objects in the world; upon that order there are imposed artificial structures for coping with aspects of that encounter, called languages. These languages become instruments for dealing with the world. They are comparatively better or worse as instruments. More can be said in Ancient Greek or Latin than in modern English because of structural refinements never achieved by the English-speaking peoples. Indeed, the sophistication of English as an instrumental language sprang from the adoption of Greek and Latin root words, and even whole words and phrases, for general use in company with the spare

---

[7]*Op. Cit.*, p 47.

Anglo-Saxon capacity for expression. Indeed, as we will have cause to examine with more depth in a moment, the power of reason depends as much upon the language of its expression as upon the neurological potential or capacity of the organism. And, this truth is no less evident relative to art as the language of emotion as it is for mathematics as the language of scientific knowings.

What we find, then, is that a primary characteristic of art is the embodiment of universal statements that derive from the logic of action, while a fundamental quality of aesthetic is the genetically conditioned dispositional response of the human psyche to those universal statements, a response which has the appearance of an archetypal idea or episode of imagery heavily charged with feeling. But, such a description of the root of meaningfulness in the experience of art is hardly acceptable to everyone.

Off in another theoretical direction are those who admit the sense of meaningfulness characteristic of the experience of art, but who deny such "universal statements" or "archetypal ideas" or anything else smacking of ideation. These are the purists. They explain expression as felt meaningfulness stemming solely from sense impression.

Purism appears more intriguing theoretically than Pater's argument for a life, and simpler in conception than theories based on the intricate role of archetypal or dispositional tendencies. The purist argues that art should be purified by purging it of subject matter so as to achieve expression through medium alone. Materials (sound, color, texture, volume, light, etc.) would be embodied in form, but form shall serve only to enhance the natural effects of materials, or as an arrangement functioning to direct or sustain attention. The aim, then, is to utilize materials for their intrinsic sensuous values alone. Materials, that is, are held to possess qualities of meaningfulness stemming from the characteristic sensuous qualities each possesses when experienced. So also do the forms of their embodiment, for the form of the material adds sensuous qualities of its own.

Fairly considered, the purist argument must be admitted to have a certain substance. The purist asserts that in our experience of materials and form per se there are sensuous flavors of meaning which are the source of the characteristic felt significance of the work. For example poetry—written to be spoken—need rely only on the sounds of words for achieved aesthetic value. Each word, the purist maintains, has its own intrinsic tonality of meaning. The forms in which the words are set also have similar qualities of meaning. Jean-Paul Sartre, a purist in his concept of all the arts except prose literature, elucidates the formal function when he observes, "For the poet, the sentence has a tonality, a taste; by means of it he tastes for their own sake the irritating flavors of objection, of reserve, of disjunction."[8] The mere sounds of words and their formal organization are enough

---

[8] *What Is Literature?* p 17.

for expression of meaning, with absolutely no need for associational values stemming from higher functions of the brain, such as are responsible for the communicative values of instrumental language.

In support of the purist argument, we must recognize that in music and painting, and even in common parlance, there is an idiom of feeling connected with sounds, words, and colors. We do indeed "feel blue" and "see red." In music we have all heard a pastoral suite as vivid as a painted landscape. Everyone is familiar with the dirge of death and the lilt of life, the dissonances of industry and the airs of martial glory. In other words, there is no possible way to doubt that certain sensuous materials – sounds and colors – by their very character and form do indeed impart a sense of meaning in our experience of them.

Because the distinctive tonalities of meaning directly experienced of materials and form are commonly experienced by men and their sensuous qualities easily remarked, these tonalities form an idiomatic basis for communication between men. From our point of view, the existence of such idiom is not unexpected. We see all sensuous materials and forms as feelings, and find that the feelings of encounter men have with the world are much the same because of both the nature of the world and the inherited structure of the psyche. Our difficulty with the purist point of view comes with their insistence upon the purely perceptual nature of aesthetic meaning, or expression. After all, the particular trick of perception – the translation of feelings into sounds and colors – is dispositional to the old brain and not the new. If there is real meaning in the event then, one would think that the higher functions peculiar to man would come into play.

By the same token, we still cannot deny that there is the suggestion of meaning resident in sounds and colors as such. There is the basis for a recognized idiom of feeling. Hung on the horns of this dilemma, the only solution appears to be that the sensuous qualities of forms and materials may indeed suggest meaning, but have none per se. In such terms, the red blaze of anger is only anger. The sound of melancholy is just sad. The sound of objection suggests meaning but has none. What we have are mere elicitations of feeling which have no more expressive value than the exposure of feeling, a point Dewey argued so well in *Art as Experience*. If so, then there is no aesthetic production possible in art guided only by puristic principles. Such art has but the status of play, an exercise in purely sensuous enjoyment, and thus open to the same criticisms as were leveled at Pater's theory of aesthetic.

The upshot of this is, then, that although an artist works directly with materials having sensuous values, and employs them for their idiomatic tonalities of meaning, the source of expression lies elsewhere. The materials and form of the "airs of martial glory" may be enlivening as such, having a distinctive sensuous character that touches a chord in our psychic makeup. The full impact of meaning, however, comes from the load of ideational affect inherent in our learned responses to the ideas and acts associated with warlike behavior. No matter the responsive chord struck upon the psyche by the sensations of the musical stimulus, the meaning idiom of the materials is as much shaped by learning in aesthetic communication as is the idiom of any other language.

The entire matter may be settled once and for all by the simple expedient of examining the nature of expression in poetry. As Aristotle pointed out so long ago, poetry is more than mere sensuous materials, titillating to the ear. The affective impact of poetry is inherent in the sound of poetry only to a minor degree. Felt sound, by itself, lacks the precise flavor of significance that constitutes expression. The affective force of poetry comes instead from what those sounds are taken to mean, even if they mean nothing. For to vocalize to say nothing also has its expression, e.g., the nihilism of surrealistic poetry.

A particular example clarifies the issue. Consider a poem written in a strange language: *The Cracked Bell* from Baudelaire's *Flowers of Evil*. Assume that we have no knowledge of the French language. We attempt to read the poem phonetically without understanding the phonics peculiar to French. We cannot even pronounce the words correctly, much less interpret them. Can one doubt the confused impression and lack of expression in our experience?

But for the sake of argument let us admit that we have given the matter a poor test when we tried to read it ourselves. After all, poetry is an auditory art. Poems are created for the sound they have to the ear, and not for their appearance to the eye on a page full of typescript. So, now let us suppose that we have a Frenchman, a skilled reader, read us the poem. Listening to him speak we now are able to gather something of the emotional character of the work. Yet, its precise emotional meaningfulness will escape us. Certainly the poem is not happy. There ought to be something dirge-like in the rhythm, full of idiomatic suggestiveness, but the result can only be emotional confusion. It lacks the felt impact of the winter wind sounding "like the death rattle of a wounded man forgotten under a pile of dead beside a lake of blood." To achieve such impact, not the sound of words – but their instrumental meaning has to be grasped. A similar requirement for intellectual apprehension is applicable to all the arts. We only find the evidence of that requirement most visible in poetry and prose.

Operant, then, in the experience of listening to the poem and achieving felt significance is the function of instrumental consciousness. With such function, feelings are translated into percepts and intellectual apprehensions of instrumental meanings are achieved. We understand sounds as words used to say something. Within the process of the experience, however, the aesthetic disposition of consciousness is enabled. Then, the focus of awareness is upon the feelings constituent of the perceptual translation and intellectual apprehension of instrumental meanings. In other words, in the poetic approach to instrumental language, consciousness dispositionally approaches its contents for the sake of tasting their affective values instead of understanding their intellectual values. In that way, one may understand the meaning of a poem to be not what is said but what is felt in the saying.

In the above description, the intervention of intellectual behaviors is seen as essential to the character of the aesthetic experience. Intellectual function is the source of the precise meaningfulness which is the mark of expression in the arts. But such meaning, while it is the product of intellectual function, is not intellectual. Meaning is grasped not as instrumental idea, but as pure affect. In the affective awareness that is expression the intellectual function attended to from the side of aesthetic tendency gives the experience meaningfulness having the preciseness if not the literally definitive nature of idea.

The crucial point of the above, relevant to aesthetic theory, is that under dominance of the aesthetic attitude, the instrumental disposition of consciousness still acts. It simply does not control, or dominate the construction of consciousness. It does not channel the tendency of consciousness toward an affective poise defined by instrumental, or object oriented, goals. Objects are indeed manipulated in ways giving the appearance of expressing instrumental, or practical values. How else does expression occur in a world of sticks and stones? Intellect still manipulates percepts and concepts and guides the confluence of ideas that one may treat as a train of thought. Intellect is an instrument of order in the world of affect no less than it is in the world of things. What is different under the dominance of the aesthetic attitude is that the results sought by these varied manipulations are oriented toward the realization of the immediate affective flavors of the experience.

For aesthetic, the function of intellect is essential, but only under the control of the aesthetic attitude. If intellect intervenes instrumentally, the aesthetic response can only be confused and even inhibited, unable to reach fruition in the affective formation of dispositional complexes which in the end grip us in the experience of the divine madness. But, when intellectual function is enlisted into the experience on the level of feeling, then there is the experience of fine art— art defined by the experience of idea. Stated otherwise, only with the mustering of the dispositional energies of the cerebral cortex, which raise the tonalities of affect to the level of idea, does the sensuous ecstasy of raw feeling, the "moving" character of dispositional complexes of the primitive brain and nervous system, and the ideational character of emotion, combine to form the overwhelming sense of possession on the level of affect that is the root experience of the divine madness.

From the point of view of language theory, the preceding presents a ground for explaining the puzzlement that the poetic use of language has always caused. In speaking of art in terms of cues and expression in terms of responses, and in understanding language to be the representation of things and acts in terms of a logic that is pre-linguistic in origin but no less rational or intellectual, the adage that art is the language of emotions achieves a new dimension in our understanding. The adage is no longer a "cute" saying. It means to convey the generalized idea that each and every medium of artistic expression trades upon a system of devices which in effect are a language providing a basis for affective communication between men, a system which involves cerebral responses such that the experience is imbued with the quality of idea.

Music is perhaps the most difficult medium to describe in these terms, but only if we fail to recognize it as a language. Recalling our work with Baudelaire's poem, we should understand that music – as a language – also needs to be learned if we are to grasp meaning from it. I have watched people read a score of music with as much pleasure as others read Baudelaire. And, just as some people advance hardly beyond the level of nursery rhymes in their enjoyment of poetry, the songs of the nursery define the limits of what is meaningful to them in music. But, because poetry trades in the devices of an instrumental language that takes hold of things and actions as structures of words, but does so with a difference, theorists fixated upon the instrumental functions of language have to be confused by poetry. But now it becomes clear in our description that poetry is language turned back upon the affective roots that gave it birth and sustain it.

Much that would pass for poetry hardly meets our description, but relates more to curiosities like two-headed calves. Here, I refer to the fad of "found poetry" of the 1960s, or the perennial experiments with the setting down of words into a form of sorts, called "concrete poetry" by some, to mention only two of the more extreme examples of linguistic gymnastics posing as verse. That does not deny the possibility of such constructions obtaining more than amusement values, but one feels that such would be accidental at best, since the usual functions of aesthetic shaping have been superceded by other criteria, or none at all perhaps in the instance of found poetry.

In the poetic use of language, the formative principle is the immediate awareness of feeling. In a life experience where instrumental language appears to dominate our understanding of what language is and how it operates, poetic language appears to be an epiphenomenon, whimsical and even alogical, a kind of further sophistication of the nature of language. Instead, as our discussion has sought to clarify, poetry is the living language of the pristine consciousness utilizing the sophisticated tools of instrumental languages in a manner that literally turns them inside out and exposes their affective forms.

Poetically, we first accept auditory energies and experience their immediate feeling idioms. These are the peculiarities of these energies as the feelings they are, sans translation into "sounds." They may have the effect of being invigorating or depressing, cheerful or mournful or whatever, but as the sheer auditory undergoing they signify nothing. Translation to "sound" is necessary for more.

We go through then to sounds and to what they have come to signify instrumentally, either as simple signs or as words replete with the load of significance entailed in achieved linguistic values. This is no subsequent, delayed event. Feeling is translated into sound with its very appearance, and the sound is immediately taken to be the word (if it is a word) that it is. In effect, we now refer to what a word does to us because it is the instrument that it is, obtaining the affective values by which a word is representative of things and actions. The affective dimensions are as broad as the history of what the word has been as an operant content of consciousness (or of the nervous system, speaking physiologically) in the structure, or logic, imposed by the language in which the word resides.

The influence of the structure of language – any language – on the construct of feeling cannot be overstated. Understand that cerebral functions associated with language are the product of cortical behaviors that are learned ways of organizing the operations of the cortical structure. The cortex certainly has fundamental physical structures and relationships between them; there are also biologically conditioned tendencies that are the bases for the powers of language. Yet in terms of the exercise of those powers, that structure is a pure potential. It is able to function in ways that we call rational, or intellectual, using the languages of intellect, because it is the structure that it is. But, its actual functions depend upon the ways we learn to use that structure, and the ways of intellectual function are objectively what we call languages. Even the pre-linguistic forms of rationalization described by Piaget are in effect languages. They are the experienced structures involved in things and actions used to rationally manipulate the structures of the brain.

Languages provide the raw materials – affective contents – for intellectual behaviors. Actualization of cortical potentials depends upon the objective structures and contents of the languages available for use in mental functions. These languages must be learned. When learned, they establish their own limits and constraints upon the actualization of the pure potential of the cortical structure. We have already remarked on the richness of the classical Greek language, a richness which one may convincingly argue to have been the basis for the flowering of civilization that the Hellenes accomplished. It enabled great thoughts that produced a wisdom unknown to other men shackled in other languages. But for the roots of classic Greek language living in our own barbaric tongue, we too would be denied our experience of the fruits of that long dead civilization.

We also noted how the inventions of the new scientific languages, embodying both scientific method and mathematical notations, worked a similar miracle and Europeanized the world. And, just as the greatness of Hellas faded upon a Latin tongue tuned to other skills, so is the golden age of European culture sinking into a quagmire of strange tongues ill suited to the great thoughts framed in the languages of Solon or Thomas Jefferson, Plato or Santayana, Heraclitus or deCartes, Aristotle or Whitehead, Thucydides or Toynbee, Pythagoras or Newton, Aeschylus or Shakespeare, Euripides or O'Neill.

There we have cited men using their common languages as languages of both knowing and feeling. What the examples demonstrate is that the affective potential of a work of art is culturally specific in the same way that an instrumental language is culturally specific. The poetry of Baudelaire and the music of Beethoven are alien, probably discomfiting to the ear of a Tibetan herdsman or an Amazonian indian. The mathematical notations of a vector analysis of the trajectory of a thrown ball would perhaps be understood as magical symbols by those same people. But for those who are culturally attuned to these aesthetic and instrumental languages, there is indeed a kind of magical power harnessed in the grasp of the forms they take. One lends to a man the taste of an adventure to the moon; another lies in the foundations of the knowings that took him there.

While the universal statements arising from biological sources are the basis for the power—the gripping force—of the language of poetic consciousness, the affective potential locked in that language of feeling is apprehended and interpreted by learned cortical responses that have roots in cultural experience. This is the effect of the broad base of learned cues and stock responses that one attains in his personal development in a particular cultural milieu. Given this biological and cultural conditioning, the experience of art, either in creation or appreciation, becomes an automatic behavior operant on the level of habit, although shaped by much deeper forces of the psyche. Only this clarifies how the character of aesthetic, likened to a divine madness, is not one of interpretive intervention of intellect, but of immediate or inspired presence of affective idea.

Because of that appearance, many authorities have held that the experience of art obtains only the pre-reflective level where biological and cultural conditioning shape our individual response to art. In fact, we agree with that point of view, but only if one accepts the perhaps paradoxical notion that intellect itself is a product of cultural conditioning to the various languages available in a given milieu. For, the power of intellect is resident in the habitual utilization of linguistic tools. Taking up these tools, which in another manner of discourse we deal with as feelings, the higher powers of the brain establish a context of feeling where the whole affective presence achieves a poise, or equilibrium, embodying a sense of meaning taken from the immediate experience of the function of those higher powers.

To the extent that meaning appears in the experience, note that we find it as the contribution of the process itself through the function of the higher powers of the brain on the level of affect rather than in the translation of feeling into instrumental "facts" of consciousness, no matter that there is such translation involved in the experience. There are, after all, visual images in our experience of a painting. Indeed, the affective contents that those images embody are as much the structure of the experience as the images are the structure of the object of art. And this description of how art functions as cue in aesthetic experience effectively is the basis for the description of the function of any linguistic medium, whether poetic or instrumental. For the single difference between poetic and instrumental language is the way in which we choose to respond. When we ignore the affective form underlying the statement, we are on the level of instrumental language. When we attend to the affective form being shaped by the statement, we are on the level of aesthetic experience and the language of art.

Enveloped in that affective form are the simple feelings of encounter, the dispositional shapings of complexes of feeling that produce tendencies that seem to point the psyche in one way and not another, and the construct of an affective poise by the higher powers. With the first, we gain affective color and enrichment, with the second the dominating force and power of the ancient Muse, and with the last, we find meaning.

So, we have set down a final footnote to the fairytale, which in its own way said at the outset all there is to say about expression in the arts. Certainly, others will append many more such footnotes on the subject, using instrumental language for further definitions and descriptions of the nature of the characteristic response people have to a class of objects that they approach with the unique attitude of consciousness called "aesthetic."

REFERENCES

Addison, Joseph: The Pleasures of the Imagination; The Spectator, 1711-12, Essays 411-421.
Anderson, F. H.: The Philosophy of Francis Bacon. Univ. of Chicago, 1948.
Anokhin, P. K.: Chemical Continuum of Brain as a Mechanism of Reflection of Reality. Publication 51176, Joint Publications Research Service, Springfield, Va., 14 August 1970.
Ardrey, R.: Social Contract: A Personal Inquiry into the Evolutionary Sources of Order and Disorder. Atheneum, N.Y., 1970.
Aristotle: Basic Works of Aristotle. R. McKeon, Ed., Random House, N.Y., 1941.
Arnold, M. B.: Brain Function in Emotion: A Phenomenological Analysis (In Physiological Correlates of Emotion. P. Black, Ed.)
Ausubel, D. P., et al: Prestige Suggestions in Children's Art Preferences. Journal of Genetic Psychology; 1956, 89, 85-93.
Ban, T. A.: Conditioning and Psychiatry. Allen & Unwin, London, 1966.
Barron, Frank: Personality and Perceptual Choice. Journal of Personality, 1952, 385-401.
Bate, W. J.: Criticism: The Major Texts. Harcourt Brace, N.Y., 1952.
Baumgarten, A. G.: Meditationes Philosophicae de Nonnullis ad Poema Pertinentibus; Halle, 1735. (Reflections on Poetry; K. Aschenbrunner and W. B. Holther, Tr. & Ed. Univ. of California, Berkley, 1950.)
    : Aesthetica; (2 vol.) Frankfurt an de Oder; 1750-58.
Bebe-Center, G. G.: Pleasantness and Unpleasantness. Van Nostrand, N.Y., 1932.
Black, P., Ed.: Physiological Correlates of Emotion. Academic Press, N.Y., 1970.
Borck, E.: The Code of Life. Columbia University Press, N.Y., 1969.
Bosanquet, B.: A History of Aesthetic. Meridian Books, N.Y., 1957.
Bower, T. G. R.: The Object in the World of the Infant. Scientific American, October, 1971, p. 30.
Bronstein, D. J., Krikorian, Y. H., and P. Weiner, Ed.: Basic Problems of Philosophy. Prentice-Hall, N.Y., 1947.
Campbell, B. G.: Human Evolution. Aldine, Chicago, 1973.
Campbell, W. J.: The Pleasure Areas: A New Theory of Behavior. Delacorte, N.Y., 1973.
Carmichael, L.: The Making of the Modern Mind. Elsevier, Houston, 1956.
Cassirir, E.: Rousseau, Kant, and Goethe; Tr., J. Gutmann, P.O. Kristeller, J. H. Randall, Jr. Harper and Row, N.Y., 1963.
Cavaggioni, A.: Physiology of the Retina; in Automatic Interpretation and Classification of Images; A. Grasseli, Ed. Academic Press, N.Y., 1969.
Chardin, T. de: The Phenomenon of Man; B. Wall, Tr. Harper & Row, N.Y., 1961.
Cohen, Y.: The Transition from Childhood to Adolescence. Aldine, Chicago, 1964.
Collingwood, R. G.: The Principles of Art. Oxford Univ., 1938.
Corneille, P.: Discourse on the Three Unities; W. J. Bate, Tr. (See Bate, Criticism: The Major Texts.)
Cory, D.: Santayana: The Later Years. Georges Braziller, N.Y., 1963.

Croce,B.: Aesthetic as the Science of Expression and General Linguistic; D. Ainslie, Tr. Mac-
    Millan, London, 1922.
    : What is Art? (Selection from Breviary of Aesthetic, in Bronstein, et al: Basic Prob-
    lems of Philosophy.)
Dewey, J.: Art as Experience. Minton-Balch; N.Y., 1934.
Dumas, G.: Noveau Traité de Psychologie. Felix Alcan, Paris, 1932.
Eysenck, H. J.: Sense and Nonsense in Psychology. Penguin Books, Harmondsworth, 1958.
Feibleman, J. K.: An Introduction to Peirce's Philosophy. Allen and Unwin, London, 1960.
Fessard, E. M., et al: Nervous Processes Underlying Behavior and Learning. USAF OSR Report
    67-2272, 1967.
Feigl, H., and Sellars, W., Eds.: Readings in Philosophical Analysis. Appleton-Century-Crofts,
    N.Y., 1949.
Fischer, A. E.: Problems in the Analysis of Complex Neural Function. (See Voss, Approaches to
    Thought.)
Forster, E. M.: Aspects of the Novel. Harcourt Brace, N.Y., 1927.
French, J. D., Ed.: Frontiers in Brain Research. Columbia Univ., 1962.
Freud, S.: A General Introduction to Psychoanalysis. Permabooks, 1953.
Gaito, J.: Implications of Nucleic Acid Research for Behavioral Events. Second Symposium on
    Neurobiology, Barrow Neurological Institute, Phoenix, 1964.
Garland, H. B.: Lessing; Bowes and Bowes, Cambridge, 1937.
Gay, P.: The Enlightenment: An Interpretation; Vol. 2. A Knopf, N.Y., 1969.
Gimpel, J.: The Cult of Art. Stein and Day, N.Y., 1969.
Goudge, T. A.: The Ascent of Life. Allen and Unwin, London, 1961.
Grasselli, A., Ed.: Automatic Interpretation and Classification of Images. Academic Press,
    N.Y., 1969.
Hassler, Rolf: New Aspects of Brain Functions Revealed by Brain Diseases. (See French, Fron-
    tiers in Brain Research.)
Hempel, C. C.: The Logical Analysis of Psychology; W. Sellars, Tr. (See Feigl and Sellars,
    Readings in Philosophical Analysis.)
    Heyden, H.: Biochemistry of CNS Cells During Learning. USAF OSR Report 66-0932,
    1966.
James, W.: The Principles of Psychology; 2 Vols. Henry Holt, N.Y., 1890.
    :Essays in Radical Empiricism and a Pluralistic Universe. R. B. Perry, Ed. E. P. Dutton &
    Co., N.Y., 1971.
Jung, C. G.: Approaching The Unconscious; in Man and His Symbols; Jung et al., Eds., Dell,
    N.Y., 1968.
    :Memories, Dreams, and Reflections, R. & C. Winston, Trs. Random House, N.Y., 1953.
    :Two Essays in Analytical Psychology, R.F.C. Hull, Tr. Pantheon, N.Y., 1953.
Kant, I.: Critique of Judgment. J. H. Bernard, Tr. Hafner, N.Y., 1966.
    :First Introduction to the Critique of Judgment. J. Haden, Tr. Bobbs-Merrill, N.Y., 1965.
Kristeller, P. O.: The Philosophy of Marcilio Ficino, V. Conant, Tr. N.Y., 1943.
Landis, B., and Tauber, E. S., Eds.: In the Name of Life. Holt, Rinehart, and Winston, N.Y.,
    1971.
Langer, S. K.: Mind: An Essay on Human Feeling. Johns Hopkins, Vol. 1, 1967; Vol. 2, 1972.
Laughlin, C. D., Jr., and d'Aquili, E. G.: Biogenetic Structuralism. Columbia Univ., 1974.
Lessing, G. E.: The Laocoon; Hamburg Dramaturgy; in Selected Prose Works. E. C. Beasley
    and H. Zummern, Tr., E. Bell, Ed.: G. Bell, London, 1900.
Luria, A.: The Nature of Human Conflicts. Liveright, N.Y., 1932.

Marais, E.: The Soul of the Ape. Atheneum, N.Y., 1969.

Mackay, R. P.: The Neurology of Affect; Bulletin of the Los Angeles Neurological Society, 1957, 22, 47-57.

Neumann, E.: Art and the Creative Unconscious. R. Manheim, Tr. Princeton, 1969.

Pater, W.: The Renaissance. Random House Modern Library, N.Y.

Peiper, J.: Enthusiasm and Divine Madness; R. & C. Winston, Trs. Harcourt, Brace and World, N.Y., 1964.

Piaget, J.: Genetic Epistemology; E. Duckworth, Tr. Columbia Univ., 1970.

Piéron, H.: The Sensations; M. H. Pirenne and B. C. Abbott, Trs. J. Garnett Miller, London, 1956.

Plato: The Dialogues of Plato; B. Jowett, Tr. Random House, N.Y.

Prescott, D. A.: Emotion and the Educative Process. American Council on Education, Washington, 1938.

Pribram, K. H.: Languages of the Brain. Prentice Hall, Englewood Cliffs, 1971.

Rapaport, D.: Paul Schilder's Contribution to the Theory of Thought-Processes. The International Journal of Psychoanalysis, Vol. XXXII, Part IV, 1951.

Reynolds, J.: Discourses on Art; R. W. Wark, Ed. Huntington Library, San Marino, 1959.

Richards, I. A.: Principles of Literary Criticism. Harcourt Brace, N.Y., 1949.

    :Practical Criticism. Harcourt Brace, N.Y., 1939.

Robertson, J. G.: Lessing's Dramatic Theory. Cambridge University, 1939.

Rustow, D. A., Ed.: Philosophers and Kings: Studies in Leadership. Georges Braziller, N.Y., 1970.

Santayana, G.: The Sense of Beauty. Scribner's, N.Y., 1936.

    : The Idler and His Works. Books for Libraries Press, Freeport, 1969.

Sartre, J.-P.: Outline of a Theory of Emotions; B. Frechtman, Tr. Philosophical Library, N.Y., 1948.

    :What is Literature? B. Frechtman, Tr. Philosophical Library, 1949.

Saul, L. J.: Emotional Maturity. Lippincott, N.Y., 1966.

Schilder, P.: Medical Psychology; Tr., D. Rapaport. Wiley, N.Y., 1965.

Schlick, M.: On the Relation between Psychological and Physical Concepts; W. Sellars, Tr. (See Feigl and Sellars, Readings in Philosophical Analysis.)

Schmitt, F. O.: Dynamism in Neuroscience. (See Landis and Tauber, In The Name of Life.)

Sidney, P.: An Apology for Poetry, J. C. Collins, Ed. Oxford, 1907.

Snyder, S. H.: Madness and the Brain. McGraw Hill, N.Y., 1974.

Staats, A. W.: Social Behaviorism, Motivation, and the Conditioning Therapies. University of Hawaii, Report TR-2, 1969.

Strout, C.: William James and the Twice Born Sick Soul. (See Rustow, Philosophers and Kings.)

Taine, H. A.: History of English Literature; 3 vols., H. Van Laun, Tr. Grossett and Dunlap, N.Y., 1908.

Thompson, R. F.: Neurophysiology and Thought: The Neural Substrates of Thinking. (See Voss, Approaches to Thought.)

Tiger, L.: Men in Groups. Random House, N.Y., 1969.

Tolstoy, L.: What is Art?; A. Maude, Tr. Walter Scott, London, 1918.

Voss, J. F., Ed.: Approaches to Thought. C. E. Merrill, Columbus, 1969.

Willey, B.: The Seventeenth Century Background. Columbia Univ., N.Y., 1967.

    :The Eighteenth Century Background. Columbia Univ., N.Y., 1940.

Winckelmann, J. J.: Writings on Art; D. Irwin, Ed. Phaidon, N.Y., 1972.

INDEX

171